RICHELIEU

BOOKS BY HILAIRE BELLOC

Historical:

    JOAN OF ARC
    JAMES II
    DANTON
    MARIE ANTOINETTE
    ROBESPIERRE
    HISTORY OF ENGLAND
    MINIATURES OF FRENCH HISTORY
      ETC.

Essays:

    CONVERSATION WITH AN ANGEL
    SHORT TALKS WITH THE DEAD
    HILLS AND THE SEA
    THE PATH TO ROME
    ON ANYTHING
    ON NOTHING
      ETC.

Novels:

    BELINDA
    THE MISSING MASTERPIECE
    SHADOWED
    THE HAUNTED HOUSE
    THE EMERALD
    THE GIRONDIN
    THE GREEN OVERCOAT
      ETC.

General:

    THE CRUISE OF THE NONA
    AVRIL
    THE FOUR MEN
    THE CONTRAST
    ESTA PERPETUA
      ETC.

Poetry:

    VERSES 1910
    SONNETS AND VERSES 1923

Children's Books:

    BAD CHILD'S BOOK OF BEASTS
    MORE BEASTS FOR WORSE CHILDREN
    A MORAL ALPHABET
    CAUTIONARY TALES
      ETC.

Religious:

    HOW THE REFORMATION HAPPENED
    SURVIVALS AND NEW ARRIVALS
    EUROPE AND THE FAITH
      ETC.

RICHELIEU
By Philippe de Champaigne
In the Louvre

RICHELIEU

A STUDY

BY

HILAIRE BELLOC

WITH 7 ILLUSTRATIONS
AND 4 MAPS

PHILADELPHIA & LONDON
J. B. LIPPINCOTT COMPANY
MCMXXIX

COPYRIGHT 1929
BY HILAIRE BELLOC

MADE IN THE
UNITED STATES
OF AMERICA

First Printing, October, 1929
Second Printing, November, 1929
Third Printing, November, 1929
Fourth Printing, December, 1929

TO THE MEMORY OF MY FRIEND
JAMES MURRAY ALLISON
WITH WHOM I TRAVELLED THROUGH
THE SITES OF RICHELIEU'S LIFE

INTRODUCTORY

A BOOK must have a title, and to-day it must have a succinct title; therefore this book appears as *Richelieu*. But that name might serve, not for one book, but for a library of books. One great scholar has filled volumes with the detail of the Cardinal's administrative work alone; another has produced in two vast tomes a study of his Coadjutor. In every language of Europe there are monographs upon one aspect or another of the man who so affected Christendom and remade it. Of textbooks giving all the main facts and dates of his life in outline there are perhaps two hundred; and of views upon him and criticisms and the rest, an innumerable host.

In the study to which these words are a preface, I am dealing with one matter only, but a matter of supreme importance, and one which the bulk of our contemporaries have allowed to fall into the background or have even ignored. It is by far the greatest consideration attaching to that very great name. It is the permanent deflection of Europe from his time to ours, into a state which leaves Christians divided doubly: which has broken Christendom into a mosaic of nationalities: which has erected the worship of nationality into a religion usurping the ancient religion whereby Europe came to be: and which has left a line of cleavage between the Catholic and the Protestant culture which has become a gulf increasing before our eyes.

To make clear that this was the effect of his legendary application, of his inhuman toil, that this was his success and that therefore through him came the corresponding failure of religious and cultural unity, is the business of my writing here. To explain it I have to consider the man and his surroundings, but all these are subordinate to that main issue. We are what we are, so divided and in peril of dissolution through our division, because Richelieu applied his remote, his isolated, his overpowering genius to the creation of the modern state, and, unwittingly to himself, to the ruin of the common unity of Christian life.

In the pursuit of that task I necessarily exclude a thousand details. I attempt no chronicle, but little portraiture, and I exclude what in most historical writing I would particularly enhance, the vital elements of colour, landscape, garment, gesture, feature, and all the matter of physical environment.

Were men to-day sufficiently aware of the chaos into which Christendom has fallen, such a study would be superfluous. Were their attention directed to the truth that this one man's will lies at the origin of the misfortune, this study would be but one of many. I issue it only that it may fill its place. If it be objected to me that one man can have had no such effect alone, I agree, as a matter of course. Innumerable factors combine in the inextricable complexity of our general story. One man, even the greatest, does but his part; nor is there any intelligence sufficient to estimate the proportion of that part. But it is true that the will of man directs the fate of man, collectively as well as individually, and it is true that in the perilous rapids which lie before us the will which we must consider as lying at their origins is the will of Richelieu. To exaggerate its effect is an error, but an error on the right side; for to give him but one place among many equals, as is commonly done, is to misunderstand the scale of his achievement.

H. BELLOC
King's Land
Shipley
Horsham
Sussex

CONTENTS

FIRST PART

THE NATURE OF THE ACHIEVEMENT

I	Richelieu the Founder of Modern Europe	17
II	Richelieu and Bismarck	31
III	The Political Circumstance: Domestic	46
IV	The Political Circumstance: Foreign	68
V	The Person and Character	87
VI	The Surrounding Figures	109

SECOND PART

THE PROCESS OF THE ACHIEVEMENT

I	The Approach	145
II	Find, Check, and Kill	185
III	The Valtelline	207
IV	La Rochelle	237
V	The Day of Dupes	267
VI	Gustavus Adolphus	318
VII	The Final War	350

THIRD PART

THE EXIT

373

ILLUSTRATIONS

RICHELIEU   FULL LENGTH   *Frontispiece*
      BY PHILIPPE DE CHAMPAIGNE, 1602-1674
      In the Louvre

RICHELIEU   IN BERETTA   78
      AFTER MICHEL LASNE
      Reproduced from Hanotaux

RICHELIEU   THE TRIPLE PORTRAIT   86
      BY PHILIPPE DE CHAMPAIGNE
      In the National Gallery, London

RICHELIEU   HEAD   88
      FROM A DRAWING BY CLAUDE MELLAN, 1598-1688
      Stockholm

RICHELIEU IN 1635   SEATED   92
      BY PHILIPPE DE CHAMPAIGNE
      In Musée Condé, Chantilly

PRESENTATION OF RICHELIEU TO HENRI IV   154
      FROM THE PAINTING BY GIUSEPPE AURELI

THE TOMB OF RICHELIEU IN THE SORBONNE   384
      BY FRANÇOIS GIRARDON, 1630-1715

MAPS

THE VALTELLINE AND THE PASSES OF THE ALPS   209

THE VALTELLINE   211

ENVIRONS OF LA ROCHELLE   244

FIELD OF THE EXPLOITS OF GUSTAVUS ADOLPHUS   318

FIRST PART

THE NATURE OF THE ACHIEVEMENT

I

RICHELIEU THE FOUNDER OF MODERN EUROPE

A MAN surveying Europe to-day discovers this strange anomaly: it is one great culture, yet it is at deadly issue with itself. It is still precariously what, for so long, it was triumphantly—the head of the world; yet it has within it principles of disruption which have already shaken it sorely and may destroy it at last.

Two great causes of such disruption are present within the body of Europe—the body which our forefathers better named "Christendom."

The first—the foundational and the most powerful source of internal conflict—is the division of this society into two sharply opposed cultures—the original Catholic culture and the more lately erected Protestant. Between these the Occident is torn by the action of a mutual contempt, making each sure of final triumph and, what is more dangerous, a smouldering not always conscious hatred; the worse because silence is kept upon its true sources.

But the second cause of disruption is also of great and fatal power: it may be called the religion of patriotism: the worship of the Nation as the supreme object of affection: the sacrifice of general unity to local feeling.

The tone and character of every society proceed ultimately from its philosophy, that is, its religion. When Europe was united before the catastrophe of the sixteenth

century, before the shipwreck of Christendom, one religion inspired the soul of the West. The central doctrine of that religion was the Incarnation; its custodians,
interpreters and agents were the hierarchy in communion
with the Apostolic See, supreme in Rome; its high
ritual was the Mass, whose mysteries, perpetually performed, inspired the general body of Christian men
with the actual presence of God their Saviour. The common creed and practice bred a common mood throughout society; and Europe, though long possessed of strong
local attachments, various languages and customs, remained essentially one.

Upon the ruin of that unison at the Reformation, there
succeeded (since men must worship something) a new
mystical enthusiasm—the adoration of one's country.

This new religion matured slowly; it was long modified by memories of the old European fellowship, it only
came to its extremes of ecstasy in quite modern times.
It began rather as a devotion to a Prince than to a
Nation; it proceeded to develop into an ardour for one's
own surroundings, thence in its last phase it became the
exalted service of an imaginary personality or idol representing one's country, and accompanied, after the
fashion of all religions, with ceremony, ritual and in-
violable symbols.

To-day, or at any rate in the generation immediately
preceding the Great War, this hitherto unknown exclusive worship, this idolatry of the nation, filled all
men's minds.

In the name of patriotism men were ready to persecute ruthlessly such of their compatriots as seemed luke-warm or capable of a divided allegiance; they were even ready to destroy wholesale their fellow members of Europe organised under other groups. The right of this new religion to men's complete allegiance was unquestioned. The very same men who were foremost in condemning the absolute claims of Christian doctrine in the past, and of a great Christian society defending itself against heretical anarchy from within, were the first to take it for granted that they might, with a quiet conscience, root out those who were heretic in the religion of Nationalism.

More than that: men allowed themselves at last to be driven by the million into the most dreadful conditions of suffering and isolation and slaughter, protracted over more than four years: they were willing to undergo torments of which the human race had hitherto known nothing—rather than be branded heretics to the religion of Nationalism.

From these two elements of disruption, the break-up of Christendom into two cultures—Catholic and Protestant; the new religion of Patriotism (each province of Europe preferring itself to the very life of Europe) proceeds, I say, our present doubt whether Europe shall survive, or whether we shall not shortly lose those achievements of ours, which made of Christendom not only the master but the tutor of the whole world. It is in doubt whether we be not beginning to slip into barbarism.

A single will, far more than other conscious force—one man far more than other man—lay, without know-

ing it, at the origin of this our present condition. One
man more than any other man, and more than any impersonal force (out of so many forces at work) both
founded Nationalism, and made permanent the division
between the Catholic and the Protestant culture. That
man was Armand-Jean du Plessis, Cardinal de Richelieu.

Two centuries later, after the ferment had worked to
a climax, another man of equal genius entered upon the
European scene, confirmed, emphasised, hardened,
seemed to render eternal that mortal division between
the two cultures—Catholic and Protestant—and also to
exaggerate almost to madness, in his victims and his subjects, the self-worship which we call patriotism to-day.
The name of this second great operator in the disastrous
affair was, Otto von Bismarck.

It is the purpose of these pages to examine what kind
of man Richelieu was who achieved, largely in spite of
himself, so vast a thing: to examine as well as may be,
his character and nature, the circumstances which favoured his actions, the obstacles surmounted; also, at
the outset, to consider the strange parallel between himself and Bismarck, his successor who confirmed the
work.

I propose to describe the circumstances under which
Richelieu worked when he produced and realised the
centralised nation of to-day; to portray as best I may the
man himself; to follow in separate episodes the steps by
which he did so great a thing as the establishment of a

powerful Protestantism in Europe, on the one hand, and, on the other, the making of the modern state.

I shall attempt this description of his action not as a chronicle, but wholly in reference to the soul that was at work, and particularly bearing in mind, for myself, as for my readers, this dreadful truth: that what men of such stature achieve is never confined to their original intention but increasingly exceeds it. For little men may plan out their successes and more or less conclude the programme to their own satisfaction during their little lives, and according to their own little desires. Those who are used as instruments for the vaster modification of mankind, as they are on another scale, so are they also more condemned to blindness. They work, as it were, in the summits of darkness. Nor is it they who work, but something other which drives them.

Of this sort are the men who change the destinies and the very mind of our race. Of this sort are those who, more often by writing, sometimes by arms, more rarely but more powerfully by statesmanship, and once or twice perhaps (most powerfully of all ways) by mere example, transform the world. Of this sort are their achievements: not their own.

So to present a great man and to attribute the mightiest consequences to the personal action of one human being may seem exaggerated and may need apology.

It is, or rather was, until recently, a universal habit, in the treatment of history, to belittle the effect of the individual. That habit remains strong.

It was a habit proceeding in part from reaction against

an earlier exaggeration of historic figures. This exaggeration had proceeded from the profound error of Comte, a philosopher of much wider indirect effect than most men recognise to-day. Comte in that Religion of Humanity of his, (which was unconsciously adopted by liberal thought throughout Europe during the nineteenth century) had deliberately proposed men of power as a sort of substitute for the gods. He judged that men would be ready to worship their fellow beings (that is, to worship themselves magnified) and he judged aright.

I say that the belittlement of individual effect upon history was largely a reaction against this element in Comte's system. A whole literature arose, interpreting history in terms of "great men." In this country its wildest devotee was Carlyle, and if his effect was so great that can only have been because men were in a mood to receive it. For Carlyle was not of the sort who moulds opinion: he followed it. But the vogue could not stand. Of a hundred names prominent in a period it was soon discovered that ninety-nine were well known by nothing more than some trick of advertisement, birth, or wealth or other luck. Even the hundredth, manifesting initiative and genius, was mortal in reputation as in flesh. The hero, of no matter what stature, when soberly examined, turned out to be a man—not a God; and, men being a fallen race, the hero must turn out to have much in him both vicious and ridiculous.

Such was the first reason for suspecting the rôle of great men in human events. But much more than any reaction against Comte, was the effect of physical science

—that great triumph of the nineteenth century—in belittling the action of individuals upon humanity and its destiny.

The conquests of physical science were due to minute and extensive observation conducted by vast numbers of men, and therefore, for the most part, by the unintelligent. Science attracted some few men of high culture and some even (much fewer) of strong reasoning power: but in themselves mere observation and comparison, the framing of hypotheses and the testing of them by experiment need no intellectual qualities above the lowest and are therefore an obvious occupation for those who despise or do not grasp the use of the reason. It has even been maintained that the ceaseless practice of exact measurement dulls the brain. At any rate, the business of modern physical science was not attached to, and became more and more divorced from, philosophy—and therefore from theology which is philosophy's guide.

But this, for the most part unintelligent, mass of observation, has led to astounding results. It has transformed the material side of human life. As a consequence, its prestige has risen prodigiously; its methods, conclusions, and much more, the moral atmosphere in which it works has affected every other art, and every other study; notably did it affect the spirit of history in the later nineteenth century.

Now these observations upon the workings of matter dealt with phenomena in which cause and effect appeared to be invariable, yet blind, and not immediately connected with any will.

On this account, the general story of mankind, the sequence of effects in which a particular nation was developed, the conduct and the consequences of great wars, the nature of great policies—all these—were studied through the minute examination of a vast quantity of independent facts, and under the prejudice that cause and effect would here, as in the material world, be inevitable in process and unaffected by immediate will.

There followed the depreciation of the individual human agent, and the conception that history was a process blind, necessary, and even mechanical. The individual appeared as no more than the product of things, and was, however vivid and distinct his action, but part of a universal process wherein he formed but a negligible and helpless fraction.

That this view was as false historically as were in philosophy the dogmas from which it sprang, the most superficial consideration of the past will be sufficient to show. It perpetually appears throughout history that one man achieves and is the true creator of a capital event. This event will not have the ultimate consequence he would have expected. He may have produced that event without any design beyond the immediate limits of his action, but produce it he did.

In military history the thing is glaring. The genius of Foch never expressed anything more truly or tersely than when he gave us the sentence: "It was not an army that crossed the Alps; it was Hannibal." The truth is equally apparent in every other form of human energy. The interest excited in us by the prospect of great genius may make us exaggerate the part which one will can play, but it is an error on the right side. We are safe in saying that in all notable achievements, but especially in the case of the highest, one man stands at their origin.

So it was with Richelieu. Here was a man blessed with certain opportunities without which, no doubt, he could not have acted; but, still, those opportunities weighed less than the obstacles he had to overcome.

See how things stood when he emerged. He appears, as he enters active life just after his twentieth year, upon a scene where any one of many diverse fortunes might have fallen upon Europe, and upon his own society.

For a hundred years Western Christendom had been the field of a devastating religious quarrel which had turned, during the last fifty, into one enormous civil war; a civil war which though springing from revolution in religion, was fed by opportunities for rapine, for sudden enrichment, for the satisfaction of revenge, of hatred, and of the mere lust for adventure and change which such a chaos could afford.

Meanwhile, in the midst of the chaos, a new formative principle is at work—that of nationality. Men after such a century of contradictory religious frenzies, are beginning to substitute the nation as an object of worship for the general culture inherited from the whole history of our race.

France, the particular nation into which this young man is born, has for its unifying principle, a long-established hereditary monarch for which all his fellow-citizens, even the rebels, feel at heart an instinctive loyalty, and which yet has been—for half a lifetime before his own advent, for forty years—the plaything or target of violent and confused rebellions.

Henry III, the last of a long line of kings (the Valois House) dies, assassinated in the presence of Richelieu's father while Richelieu is a baby. His successor can only be found in a distant cousin, (a Bourbon, Henry IV) who himself dies assassinated before Richelieu has completed his twenty-fifth year. The son and succeeding monarch, Louis XIII, whom Richelieu was himself to serve, is but a boy of eight at his accession on his father's murder, and grows up capricious, restricted and cold, hardly normal; there surround him a number of characters not one on a high level, whether in intelligence or morals. The most powerful is the Queen Mother, the Regent; the most dangerous, her favourites and those of the Boy King; the most disturbing the King's own brother Gaston, vivacious but incompetent, and (largely through the pressure of others) wrongly ambitious: treated always as the heir, eager to succeed, yet empty of policy and the puppet of his country's enemies.

All the first years of the new reign are taken up in the last and most violent religious rebellion against the French Crown, which, until Richelieu rose to permanent power, when the King was but twenty-three, seemed likely to submerge that monarchy.

Meanwhile, two great waves of reaction against those long years of disorder are flooding Europe.

First—and much the most important—is the reaction towards spiritual order: towards Catholicism. The ancient religion of Europe begins to reconquer the minds and therefore the policies of men, recovering from its lowest point, which it had reached some twenty years before Richelieu's birth, and daily recapturing province after province: not only provinces of territory but provinces of spiritual action. New and restored religious orders arise. The enthusiasm of the Capucins, the long, persistent, disciplined effort of the Jesuits begin to bear their fruits.

Second—second but very powerful, and more difficult for our time to comprehend—is the reaction towards monarchy, that is towards political order.

Allied with the reaction towards Catholicism, and closely intertwined with it (so closely that the two are sometimes hardly distinguishable) is the recovering power of the House of Hapsburg in its two branches. It seems overwhelming and destined to absorb into itself and dissolve the separate national feelings which have arisen. For in one branch (the House of Austria, with its capital at Vienna), its head, as Emperor, is in theory ruler over all the Germanies and over much wider territories still nominally attached to the Empire. In the other branch, that of the cousin monarchs of Spain, its head is unquestioned ruler of the Western Mediterranean, half the Italian lands, all the New World of the Americas. These two cousins between them, the King of Spain, the Emperor, dominate the world, (with minor districts and towns, such as Venice, the Papal States, the Scandinavian countries, etc.) all is Hapsburg: and though the Spanish half of the great house has proved

itself vulnerable at sea and has failed to reduce the Northern Netherlands yet it has still a mighty name, and in
particular, surrounds French territory in a ring of hostile
ground: by the Pyrenees.

Within the French monarchy are powerful forces—
the religious orders, the common religious feeling of the
people, the desire for authority and peace after prolonged
disorder—supporting the great Catholic reaction, and
there are many of the ruling families and more among
the officials who (commonly from petty motives) are
on the same side. But the great nobles are still half independent and the best captains among them, with armed
forces in the field, levy war upon the king. They act on
the anti-Catholic side, some sincerely Protestant, many
mere political rebels making religion their plea but all
with some national excuse for their attitude, because the
encircling power of the Spanish Hapsburgs all around
the French frontiers and the menace of the Austrian
Hapsburgs beyond to the east, stands for the ancient
creed of Christendom which Protestantism opposed.

Such was the confusion of interests and powers when
Richelieu arose.

Is it not clear that from such a welter, any one of many
diverse consequences might have flowed?

We might have had a Europe consolidated to-day once
again as a homogeneous Catholic thing—but under the
rule of one Hapsburg family. We might have had (less
probably) a Catholic Europe confederate of several provinces, but reared upon the extirpation of the heresies
which had threatened the very existence of civilisation.

We might have had, on the contrary, the triumph of extreme Nationalism throughout Europe long before its final date of development in our own time, and with it the destruction of Europe long ago. In connection with this we might well have had a new France turning rapidly Protestant, organised in feudal fashion under the great French Protestant nobles who were the best commanders and led the best armies in their time.

What *did* result, was not one of such various possibilities but the thing we know.

There resulted the check of the Catholic reaction just as it seemed bound to reconquer all the Germanies and to impose itself upon the mass of Europe.

There resulted, from that check onwards, the first decline of the imperial power and of the House of Austria, which decline continued uninterruptedly until the tragedy of the Great War in our own day.

There resulted the downfall of Spain; the wounding of that power; the bleeding of it; the final loss of the Northern Netherlands; of its passage down the Rhine basin; of its unquestioned power to the Mediterranean.

There resulted (at first the process was hidden), that decline in direct Spanish rule over the New World which was to end, two hundred years later, in its separation from Madrid and the establishment of the South and Central American Republics.

There resulted the saving, the strengthening, and the growth of the Protestant culture throughout all the North; the abandonment of Ireland; the first perils of Poland—which were later to lead to the murder of that

Catholic outpost; the beginnings of Prussia and the gradual absorption and control by Prussia of more than half the Germanies.

There resulted, above all, a new highly-organised modern nation in the midst of Europe, subject to one strong central monarchical power, reaching rapidly to the very summits of creative art in letters, architecture, painting, sculpture and military science, and forming a model upon which the new ideal of Nationalism should frame itself.

That new organised nation was France. The man who did all this was Richelieu. He was the man without whom these things would not have been. He it was who, by subordinating every other consideration to that of the monarchy he served (and therefore to the nation), consolidated all under the crown. He did so at home by tolerating religious differences in order to preserve national unity. He did so abroad by setting up Protestant power against the Hapsburgs. He it was who securely founded Protestant Europe by actively aiding the anti-Catholic forces of Germany and Sweden, used as allies against the temporal Catholic rivals of the French king. He it was who achieved directly, by his immediate will, the settlement of the seventeenth century, but also, in spite of his immediate will, the Europe of yesterday.

Through him modern Europe arose; until there came, two hundred years after Richelieu, to confirm its divisions, and to render apparently irreparable the schism in our culture, the corresponding genius of Bismarck.

II

RICHELIEU AND BISMARCK

WERE Plutarch to return he would find no better modern subject for a parallel of lives than those of Richelieu and Bismarck.

Each born in the nobility of his realm, each some distance from its highest ranks, each rose to be the chief in title.

Each served a dynasty, and each died leaving his crowned master at the very summit of power.

Each constructed and consolidated a realm, and each triumphed through a combination of diplomatic, political and military qualities.

Each left, as the immediate fruit of his genius, a great succeeding epoch: Richelieu, the "Siècle" of Louis XIV which directly inherited from his labours: Bismarck, that Prussian hegemony over Europe, and that rapid expansion in wealth and numbers of his "Reich" in which expansion was the salient political fact in Europe over almost as great a stretch of time as the glory of Louis XIV. For the "Grand Siècle," beginning about 1660, is in full decline by 1710, that is in fifty years; it faded out before sixty had passed. Bismarck's Prussian hegemony over Europe is apparent in 1866, fully established in 1871 and endures to near the end of the Great War in 1918.

But there is a significance in the juxtaposition of these two men far deeper than the resemblance of their careers.

For, as I have said, the one founded what the other completed. There is a succession between them, and the link of common agency in a mighty effect which the first had not foreseen nor the second directly designed, but to which both acted, the one as an originator, the other as a concluder, under the direction of powers far above human purpose. That mighty effect was the two-fold thing we have been watching: the emergence of Nationalism as a chief motive for action in men and the consequent or accompanying reduction of the Catholic culture to the defensive under the supremacy of anti-Catholic and mainly Protestant forces.

The united and organised French state, given as a model by Richelieu to the world, was followed by the complete moral unification of England through the extirpation of a Catholic religious minority therein and of the Stuart dynasty protecting it. This twin example of French and English Nationalism slowly affected all Europe. The new Russian state of Peter the Great derived from that example. The idea of Nationalism became familiar, though not yet of effect, in the divided Germany and Italy of the eighteenth century. Prussia became almost as much a nation as a system. The Scandinavian victories leave a similar heritage for Sweden. With the French Revolution that idea took fire and became the religion around us to-day, and, as an effect of it all, the mid-nineteenth century is full of "nations struggling to be free" in regions where such a conception has hitherto meant nothing. The modern Italy is formed.

Hungary asserts itself. The long established partition of Poland does but emphasise the Polish demand.

At last comes Bismarck, who with unique dexterity uses the new ideal to strengthen what would seem its very antithesis, the Prussian Crown and the domination of Berlin over the lesser units of the Northern and Central German peoples.

He creates an artificial nation so successfully that we have come to call it "Germany" within thirty years of his death, although its very principle is the denial of German unity and the exclusion from that "Germany" of whatever among Germans could outweigh the power of the Hohenzollerns. He relies upon this new Religion of Nationalism to inspire, give unity and life to what began as a mechanical and artificial arrangement. He amply succeeds; and the next generation will die gladly for their new "Reich," indifferent to the body of Germanism external to it. At the same time, by his treatment of the French after his victories over them, by his increased harshness to the conquered Poles, he inflames Nationalism to the east and to the west of his new frontiers.

In the concomitant reduction of Catholic influence the same process is apparent. Richelieu by his toleration of the wealthy and numerous Huguenot body renders familiar to the French mind the conception of religious division within the state and the continual adverse discussion of its established worship: hence the growth of the sceptics, the strength of their propaganda, the rise of the anti-clerical spirit, until the official dominance of the Catholic hierarchy in France and its privileges become an anomaly. The Revolution resolves the problem with violence. Acute moral division within the remaining Catholic culture of Europe becomes everywhere the rule, and Nationalism reinforces the quarrel. France after her defeats in 1870, the new Italy risen on the abandonment of the Papacy, foster the decline of the Church, its morals and spirit. Meanwhile, eighteenth-century Britain having extirpated Catholicism within her own boundaries, reduces Catholic Ireland to servitude; Holland is confirmed as a permanent power keeping under its rule a large Catholic minority. Turn where you will in Europe, when this process was in full power during the nineteenth century, you find everywhere in the Catholic provinces profound moral dissension, in the non-Catholic the rule or supremacy of hostile powers over Catholic minorities; never the reverse.[1]

Bismarck put the crown upon the edifice. He divided the Catholic forces of the Germans, swept into his net so much of the Catholic body as would cripple the rest without being large enough to endanger the moral mastery of their opponents. To the historical ideas and general culture of Protestant Prussia that Catholic body gradually conformed, so that now the Reich, with a third of its people Catholic, counts as a Protestant power;

---

[1] A belated example of this system, probably the last we shall witness, was the precarious erection of the "Six Counties in Ireland." There, by careful calculation, a Catholic minority was cut off and left subservient to alien rule; a Catholic minority withdrawn from the support of its fellows in the rest of Ireland and made as large as was compatible with the maintenance of its subjection and impotence.

the name "German" has come to connote such a power,
and the fact that one half of German speaking families
are of the old religion is lost, in effect, upon the modern
world.

Thus may we follow the way in which the work of
these two men followed and completed the one the
other. The parallelism and the succession are apparent.

But the contrast also must be noted; the contrast in
character and the contrast in the respective advantages
and disadvantages which aided and hindered them.

In physical appearance that contrast is glaring. No
two figures are more opposed than the square, full
blooded, blunt face of the one, the pointed chin and
finely cut, pale features of the other; the subtle fire and
readiness to restrain or spring which Richelieu's face con-
veys, the deceptive mask of brute simplicity which covers
Bismarck's. The bodies are in similar opposition. It is
the Ox and the Leopard.

In the one, Bismarck, the supple spirit is hidden under
an external directness and rough assertion which are
not all put on, but derive, in part, from the blood of East
Elbe squires. In the other a spirit as supple is expressed
in every restrained gesture and in slight movements and
glances of an exquisite delicacy. It has been said that the
one might be likened to strong ale, the other to a rare
brandy. It may be so to the taste, superficially, but in
effect, in the nourishment of a political plan, both were
like a profound and rich wine. There appears in the one
no visible reserve at all; in the other all seems reserve.

But, in truth, both were exercising with full power all the interior discipline required to achieve his full effect.

The advantages in common to both were many. There was for both the continued support of a royal master whom each so devotedly served. There was the incompetence of that master (a negative quality very valuable to a servant). There was also the recognition by that master of his own incompetence (a positive quality more valuable still). Both enjoyed good fortune at critical moments, but Bismarck more than Richelieu. For Richelieu created his own success in every crisis—as for instance, on the famous "Day of Dupes," or again at Casale; while Bismarck had sheer luck time after time. Thus Bismarck was able to use Bavaria at will because the King of Bavaria was mad, and Bismarck had, without having to manœuvre for it, the neutrality of Britain; while Richelieu could count on no neutrality he had not himself engendered, and all his allies were on the alert for their own ends.

Both possessed an incomparable secret service which each had to create. Both had ample resources, though these could only be obtained by Richelieu at the expense of difficult and excessive taxation. Each stood in geographical situations central for his time, and each was aided by the increase of mechanical invention and science during his period of action.

Both had the service of good subordinates, but Richelieu had here far greater fortune than Bismarck. For Richelieu had ready to hand a whole group of competent and devoted men like Charnacé, and, above all the invaluable inspiration of Joseph du Tremblay, while Bismarck had no lieutenant worthy of his great task. Both managed to preserve their loyalty and service unbroken through all the useful years of life.

Of common disadvantages there were many. Both had to deal with jealousies at Court, though this in Richelieu's day was a far more powerful obstacle than it was in the nineteenth century.

Both had to meet severe domestic opposition, both were hampered by religious and political differences in the area they intended to consolidate.

Both were condemned to considerable periods of apprenticeship and delay.

In other disadvantages they differed. Bismarck had the high advantage of physical health—at least, in all the active part of his career, while Richelieu was an invalid suffering more and more as the years drew on. Bismarck was secure in one frontier and could make reliance on Russia, the corner stone of his building. Richelieu was secure in none, but spent his life repelling and overcoming a ring of hostile forces.

Richelieu had to create from nothing and against fierce opposition, the naval and military instruments of his policy; and each was doubtful in quality. Bismarck needed no navy and had inherited a superb instrument of war in the Prussian army, with traditions of two centuries behind it. To this great gift of fortune he owed those two dazzling campaigns against Austria and France, which established his power, as by magic, in four short years.

But while Bismarck had over Richelieu the very great advantage of immediate, overwhelming military success, with all the moral prestige it gives, and all the material power, he had one very bad handicap from which the Cardinal was free: he had to work under a secret divorce between his real and his ostensible aim.

Richelieu was impeded by no such spiritual chasm in his road. He openly desired the unity of his country, the strength of its central government, the attainment of its natural frontiers, the toleration of its religious divisions, the suppression, however, of a religious "State within the State."

In the details of Richelieu's diplomacy there was, of course, as there is in the details of all diplomacy, a great measure of insincerity. In order to over-reach his opponents he had continually to be pretending to desire this or that when he was really desiring something else. He had continually to be presenting to allies their supposed advantage when really he was following the advantage of his own people. He had, as have all such, to master enmity, foreign and domestic, by strategy as well as by force.

But all that sort of duplicity is an essential in any handling of men by methods other than direct authority. It remains true that, on the large lines Richelieu could afford to be sincere, Bismarck could not; and to be compelled to insincerity in the large lines of your action is a heavy burden, a large tax upon energy. Bismarck had to appeal to the strong German desire for racial unity when all the while his whole effort was aimed at the destruction of that unity for the aggrandisement of one section over the rest, and for the service of Prussia alone. Again, from that fact that the military instrument was so essential to him, Bismarck, upon what was perhaps the most important point in the whole of his policy, allowed himself to be overruled. Richelieu was never overruled.

Bismarck was overruled in the matter of Metz.

He had proposed to draw the new frontiers, after the victories of 1870, so as to include whatever was, (much as it detested Prussia) German-speaking (and in social life and custom German) upon the eastern frontiers of Napoleon III's Empire. He would have taken all Alsace, but of Lorraine only the German-speaking portion. He would have left Metz unannexed, and still attached to the French culture of which it forms a part. For Metz in 1871 was as French as Canterbury is English. Its architecture, its social custom, its civic language (allowing, of course, for the fact that many German-speaking people from a few miles away would come into the town) were all French; and indeed, there is no more striking example (within my experience at least) of the power of the modern state, with its crushing machinery of universal compulsory education, than the transformation of Metz into a German-speaking town. I have myself seen the process going on decade by decade during my own lifetime, and it has been of absorbing interest. For here you now have a population transformed in fifty years. Metz is to-day in the main German-speaking and reading its papers in the German tongue, yet inheriting social traditions wholly French and living in houses and worshipping in churches as French in spirit and design as those of Amiens and Beauvais.

Well, it was a fact that Bismarck allowed his wisdom to be overruled by the folly of the generals which ultimately led to the German disasters after his death. For though the proposition may be vehemently denied, I cannot but judge (for my part) that if Metz had been left French and the Prussian annexation in Lorraine had been confined to the purely German-speaking districts, time would have consolidated these with the rest of the Reich; and this, even when we have allowed for the incapacity of the Prussian official to govern. For he suffers, as do most good administrators, from a singular insuccess in ruling; ruling is based upon persuasion but administration upon mechanical order.

Now in nothing of such importance was Richelieu ever overruled. He was not overruled for instance, in the matter of Catalonia. It is due to him that the southeast of France has its frontier at the Pyrenees. He would not give rein to the dangerous jingoism which wished to stretch beyond the mountains, and it was through his influence that, long after his death, the Treaty of the Pyrenees established natural defensible frontiers for France.

He was not overruled in the matter of the left bank of the Rhine. He suffered sharply in taking the decision to restrain French influence there, and to restrict it to the frontiers of his choosing. He did not so decide until after consultation with Père Joseph, and perhaps at the suggestion of that other; but he was not overruled by that other.

He was not overruled in the matter of Gustavus Adolphus. He did not get all that he wanted, nor had he previously been able to get all he wanted, for he could not get the Swedish captain (any more than he had previously been able to get the Danish King) to work with the Catholic League. He had to take second or third best; but he had not to suffer the imposition of another will.

With that word "will" I am led to one last consideration upon these problems, which is not only curious but important to their comprehension. I have said that Bismarck's fatal decision in the case of Metz was due to his being overruled by the Army. Was there not behind that submission some defect of the will?

I think there was. Among the many and sometimes violent contrasts between these two strangely parallel lives, you find a contrast in moral texture which extends to the region of the will. Bismarck's will had not that incisive, rapier quality, that quality of highly tempered steel—flexible, unbreakable, of mortal effect, decisive, a sword—which had Richelieu's. Bismarck's will had rather the quality of a crowbar, sometimes to be used as a bludgeon. In the government of self, Bismarck's will broke down from time to time, as Richelieu's never did; and, after all, the government of self is the supreme test of will. Bismarck quarrelled, often foolishly, in private matters; under rebuff he was even peevish. I am not suggesting that his will was not strong: it was very strong;

and the metaphor I have used of the crowbar and the bludgeon does not suggest weakness. But it lacked temper. Of Richelieu I think you may say that it was the most highly tempered will in modern history.

But on another side of character Bismarck seems to have had the advantage. I hope I shall not be called paradoxical if I say that in the mere use of the *intelligence* he would seem to be somewhat the superior of Richelieu.

Richelieu's judgments upon men and situations were excellent, his political maxims were wise. He admirably adapted himself to his needs. But I cannot help observing, in sayings of his which are authentic, and even now and then in deeds, a certain narrowness of thought— perhaps the inevitable result of so much concentration. With Bismarck, when the intelligence alone is at work, you are watching an instrument of somewhat more general power.

I come to a last consideration in my comparison of these two: the permanence of the structure built by each.

The permanence of his achievement is perhaps an unjust test of greatness in a man; but inevitably we ephemeral creatures born to an immortal destiny turn to permanence as a measure of success. We can but ask "has the work lasted?" The boundaries of Diocletian define ecclesiastical dioceses and civil provinces to this day. The calendar alone is a testimony to Cæsar. The commandments of Mohammed are still obeyed from the Atlantic to the China seas—and we judge by such things.

It might be said of both men that at first sight their

achievement was not of lasting quality. The absolute monarchy which Richelieu erected crashed, to all appearance, in less than 150 years, and the supremacy of the Hohenzollerns over the new state which Bismarck called into existence was destroyed in less than sixty.

But these failures are only apparent. The real work of both men has proved far more enduring. How long that of Bismarck may survive we cannot tell, but it is fair to say that after it had stood firm through the better part of a lifetime its essentials have so far survived the mortal ordeal of the Great War. Bismarck's Reich may well prove to have taken root strong enough for indefinite duration. I will discuss this in a moment.

The Hohenzollerns have disappeared, perhaps permanently, but the Reich remains. And its specific character, its essential (which is the subordination of a large Catholic minority to a government centred in anti-Catholic Berlin) is as apparent to-day as it was fifty years ago.

In the same way the achievement of Richelieu was the consolidated unity of the French people and not even the destruction of the Capetian monarchy has, as yet, appreciably affected that result. It is not time, therefore, to say that the work of either of these great men has been undone.

But there are present in the achievement of each certain forces which, if they continue uninterrupted and increase in power, will destroy either or both creations.

In the case of Bismarck's creation, the destructive act would be the union of the German race. Even a loose federation would be sufficient to undo Bismarck's work. The inclusion of the Germans of the Middle Danube and of those of the Alps into the same federal system as has hitherto been confined to the Germans of the Rhine, the Upper Danube and the Northern plains, would be the dissolution of Bismarck's achievement. It would restore the old balance which he destroyed; it would restore the German Catholic culture; it would create at least three centres of energy, upon the Danube, upon the Rhine and in the Northern plains, instead of leaving all dependent, as at present, on one pole in Berlin. It would probably reawaken that age-long instinct of the German people for separate local systems and for a sort of tribal diversity. But that union of the Germans has not happened yet and it may not happen at all.

As for Richelieu's achievement, what would destroy it would be a pushing of the religious quarrel among the French to such a limit that either the sentiment of national unity should disappear, or the Catholic culture itself should perish from the land. To-day such an extreme seems impossible, but there are already apparent the symptoms of some such possible catastrophe. We have in these last few years seen the hatred of the Catholic Church among its organized enemies in France preferred to the financial and political security of the country. We have seen it nearly ruin the attachment of Alsace and destroy, in a brief ten years, the enthusiasm of the recovered province for its old comrades. We have seen the financial stability of the country grievously endangered by men who are chiefly concerned with the suppression of the religious orders because they know that the religious orders are the strongest force for preserving and protecting the Catholic faith; and daily we can perceive compulsory state instruction in the schools eradicating from the mind of the French masses the roots of the Catholic culture. Now with the loss of that culture France will cease to be what, historically, we have known. The effects are already beginning to show in French architecture—which is growing repulsive—and in French prose—which is growing turgid. Such ulcers point to causes deeply affecting the whole body of society.

It would be a strange Nemesis, in the case of either Bismarck or Richelieu, if such a fate should fall upon their work. It would be a piece of historic irony of the first class, for it would be the destruction of a man's edifice by his own instruments of construction. What was Bismarck's chief moral instrument in erecting his "Reich"? Why, of course, the cry of "German unity." And yet the one thing most perilous for his work would be the restoration of a real German unity.

What was Richelieu's guiding principle in the attainment of an indivisible France? It was the permission of deep religious cleavage in the French nation as the price to be paid for preserving that political union by which, as he thought, the national soul could be alone (and sufficiently) preserved.

In the one case as in the other, what may undo all the builder did is the very moral force he originally relied on.

III

THE POLITICAL CIRCUMSTANCE DOMESTIC

THE circumstance under which Richelieu lay in his public action consisted in two great departments, a domestic and a foreign: first, the rebellion against the French Crown at home; secondly, the pressure upon the French Crown abroad, through the power of the House of Hapsburg, which surrounded it on every side. The rebellion against the French Crown at home was aristocratic in motive, religious in colour. Its main driving motive was the desire of the nobility, especially of the greater nobles, to enfranchise themselves from the central power of the King—that is, from popular government: for the King of France stood, of course, for the people. Its complexion was Calvinist.

The nobles desired thus to enfranchise themselves to the utmost from the power of the King, partly because it would give added power to themselves, more because it would give them greater wealth. Their action was part of that action which their fellows had taken all over Europe—in Germany, in the Netherlands, in England, in Scotland, and which everywhere had been the appetite supporting the Reformation. Their atmosphere was that of the violent religious enthusiasm which imagined that, in the ruins of Christendom it could erect some ideal, though terrible, new Europe.

This twin force had desolated France for a lifetime;

46

the wars it had provoked had ended, not in a victory for either side, but in a compromise, of which Henry IV, originally a Huguenot leader and a great rebel noble, afterwards converted to Catholicism and legitimate king, was, by his dual fate, the symbol.

Henry IV represented that truce, I say, and after his death, with his son Louis XIII a minor—indeed, a child —only nine years old—the menace reappeared. The great nobles were about to make war once again on the King of France, and with that rebellion was to be mixed up the Calvinist religion, because in the truce for which Henry IV stood, the Calvinists, that is the great rebel nobles, had been, by the Edict of Nantes, left half independent, a state within the state, permitted to hold strong cities, to summon parliaments of their own, and to rule themselves, largely independent of the monarchy.

It lay with any one man who should be faced with this problem to decide which of two policies he might adopt. He might concentrate upon the salvation of French culture and therefore of the Catholic faith in France; he might even, with a more exalted view, concentrate upon the Catholic faith throughout Europe by the action of France, and make it his chief business to attain religious unity. To do that was to risk the monarchy. It was to play "all out." It was to challenge every fierce opponent of the throne: not only the political power of the great nobles and their wealth, their armament, their independent jurisdiction, their retainers, but also the moral power of the sincere Calvinists, of whom there were many hundreds among the smaller nobility, a few perhaps among the greater, thousands among the lawyers and merchants, and hundreds of thousands among the yeomen, the better class artisans, and the lesser professions.

He might do that. He might take up the full Catholic cause and play the hazard: he might aim at a double victory, the salvation of the monarchy in France and the complete success of Catholicism throughout Europe—a result difficult indeed to obtain: or he might concentrate upon the salvation of the French monarchy *only,* and lighten the task by throwing overboard the attempt to achieve a complete Catholic victory.

Richelieu—as might have been predicted of such a man and of such a character—decided for the second policy, and pursued it all his life. To the Huguenot as rebel, to all rebels whether Huguenot or not, he was ruthless. To the Huguenot as privileged and therefore forming a state within the state he was an implacable enemy. He would allow no such division of temporal power. To the Huguenot as a great noble with a sort of sovereignty over his own land (hitherto possessed throughout French territory after a fashion unknown in England) he was a determined master and debaser. But to the Huguenot as a man destroying the moral unity of Europe—and the moral unity of France at that—to the Huguenot as a schismatic and a heretic, to the Huguenot as a man breaking up spiritual, but not immediately breaking up political, society, he was wholly indifferent. On that side he proposed to secure the unity of the kingdom by a complete toleration.

Let us note here the contradiction between the policy in England and in France, and the causes of that difference.

In England, where there had been no popular movement against the Catholic Church, where a Reformation settlement was imposed with difficulty upon a reluctant people, and with every precaution not to push it too far, one fixed principle guided first of all the Cecils (William and Robert, father and son), and after them their successors the spokesmen of the rich nobles and the merchants until the end of the seventeenth century. That fixed principle was the achievement of moral unity for the English state through the destruction of the Catholic Church therein.

The Cecils first, during their long reign (1559-1612) reduced, by government action, by slow relentless official pressure, horrible but unremitting persecution, torture, mutilation, financial ruin and death, those who sympathised in any degree with the traditional national religion. From the great majority which they were throughout most of the reign of Elizabeth, they fell to something like half the nation at the accession of James I. Later on the class of squires and great merchants who ruled England continued the extirpation of Catholicism and those who sympathised with it were fallen to be but a quarter or less of the nation under Charles II and his brother. At last in 1688 their triumph was complete. A violent effort spread over a century and a half had torn up by the roots the traditional religion of the English, and the nation entered the eighth century, a homo-

geneous strongly anti-Catholic nation with no more than
a remnant of alien distracted and divided Catholics in
its midst, who were shortly to sink to a negligible and
wholly cowed fraction of less than one-hundredth of the
people.

The original motive of this tenacious policy upon the
part of the Cecils was the preservation of the loot their
class had seized from the endowments of the Church,
monastic and secular. That class, of which the Cecils
were the spokesmen, had seized all the monastic lands,
nearly all the hospitals and other charitable and educational foundations, and much of the endowment attached to bishoprics, colleges and even parish clergy.
Thus the natural leaders of any rebellion against the
artificial government eradication of Catholicism had
been bribed by the loot, and their interest was to stand
aside. Therefore the popular rebellions against that policy, vigorous and courageous though they were, in Kent,
Sussex, Devon, Cornwall, Norfolk and Suffolk, Oxfordshire, Nottinghamshire and in general the Midlands,
found no support in the only class which could have led
them to victory, and when the last great effort was made
in the North, the Midlands and South having been
beaten flat by wholesale execution—notably through the
Russels—though leaders of the gentry were to be found,
they were not to be found in sufficient numbers, and the
Cecils put down that last rising of the English people
in a fashion so thorough that none other has been known
since.

But in France it was quite otherwise. In France there

had been no dissolution of the monasteries, nor any general loot of church land, because a bargain, much to be blamed but existent, a bargain purely political in motive, had been driven before the height of the Reformation storm was reached between the King of France and the Pope.

By that bargain (called the Pragmatic Sanction) the King nominated as he willed to bishopric and abbacy and the rest. He could hold at will or cause his favourites or bastards or relatives to hold for life, the main part of the Church revenues *in commendam*. And while this produced in the wealthier French classes an angry motive to possess themselves of the loot which their brethren in England and North Germany had acquired, it left the Crown free to pursue the old national tradition of Catholicism and to be the natural head of the national resistance to religious change.

Therefore, while in England the Crown sank to be but the servant of the wealthier classes (so enormously enriched by the Reformation) and was at last conquered by it, in France the Crown survived. In France, the Crown not only survived by its successful struggle against the cupidity of the wealthier classes: it vastly increased in power. It had the people at its back. It did not fall into subservience to the nobles and the rich lawyers, but after a hard fight to maintain its position, a fight the victory in which was won by Richelieu, it became absolute.

Richelieu decided that the struggle to achieve *two* ends, to keep the Crown supreme and also to create

a moral homogeneity, such as had been created in England, would be too arduous, and too risky. He was content to destroy the political power of the great nobles
and to leave the nation divided in religion. He thought
political unity sufficient in spite of religious disunion to
secure the monarchy and the cohesion of the state.

He was half right and half wrong. He was right in
thinking that this policy would secure cohesion of the
state in all external things, and would create earlier than
was created elsewhere (much earlier than was created
in England) a centralised homogeneous nation—homogeneous in all temporal matters. He created the complete unison of France, and it has endured to our day.

But he deliberately sacrificed the ideal of a complete
moral unity such as England achieved. He left the seeds
of philosophic dissension vigorous in French soil.

When, half a lifetime after his death, Louis XIV tried
to found a united Catholicism and to uproot religious
discussion, it had taken too strong a hold. There followed the scepticism of the eighteenth century and the
rending religious quarrel of our own day, which, while
the external unity of the French people is preserved,
makes of them, in the things of the soul, and therefore
in fundamental character, a nation divided against itself.

It is essential to remember in our appreciation of
Richelieu's decision so to act—to leave France divided
against itself, to leave the seeds of disunion vigorous in
Europe, to permit what later became the ruin of our

common civilisation—that no man, whatever his diplomatic genius and foresight, can conceive the future.

At the moment in which he lived, the preponderance of tradition (and therefore of civilisation) seemed assured. The great monarchies—and that which he himself served—were the secure guardians of the time to be; and if he, to the scandal of contemporaries whose Christian instinct was more sound (though their intelligence was more confused) than his own, compromised with the sacred principle of unity by which things *are;* if he, in that much, betrayed Europe, he did not know that he was betraying. He thought that he was but preventing the absorption of French effort by a mixture of Spanish and German: that he was preserving one of the spiritual factors of Catholic Europe, and that the one factor to which he was in duty bound. That France could ever cease to be mainly Catholic was as remote from his conception as is from ours the picture of a world without America. It must further be remembered that there was, more illuminated, more inspired, and perpetually at his side, that great monk du Tremblay with whom I shall deal in a moment: a monk who dreamt of Crusades, and who could not conceive of Christendom without the Gallic sword.

There are further to be considered in the political circumstance which Richelieu found at home, three characters quite unfamiliar to our time. Justice and administration were but indirectly connected with government; the armed force of government was not permanent but occasional; the revenue of government from the *taxes* was not regular but capricious and exceptional.

In the modern state—at the origin of which Richelieu lies—we take the *opposites* of these characters for granted. Justice and administration are directly connected with whatever governs; the armed forces, police and military, form a large permanent body wholly subject to that which governs, a weapon which renders that which governs almost invincible; whatever revenue that which governs needs for its action is gathered as a matter of course, regularly and continuously, its amount is fixed by authority, the taxpayer has nothing to say to it, his only function is to pay.

In every highly organised large community to-day there is an all-powerful prince, whether his name be dictator, hereditary king, elected president, civic mayor, state governor, a complex of financial and political magnates or a ruling class. His or its will directly commands justice and administration, army and police, continuous annual taxation.

Three hundred years ago it was not so anywhere in Europe among the greater nations. It was Richelieu's task to originate those conditions in France and so to found the modern state; but, at the inception of this task, all was lacking to him. His overcoming of such difficulties is the monument of his genius.

Justice and administration were removed from direct control in three ways: First, the main legal courts, criminal and civil, were in the hands of corporations called *Parlements*,[1] of which by far the most powerful, affecting nearly half the kingdom, was the Parlement of Paris: Secondly, provinces were under the administration of great nobles called "governors" who had something like sovereignty over their districts, while below them lesser areas, in a confused mass, were subject to their lords: Thirdly, the social structure of the time, a remnant of feudalism, obstructed direct action by the central power; for even petty nobles had their retainers whom they could arm, while the greater ones could raise forces large enough to take the field, and the hereditary rights of the whole caste were deeply rooted.

The great lawyers of the French Parlements were also a caste, already becoming hereditary. In that agony for money which had afflicted all governments after the huge inflation of currency during the sixteenth century, the French Crown had (in 1604 when Richelieu was but nineteen) sold judiciary posts for an annual charge to the great lawyers and so made most of them hereditary: for a man could leave to his son the post and the duty of paying the corresponding annual charge. In

[1] The word is the same as our word "Parliament." A Parliament in Christendom meant originally "The king in conference with his nobles, judges and occasional representatives of the merchants and squires." Of that institution the legal side preserved the name in France, the nobles and squires assembled preserved it in England. Thus by the seventeenth century the word had narrowed down in France, to mean occasional gatherings of nobles, squires and merchants called the House of Parliament. There were eight Parlements at the beginning of Richelieu's power—the "eight pillars of the realm" as they called themselves—Paris, Bordeaux, Dijon, Rennes, Rouen, Toulouse: two more, Metz and Pau, were added by the middle of the seventeenth century.

practice the magistracy was none the worse and Richelieu knew its virtues well, for his mother was the daughter of such a high jurist; but in theory, both the sale and the inheritance of judicial power shocked Roman tradition. The legal caste so formed was learned and conscientious—but it could oppose the central power of the Crown. It could refuse to give statutory force to the King's taxes. It was a perpetual interference with his power. It could refuse to restrain by punishment those whom the prince desired to restrain. It could punish those whom he could absolve or leave undisturbed.

The power of the lawyers was not absolute—far from it. The King by exceptional action could compel them to do his will. But *normally* they could—and often did —act independently of him; and they were irremovable.

This exception in the unity of the state Richelieu never eliminated, as he did the others. The strengthening of government in all other ways, which he achieved, left the lawyers less daring: but they continued to be a caste and to resist the central power on occasions, right up to the Revolution.

Nor was Richelieu able to simplify the confused mass of lesser tribunals below, with their overlapping areas and claims to try cases: of Seneschalries, Bailiwicks, Court, Ecclesiastical, Maritime and Martial, Guild and professional jurisdictions. Here again—right up to the Revolution—*half* the business of the higher courts consists in deciding under which jurisdiction among the lesser courts a particular case might fall. (One of Robespierre's first briefs, 140 years after Richelieu's death, deals with a dispute of jurisdiction between an Abbot, a Bishop and a lay Lord). We may say that the failure to secure unity and simplicity of action in the matter of law was Richelieu's one (or chief) failure. But no one else could have succeeded.

For the rest, in administration, his work was thorough. He found administration submitted to half independent nobles small and great, with the noble governors of provinces formidable against the Crown. He left it an affair of "intendants," middle-class (and most efficient) civil servants of the Crown. Nominally envoys to observe or aid, really rivals to and with more real power than, the governors: who hated them but whom, in the royal name, they could override. It was these "intendants" who, in the next three generations, fixed on the face of France that stamp of monarchy which survives so strongly in the great public buildings, main roads and harbours of the seventeenth and eighteenth centuries. They survive in masonry and sculptured emblems everywhere.

Neither the name nor the office of intendant were of his creation: the name dates June 1551, thirty-four years before his birth, and the function (small and tentative) from the succeeding years. But it was Richelieu who made the intendants what they mean in French history, —great departmental salaried officials taking over the public works of a province—who increased their numbers and vastly increased their powers. His contemporaries judged rightly in identifying the new machinery with his name.

The standing army and navy of a modern state were equally his work. Throughout Europe armies, before his advent, were chance gatherings of men hired by the month or year, giving rise to an exceptional charge on the treasury during their incorporation, disbanded as soon (or sooner than!) their purpose had been accomplished. Europe was full of out-o'-works whose trade had been fighting. The religious wars had seen to that. But it had no Regulars, save little bodyguards about the kings, and here and there a few troops of horse.

It was from Richelieu that his successors inherited the idea of regular regiments, to be kept in being even during peace.

The same is true of the navy. There had been in England a certain number of "King's ships" at all times, but nothing like a regular fleet. In France there was not even the nucleus for such a thing. When Richelieu undertook the first struggles at sea, in connection with the Protestant rebellion, he had to hire ships from the Dutch and from England herself. It was not until his power was fully established that he began to create a true navy; but having once begun it, he left that also, like the army, as an inheritance to posterity, and he is the true creator of that force which held the sea, disputing the command of it for the next hundred and fifty years, until, after its success in detaching the American Colonies from England, it was destroyed by the Revolution.

It was indeed against the menace of Richelieu's newly created regular fleet that the Stuarts of England made their most gallant effort. Charles I had the wisdom to levy ship-money; his wealthy subjects the unwisdom to refuse or grudge it: that ship-money was the necessary price of a fleet which was vital to England in the presence of this new menace and which handed on its tradition to the navy of the Commonwealth. But a naval effort comparable to that which Richelieu undertook was not made upon this side of the Channel till much later, not even under the despotism of Cromwell, when the wealthier classes were silenced in their opposition to taxation by the dread of their chief representative who governed by brute force alone. The true beginnings of the English navy come later, and the creator of that force is James Duke of York, later James II, the great sailor and ardent defender of sea-power from whom, as the founder, British maritime policy has descended.

Thus to some extent in administration, though less in control over the courts of justice, Richelieu began the model of the modern state, making of the French Crown a true central government. Thus did he also act in the matter of his armed forces, without the control of which no modern government could act. But the necessary support of all this is a large and regular revenue from taxation, and it was the creation of *this* for the first time in Europe since the days of the pagan Empire that was Richelieu's most remarkable particular achievement in the general achievement of the Cardinal.

There is nothing, in the contrast between the Europe of the Middle Ages and the Renaissance, and the Europe of our own day, politically more striking than the contrast in the attitude of the public mind towards revenue. When the central government of the Roman Empire began to break down, its revenue, which was of the true modern type (that is, drawn from taxes which had been imposed upon the citizens without their having any say in the matter), and which was also of the true modern type in being stretched to the very limits of what it was possible to pay (and more), rapidly declined. In its place there arose in support of the local kings who had taken over the old Imperial Government great incomes drawn from rents on land. These incomes of the Kings were regarded as their private incomes, drawn from the rents of their private properties. Government after a few generations of this process was not regarded as a function which had any right to take part of a free man's revenue, but as a function which must be supported *out of its own endowment;* therefore through the Dark Ages and right on into the Middle Ages, it was taken for granted that the King ought to "live of his own." He had a vast *personal* revenue from his own lands, the lands of which he was direct lord, and from the feudal dues of his vassals and towns.

In times of exceptional strain, especially in times of royal wars, he would be compelled to ask for extra money, over and beyond this regular private income; but the "aids" so requested showed by their very name that they were regarded as exceptions. A tax everywhere remained, until the very beginning of the seventeenth century, an anomaly, and a sporadic thing. It was never taken for granted as regular and necessary. There was always the idea that it was a temporary strain, which should at last be relieved. Indeed, it was the impossibility of founding a regular system of taxation against the opposition of the wealthy which proved the undoing of the English monarchy. It was Richelieu's success at that same task which made the French monarchy supreme.

But the difficulties in the way of establishing the innovation were formidable, nor would it have been possible to have done it had not Richelieu begun by crushing the power of the richer families by force of arms and ended by being able to plead a great foreign war, during all his later years.

The chief difficulty was that in a country which had not felt the full effects of the Reformation the peasantry remained possessed of the land. They were subject to feudal rights, but not to competitive rent. Therefore any very great bulk of revenue, even when allowance had been made for feudal receipts from nobles and for very large grants by the Church, had to press heavily upon the whole mass of the people; and in nothing was the unpopularity of the Cardinal more emphasised than in the hatred the great mass of an agricultural population of small owners felt for his fiscal policy.

He left France with a regular revenue, and a large one—the French Crown possessed for good of that fundamental instrument. But he did so at the expense of crushing, not indeed out of economic existence but to anxiety and strain, the millions of small farmers upon whom the French state reposed.

There is here a notable difference between the revenue to be gathered from a capitalist industrial state,

such as is ours to-day, and a peasant state, such as was
that with which Richelieu had to deal. A capitalist industrial state can yield to the government a far larger
proportion of its total annual income than can a peasant
state. In a capitalist industrial state the great mass of the
so-called citizens are wage-slaves, who can pay no direct
taxation because they are already on the margin of living.
The surplus wealth of the community is in the hands of
a few, who can be fleeced of large percentages of their
incomes and still remain rich. But where a peasantry
retain in their own hands the bulk of the surplus wealth,
the proportion available is smaller. From a man with a
hundred thousand pounds a year employing five hundred men at two hundred a year, you may take half
his income and so get a revenue for the state of fifty
thousand. But distribute his surplus wealth among his
employees, and you will not get from that body of small
men at now four hundred a year half *their* incomes, nor
a quarter. The relative sacrifice in their case is too great.

Thus it is that the political custom of a regular revenue
acquired from imposed taxation, once it has taken root,
will leave the government of a peasant state, or any state
in which property is well divided, less powerful finan-
cially than the government of a country where wealth is
in few hands.

Richelieu originated that political custom. He re-estab-
lished after so many centuries that impersonal arbitrary
and large volume of taxation, not granted, but imposed,
perennial, calculable, which England was not to enjoy
till the eighteenth century, but which all nations fol-

lowing upon Richelieu's plan have to-day erected. Yet
the nations which took it up later, notably England, as
they ceased to be agricultural, and became industrial and
capitalist, improved upon the figures of those whom they
copied, and procured a public yearly fund which the
agricultural country could never equal. At the present
moment the national taxation imposed in England, apart
from the very heavy local taxation, produces about
double that imposed upon France; in each country the
limit has been reached; yet in total real income or power
of demand among the citizens there is no very great
difference.

It is a last consideration, and one of a sort which historical irony perpetually presents, that even while
Richelieu was setting out to make the French monarchy
supreme at home and turn it into the first true central
government of modern times, and even while in England at the same time the squires and merchants were
preparing to destroy *their* monarchy for ever, to the out-
ward observer it was the English Crown that was the
more firm.

It is characteristic of the contrast between the landed
classes under the French and under the English monarchies at this moment, that the externals of power
were far more striking among the upper classes of
France, the country where the political strength of the
noble class was shortly to break down, than they were
in England, where the upper classes were shortly to
pull down the throne; and that the externals of power
in the Crown were correspondingly more striking in

England, the country where the Crown was rapidly sinking, than in France, the country where it was about to be raised to complete dominion.

The French nobility in this first third of the seventeenth century had proved able to levy war against the Crown openly for a whole generation; their more important members were like little kings in their own districts, and their class overlapped with many of their own sort, who were completely independent: for instance, the Duke of Bouillon, or the Duke of Lorraine.

Many of the smaller squires and most of the larger ones had the right to private jurisdiction; the number of nobles with the right to put a man to death upon their own estates was appreciable, and there were even some left who had the right to coin money.

Contrast this situation with that of the landed classes in England at the same date. Only one attempt had been made within living memory to raise a powerful force against the Crown; that had been the revolt of the Northern Earls in 1569. It had been crushed, and there could be apparently no question of success for any further venture.

When we turn to the other side of the picture, it is the same thing. We, who know what was going to happen, who know that the wealthier classes in England were about to levy a successful civil war, to put the King to death, and to destroy active monarchy in this country for ever, have difficulty in appreciating how, (judging by externals only) things looked to a contemporary.

For a whole lifetime (1560-1620) out of five kings of France not one had exercised undisputed power and the two last kings (Henry III and Henry IV) had died assassinated. In England, an uninterrupted reign of nearly forty-five years (that of Elizabeth) had been followed by a quiet, legitimate succession, undisturbed by the least public movement.

Even by points of ceremonial, contemporaries would naturally have judged the English Crown to be far the stronger. At a time when Henry IV of France was little more than a partisan chief, among a number of equals, and in peril of losing such hold as he had, the ageing Elizabeth of England was being treated with a religious ceremonial such as might be paid to a divine being. Though she were absent from the hall—indeed, even before the state dinner was set out—the ladies and gentlemen who set the table genuflected three times to the empty royal chair.

Or again, read the claims and speech of James I; read the terms in which he was addressed. One would think one was dealing with a sort of god on earth.

Or again, consider the restraints and limitations of the two monarchies. The judges in England were at the discretion of the Crown; they were no more than its servants; they were nominated by the King or Queen, and they could be broken by him at any moment.

In France, the Parliaments, that is, the highest legal corporations, could hold up any legislation—could refuse to give it final sanction, and only in the gravest cases and by an exceptional procedure, could be submitted to the royal will.

Or consider revenue. The English change which ultimately put the control of public expenditure into the hands of the squires, of the great merchants, and their dependents in the House of Commons, had just begun to mutter, in 1610-1620, but it had as yet no formidable aspect, nor had men hitherto recognised it for what it was. When the King raised his tolls on foreign merchandise the courts still decided in his favour, and indeed, the rightful exercise of the English royal power in this matter had been taken for granted for at least 200 years.

When the King of France—at Richelieu's first appearance—could not raise enough money to build the smallest fleet, and had to hire merchantmen as best he could, or foreign ships for his wars, the King of England was able to pay for the beginnings of a formidable navy.

Fifteen years later one King of England was put to death, an impotent victim, by his more powerful subjects. After he had lain buried a short while his son returned as their salaried puppet. The King of France was Louis XIV, the greatest royal figure, the most powerful single man, since Charlemagne.

And so it is throughout the revolutions of human affairs. The great changes are sudden in their manifestation, unexpected, unprophesied. When they are fully accomplished we pretend to discover their causes and to see them approaching before they appear indeed. Contemporaries never perceive such portents, and we to-day are preparing for, arming against, prophesying a future which will never be; and have looming over us some other Europe of which we know nothing.

IV

THE POLITICAL CIRCUMSTANCE
FOREIGN

WHAT was the situation of Foreign affairs when Richelieu attained full power in 1624—a power which he maintained unbroken for more than eighteen years, to his death at the end of 1642?

It consisted, as I have said, in the presence upon every frontier of France (save that of the Alps) of the House of Hapsburg in its two branches: The House of Austria at the head of the Empire, and the Crown of Spain.

The two branches of one dynasty, of one family—their monarchs were close cousins—worked without rivalry and with a common twofold aim: the complete restoration of Catholicism throughout the continent of Europe, and the establishment of absolute central government throughout their dominions.

These two sides of their united effort were, unfortunately for Europe, inseparable. Had Austria aimed at no more than the spiritual recovery of all the Germanies, of her Slav states and of Hungary, had Spain cared only for re-establishing the Faith throughout Christendom, the problem presented to the Crown and government of France would not have existed. There would have been no reason why the minister of Louis XIII—a King profoundly Catholic—acting in a nation the bulk of whose numbers (though less of its wealth and armed force) was Catholic, himself a Churchman and a

Cardinal of the Church, should not have made common cause with the rising effort and appeared as an ally of the Hapsburgs in that cause; helping Spain in her struggle with the Calvinist oligarchy in the Northern Netherlands, helping the Empire in its attempt to restore the looted Church lands throughout its jurisdiction, and to re-impose the creed upon the ruins of the divided Protestant states.

But no such simple action was conceivable. It was not possible for the government of Vienna to achieve its spiritual task—in which it was sincere—save with the instrument of complete political dominion, and should it succeed—as it so nearly did—in restoring a united faith throughout Germany, it could not but emerge from that religious victory an exceedingly strong temporal power holding all central Europe and permanently founded: something over against which the French people would have stood permanently weak, open to invasion and subject to continual interference.

Still less was it possible for the government of Madrid to disassociate its religious with its political policy, nor had it any desire to do so. In the case of Spain the idea of dominion was at least as strong as the zeal for religious unity. Unlike his cousin the Emperor, Philip III of Spain inherited a tradition of almost unchecked power, a monarchy already strongly united and now covering all the Peninsula. The Emperor started with a long tradition of incoherence and failure, of successful rebellion everywhere against his nominal supremacy over the German states, of well-established precedent for independence in his nominal subordinates. The King of Spain started with a complete practice of autocracy established and rooted from long before his accession, or his father's.

Had Spain so rallied as to recover the Northern Netherlands and to triumph in the religious aim which she shared with Austria, she would have established all round French territory the garrisons of the best army in Europe—on the Jura, along the Pyrenees (with gates for invasion at either end of the chain, upon the Atlantic as upon the Mediterranean) and in full force upon that open North-Eastern plain of Flanders and the Artois which remains the most vulnerable front of France. And in that position the court of Madrid, unlike that of Vienna, would have thought more of temporal aims than of ecclesiastical. Between them the French monarchy would have lived at their mercy.

Therefore it was that Richelieu was to decide—against the violent upbraiding of his own communion and the indignation of all who, in France as elsewhere, made the restoration of religion their chief concern—to manœuvre with all that opposed either branch of the Hapsburg House. He was led by his policy, step by step, to support the German rebels, first through their Catholic members, then openly through their Protestant champions native and foreign: he was led by it to support, indirectly, the Calvinist oligarchy entrenched against the Spanish power in the Northern Netherlands; he was led at last to open war against both rivals, and, after a most critical five years, to die, at the end of two more, victorious over both; leaving the great scheme of a United Catholic Empire in Germany ruined, and the Spanish Crown finally stripped of its last hope on the North Sea and deposed for ever from its claim to supremacy in the West of Europe.

Richelieu died with his end accomplished, his monarchy already free from either pressure, and soon to be by far the strongest in Europe; but the religious schism in Christendom rendered permanent, and the beginnings, already apparent, of that Protestant ascendancy which till recently was the mark of our time.

The position of Austria had passed through these stages:

At the moment when Richelieu first appeared (for but a few months) in the Government, that is in 1616, all was moving among the Germans towards the crisis which broke, two years later, in the opening of the Thirty Years' War: the climax of the quarrel between the Emperor with his seat at Vienna, in theory overlord of all the Germanies, and those who were technically his subordinates, the Princes and Free Cities, had come. The rivalry was closely interwoven with the claim of so many among those princes and senates to exercise the Reformed religion in their states, to exclude or keep down the Catholics, and—above all (this was here, as throughout Europe, the key of the business) to keep the masses of Church land and revenue which they had seized at the Reformation.

Ever since the first Lutheran movement, a hundred years before, the local powers had become more and more independent of the imperial tie. They had been really independent long before, but the religious quarrel gave them all—Catholic as well as Protestant—the opportunity to emphasise their freedom.

Meanwhile, under the advantage of this paralysis in government, the revolt from Catholicism prospered and spread. It so affected all the states that there was a movement, in the latter part of the sixteenth century, when it looked as though all German-speaking land would be lost to the traditional culture which had moulded it since Charlemagne. What saved the situation and turned the tide was the work of two fervent, disciplined and ubiquitous bodies of religious: the Jesuits, of recent foundation, and that reformed and zealous order of Franciscans known as Capuchins.

Both bodies had a single aim—and a single aim is the prime condition of success: for success can only be measured in terms of desire, and conflicting desires are not realised. That aim was the recovery of Christian unity. Both concentrated upon the Germans because the Germans were the uncertain, swaying mass in which the break-away from Catholic Europe had begun, and in which the result remained undetermined. The religious wars in France had ended with a compromise, indeed, but with the government finally established on the side of tradition. In Germany there was no such central power, and right up to the gates of Vienna and beyond, in Transylvania, in the Hungarian lands, the revolt was powerful.

For it must not be imagined, because Germany was

ultimately settled into what is very roughly a Catholic South and an anti-Catholic North, that the problem of the sixteenth century was of this simple territorial nature. Distance from the seat of Empire at Vienna was one cause of the form the ultimate settlement took; the opportunities which the foreign enemies of the Austrian House therefore had to support rebellion in its outlying dependencies, was another cause. But the main cause was, as will later be seen, the launching by Richelieu, under French subsidy, of a military genius, the King of Sweden, into the battle upon the Protestant side; and his effort, directed from the North, determined more than any other factor the geographical form into which the division between German Catholicism and Protestantism finally crystallised.

But the spiritual battle hung undecided in those early years of the seventeenth century. The Danube valley was, at that moment, as much a field of conflict as the centre. Austria swarmed with excited and angry men pledged to destroy the Church. In Bohemia the national (and Slav) feeling swelled the rebellion and led to those violent reprisals against the Imperial authorities which were the first acts of war.

The Emperor Matthias, a weak elderly man and childless, who had attempted to cajole the anarchy by yielding to it, died in 1619, and there succeeded to his hereditary lands his cousin, Ferdinand ruler of Styria.

Ferdinand—known in history as Ferdinand II—was a man of very different calibre. It should be impossible to read of him without admiration. In the full maturity of his power (he was forty-one) he set out with direct aim and disciplined will on the mighty task of restoration. After a few months of desperate peril he got firmly into the saddle. He was elected Emperor, crushed the Bohemian rebels completely at the battle of the White Mountain, and proceeded from strength to strength. Philip III of Spain, his relative, helped with money and men, and, after his death in 1621, his young son, Philip IV, continued the same policy.

The zealous and intelligent Duke of Bavaria was wholly with him. The Rebel Palatine (son-in-law of James I of England) who had had the folly to attempt the Bohemian Throne, having been ignominiously beaten, his principate was forfeited, and the Duke— now Elector—of Bavaria installed in his stead. By 1623 the last fortress of the Palatinate, Frankenthal, was reduced. The Protestant pretender to Hungary shamefully allied with the Turks—an adventurer from Transylvania called Bethlen Gabor—was defeated in his turn and made peace—already the victory of Stadtlohn had destroyed the last opposing rally in the Bishopric of Münster. All this was accompanied by the firmest handling of the effects of victory: wholesale confiscation from the rebels, stern executions. Everywhere the looted Church lands were recovered. The thing went in a flood, and by the end of 1624 it looked as though what we now call "The Thirty Years' War" was over and the triumph of Ferdinand complete. His troops were quartered even in the North. Germany was in his hands. But it was the moment when Richelieu entered the Council for the second

time, and this time to be its head and the master of
French policy.

Such was the situation of the Austrian half in that
twin problem which faced the Cardinal. I turn to the
Spanish.

In the double pressure against which Richelieu was
about to frame his policy, the matter upon which the
modern reader may be most easily misled is the position
of Spain.

What a united Germany under one monarch, whether
at Vienna or elsewhere, could mean in the way of peril
to the French house and its dominion, we of to-day can
easily understand. We have been familiar with increasing menace of the same kind for more than 150 years;
but, with a corresponding menace from Spain, we are
to-day quite unacquainted. The matter is further confused by the perpetual recurrence in our general his-
tories of phrases describing the Spanish power as paralysed at almost any moment of its existence during two
centuries and more, from the conquest of Granada to
the Bourbon claim. Spanish military power had sunk
to its lowest at the very moment when the nineteenth
century school of anti-Catholic historians was flourish-
ing; they were aware of Spain's ultimate decline; they
would therefore discover at almost any moment in the
life of that power the presence of disease. They missed
the continued, though failing, greatness of that Empire.
The error was further emphasised by the exaggerated
prominence given to the subordinate episode of the
Armada in 1588, (which was represented as a decisive

action and turning-point in the whole process of Spanish history) and by the pretence that the Calvinist millionaires of the Northern Netherlands were able to defy Spain single-handed: the obscuring of the truth that, but for their support by the great rivals of Spain, they had not a chance.

Thus we are told, with the first outbreak of rebellion in the Netherlands, that Spanish power was becoming negligible. We are told the same thing twenty years later, when the attempt to invade England fails. We are told the same thing thirty years later, when a Spanish marriage with England is broken off. We are told the same thing (more truly) twenty-five years later again, at the peace of Westphalia. We are told the same thing half a century later when the Bourbon claim to the Spanish succession is advanced. We are even asked to wonder that Louis XIV should have made such efforts to acquire a thing so worthless as the Spanish Throne for his grandson.

It must strike every critical reader that this perpetual succession of final dooms, unperceived by contemporaries, has something strange about it; it can hardly correspond with reality. Nor does it. The truth about Spanish power between the mid-sixteenth and early eighteenth centuries is briefly this:—

It was never adequate to the maintenance of its immense territory, but the loss of its hold upon so much revenue and military power was gradual and slow. The Spanish Crown was at any one moment in the process far more formidable than we, looking backwards from a time in which the old Spanish might has disappeared, can easily appreciate.

On the other hand, contemporaries always tended to exaggerate Spanish power at any given moment, and the Spanish Crown tended to exaggerate its own estimate of its self at any given moment.

There is always a "lag" in the public appreciation of real political power: a "lag" corresponding to the "lag" between the real gold value of a debased currency and its immediate purchasing power.

There is, in other words, when one old political factor is failing and a new one rising to take its place, some interval, longer or shorter, between the real advent of the new state of things and the appearance and full recognition of that state of things.

It was so, for instance, during the decline of the English monarchy and the rise of the Houses of Parliament —that is, of the gentry. Men went on thinking in terms of the old strong monarchy even beyond the date 1700. The monarchs themselves retained something of the illusion; even the conquering Parliament retained that illusion in some degree, and hardly ever acted as strongly as it might have done. Similarly to-day, with Parliament already almost negligible through the decline of the gentry and with its replacement by international finance, men continue to think in the old terms, and the new power itself is still deferential to politicians.

This "lag" between reality and appearance was more prolonged in the case of Spain than in any other modern example. As late as 1661 not only did the Spanish monarchy regard itself as superior to the French, but the French monarchy itself half admitted the claim.

The young French King proceeding to meet his bride, was proud to notice that the Spaniards permitted the marriage to take place upon the frontier and could not compel him to attend their Court.

A lifetime later all Western Europe was stirred with the fear that the Bourbon monarchy in Spain would mean an overwhelming power in the hands of one family.

The fact that these "lags" were so prolonged in the case of Spain, was due to a number of causes, a consideration of which will explain why contemporaries felt as they did.

In the first place, there was that powerful instrument, the map. We to-day know well enough of what effect the mere map can be, and how those who can use it to enhance their prestige do so use it most vigorously. Though we control, or half control, but a thread of fertile land trickling through a vast expanse of desert (as in Egypt), the whole desert is triumphantly coloured red. Though the real hold over what was once a colony be obsolescent or actually denounced (as in South Africa), the colour on the map remains the same as though the district were an English country.

Now, in the case of Spain, even as late as 1624, when Richelieu takes the helm, you can see upon the map what was, in those days, virtually the whole of the new world coloured Spanish; especially after union of the Spanish and Portuguese Crowns: all Central and South-

RICHELIEU
AFTER MICHIEL LASNE

ern America (the North as yet was quite negligible), all the Eastern trading centres and Pacific Islands.

Then there was all Southern Italy covered by the same power: Sicily and Sardinia as well. In the North the all-important Duchy of Milan. There were the whole of the Southern Netherlands, and even the independence of the Northern Provinces was not absolute and regular as yet. There was Luxemburg. There was the Franche-Comté (that is the Jura: Spain controlled Gray, Dole, Besançon—a whole province of Eastern France). There was something like a Protectorate over Genoa by which port Spain held its communications with Milan.

We have to consider the visible wealth, and the way in which it affected Spanish prestige.

It is true that the Spanish Crown was always embarrassed, perpetually in debt, often compelled to repudiate. That was because its financing demanded revenue far in excess of what could in practice be gathered, in days when the State had little of the tyrannical power it has since acquired over its subjects. The precious metals came in a steady stream from America direct to Spain, but its mere metallic currency is nothing compared with the total wealth of a community, and even that currency perpetually sank in value as more and more gold and silver poured in. But still there was the striking spectacle continuing for centuries of the precious metals entering Spain from Central and South America, and of a trade which covered the Atlantic and the Mediterranean. In the presence of that spectacle who could fail to fear and admire the Spanish Empire?

Next, there was the prestige of the Spaniards in arms, especially in infantry. They had by far the best and largest trained body of footmen in the world, and the tradition informing that body was an ancient and strong one. The superiority of the Spanish soldier was unquestioned until the end of the Thirty Years' War.

At sea, though insufficient to protect the huge mass of commerce, or rather, protect a monopoly in it, Spain remained formidable for two centuries, and had to be calculated with until the end of the third. It was not until after Trafalgar that such calculation was no longer necessary.

Lastly, let it be noted that the Spanish power did not suffer invasion, nor did it ever meet with any one decisive defeat. One cannot point to any one famous battle in which the Spanish power went under, nor to the prostration of the country before any invading and conquering army.

Now nothing more affects the prestige of a power than its dramatic and rapid defeat in the field, though the real effects of such an action are often less than the effects of a long series of petty losses. And the example of a country suffering invasion, even though it conquer in the end, wounds its prestige as heavily.

It is all these things put together which maintained the nominal position of Spain at a level superior to its real power, and meanwhile we must remember that real power was always greater at any given moment than modern history is inclined to grant.

When Richelieu's effect first began to be felt after

the success of the Valtelline, the preponderance of the
Spanish Crown over the French was still very great. The
causes of this real strength of Spain in 1624, when Richelieu is about to take the helm in France (as distinguished
from Spain's far more striking apparent greatness),
were, in the first place (what is not to be despised) her
moral value; in the second, the continued excellence of
her armed forces by sea and by land; in the third place
her great tradition of continued predominance and uninterrupted empire, coupled with that most powerful
of politically dominating effects the unquestioned maintenance of unity.

As to the first of these, the serenity and splendour of
the Spanish Throne, the magnificence of its externals,
expressed in ritual, in every detail of comportment, still
more in architecture, profoundly affected the mind of
Europe: and rightly so; they remain to-day to astonish
us. I may be thought extravagant if I say that the
Escorial, that huge block of dark granite unearthly pro-
portioned, is a parallel to the Pyramids. I do not myself
feel the parallel to be extravagant. At any rate there is
nothing else in Europe which so presents the eternal and
the simple combined. It is never forgotten; and I
suppose it should endure when all more complicated
effort at expression has weathered and perished to a
ruin.

I can believe that when our civilisation has so completely disappeared that men retain no memory of it,
this tremendous thing will stand as the testament of

magnitude, and the barbarians of that day will cry: "Here was a great king!"

But the Escorial is not a mere symbol, still less a façade; it is the very soul of the imperial name. It could only have been raised and inhabited by kings who were believed by themselves to be, and were believed by others to be, the chief on earth.

That the armed forces of Spain were in quality and numbers the greatest, even in so late a phase as that of the early seventeenth century, should be a commonplace. They failed, for the tasks they were set were beyond human power. But though in the north the occasional expeditions by sea could not raise the blockade of the Netherland ports, nor support the Catholics of England effectively, yet it is wildly bad history to think of Spain in those days as failing by sea. The great transports held the Atlantic, conveyed the wealth of the Indies with losses insufficient to affect the main strength of him who owned them, and Lepanto, the theme of our finest modern ballad (I mean Mr. Chesterton's) was not an accident but a seal.

As for the land forces, not only was that infantry of which I have just spoken still the terror of its enemies, but it was still capable of digesting and training an increasing proportion of alien recruitment. While the population of the Peninsula was declining, the Spanish army was maintained at full strength by such methods of absorption, and as yet none could meet it with permanent success. Not indeed that it was a regular and standing army; it was produced for the purposes of war, and

destined if the wars should cease, to disappear. Nor did
Spain initiate, rather did Richelieu initiate, the modern
idea of a regular force. But since the military effort of
Spain was continuous, its armed force was perpetually
growing, and in that early seventeenth century when
you used the word "soldier" you thought at once of a
Spaniard. The Spanish organisation for war had the
best marching power, the best artillery for siege work,
far the greatest proportion of guns, far the greatest experience in action. If the cavalry was heavy, yet shock
was the tactic of the time, and in precision and co-
ordination the Spanish captains had no rivals.

One may by a metaphor compare the Spanish armament which faced the French Crown when Richelieu
undertook its new fortunes, to strong ice over a great
lake at the end of winter. The ice still bears like a rock,
the water beneath it is warming with the spring, it is
thawing from below, but to the eye, to the foot, for all
apparent purposes, it is as solid as ever. No crack has yet
appeared.

The third factor in the continuing preponderance of
Spain, her tradition of continued uninterrupted empire,
affected every mind in Europe, as did that most striking
aspect of it, the unchallenged discipline of the mighty
body which stretched right round the world: unchallenged save on that cancer point of Holland, whereby the
huge organism was poisoned and broke down.

It is strange that our time should not appreciate the
effect of unity upon rivals. Autocracy, though now returning, is still a novelty to us. The unity of the Spanish

Empire was autocratic. But whether unity be achieved by the aristocratic spirit (as in that older England whose chief legacy to ourselves is the solid social tissue which aristocracy produces and which we still enjoy) or by enthusiasms such as those which, in the worship of a tradition, give unity to the North American Republic, unity it is which, more than any other cause, impresses, and rightly impresses, contemporaries. Now the unity of the Spanish Empire in the early seventeenth century was, in the eyes of its contemporaries, that of a vast mountain rising from the plain in single outline against the sky. It had no legacy of civil wars. The mortal peril of the Jewish and Mohammedan conspiracy had been destroyed (at what an effort!) by the Inquisition. It seemed as though the fully organised structure linked in every part could never fall into fragments. Even the distant effort in the Netherlands had not yet been abandoned, and the rest seemed wholly secure.

Such was the prospect of Spain when the French monarchy slowly and carefully under its great minister, with every precaution, safeguard and even hesitation, was ready to begin the challenge.

For many years that challenge, though present, lay silent. There was family alliance, the King of France had been married from boyhood to the sister of the King of Spain, the King of Spain to the sister of the King of France. There was no direct antagonism. There was in France no such continuous hostile policy against Spain as against the peril of a united Germany. Still, it was essential to Spain to hold communication with the great taxable wealth of the Low Countries. She was even about to renew a last effort to recover Amsterdam itself and the Ports and Senates which had thrown off her rule on the extremities of the North Sea; she needed passage up northward through the basin of the Rhine, which left her perpetually upon the flank of France. What was more important, she could and did support Austria through that passage of the Valtelline whereby troops could march across the Alps from the Spanish Duchy of Milan to the aid of the Empire—and what that meant we shall see when we come to view in more detail this famous avenue through the hills.

Lastly, there was opposed to Richelieu on the further side of the Pyrenees a character wholly different from, but worthy of, his own: that of the dark, broad-shouldered, intense, commanding, laborious Olivares, a tamer of horses and of men. He, a master in the forties, controlled and stood for Philip IV, who had come to the throne of Spain but a few years before as a boy, and who was in his twenties still. That lad, gay, highly instructed, an excellent patron of all arts, wisely left everything to such a minister, as on the north of him everything came to be left, as wisely, by the French King to the Cardinal. One may regard the long business of Richelieu's eighteen years as a duel between his own soul and that of Olivares. His own type of tenacity, courage and intelligence were pitted against the contrasting tenacity, intelligence and courage of the Spaniard—who did indeed incarnate his people; and if Olivares lost that duel, it was because the age and its gods were against him.

Who does not remember the final day when that captain came to announce in the royal palace the fall of Perpignan, and the great Sign of the Cross made against the sky by the Commander of the garrison surrendering with his starved skeletons after so noble an endurance? France had reached the Pyrenees. Olivares on his knees, in a voice hardly audible, broke the news to his king, who answered, "It is the will of God." That king was then himself approaching age; Olivares had long entered the last passage to the tomb, and within some few weeks Richelieu, the victor, was to die.

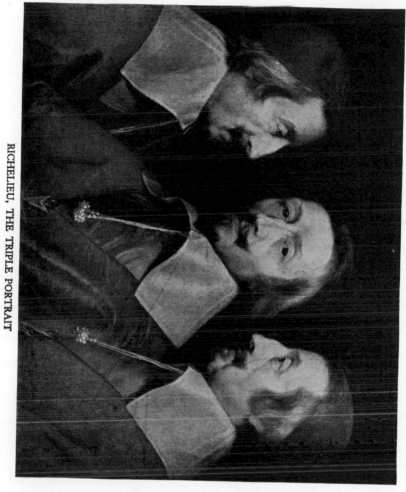

RICHELIEU, THE TRIPLE PORTRAIT
By Philippe de Champaigne
In the National Gallery, London

V

THE PERSON AND CHARACTER

WHEN Richelieu, at his height, chose the Jansenist Philip of Champaigne for his official painter, he did well. The alternative was Rubens, and it has been said that if he set Rubens aside, it was out of rivalry with the Queen Mother, whom Rubens served. But it was more than that: it was an appreciation of the Arts and of men. For Rubens could never have painted Richelieu. Philip of Champaigne has fixed him for three hundred years.

Of his portraits, the choice between the National Gallery in London and the Louvre lies with the Louvre. The famous triple aspect in London, the two profiles and the full face, would have been sufficient for posterity had the masterpiece of the Louvre been lost: but, possessing that masterpiece, we have an even higher record.

It is a thing on which to meditate. A man who knew no more than the name, or not that, would pause before it to wonder. A man who has read all he may on the Cardinal, does not know him till he has seen that canvas, and, when he has seen it, has all his book knowledge illuminated as though by contemporary and personal acquaintance with the man.

He stands there in his red robe, the delicacy of his fingers enhanced by the slight weight of his beretta, and is in the act of attention, as though at audience: the spare figure seeming taller than it is, through a certain

air of concealed dominion: the carriage erect and yet
ready to be bowed somewhat by the weight of thought:
his sparse hair long and dark against the exquisite fine-
ness of his pallor: the brows arched exaggerated and
steeply into the broad forehead, so that "he seemed fixed
in surprise"—but beneath them, those eyes. How shall I
describe those eyes?

There is in them a discretion but a reserve of power,
an acceptance without advance, an observation without
admittance (windows, not doors), which, as you watch
them, increase upon you as might the expression of the
living man. They are a sheath to a sword; but a sheath
transparent. They are watchers not hidden though
guarded, and guarded by nothing more apparent than
a kind of neutrality which is much more than
indifference but less than vigour. It is as though they
were designed to convey all whatsoever to the mind inwards, but, from that mind outwards to give no more
than the giver intended, whether of measured courtesy
or exact blame. It is difficult to conceive in them anger
or any other intensity, for all that lives behind them
lies far within. Those eyes are large and almost prominent. They are mild in contour. There is nothing secretive in their somewhat melancholy gaze. They are
fixed and their glance must have been slow. But from
them, as from the firm slight lips between the military
moustache and beardlet of that pointed face, with its
fine arched nose and drawn lines at the mouth, came
decisions unchangeable and orders which moulded a
world.

RICHELIEU
FROM A DRAWING BY CLAUDE MELLAN
STOCKHOLM

So he stands and is seen in the last maturity before there began in his frail body that last physical breakdown of which his spirit was contemptuous and to which it never yielded. It is but an external vision of him. To know him we must consider his descent and the aids and hindrances surrounding his puissant spirit.

In blood Richelieu came of a father loyal, passionate, ugly, brave, perhaps diseased, embarrassed in fortune: a man of the Poitevin gentry who had killed in boyhood the slayer of his own father, who had wandered in exile, who had shown devotion to the King his lord and had died early, encamped during the civil war, high in the service of the Crown. Such was the father. The mother was from the higher middle classes, the lawyers, a woman gentle, prudent and absorbed during an impoverished widowhood in the re-establishment of her sons.

She had borne him late—at the age of thirty-five—the fourth of her children, a baby whom they thought for months might not live; and growing up into a boyhood already stricken, a manhood never free from grievous nervous trouble and a tainted blood.

His head ached continually—sometimes so severely as to incapacitate him altogether. All his life he was afflicted with boils and other troubles of the sort which ultimately killed him, and, apart from the neuralgic pains which tortured him, he must have inherited a weakness of the nerves which, in one brother at least and one sister, appeared as feebleness of intelligence at the best, madness at the worst. In his own case—side by side with a vigorous understanding—this weakness appeared as an occasional mechanical instability which may have been epileptic.

There is in connection with this surmise a tradition of his epilepsy which can only be cited *as* a tradition (for I believe it is without contemporary documentation) but which (since tradition is essential to history) must be mentioned.

The same thing has been said about many men of genius. Perhaps the origin of it lies in nothing more than the strain to which high capacity and high achievement put a man of delicate health.

Not only is there this tradition of epilepsy, but there is a further addition to it of occasional aberration.

The tradition was still strong when Madame, the coarse German widow of Louis XIV's disgraceful brother, left it behind her in writing. Her "Letters" lay unpublished for a century, and she herself wrote nearly a lifetime—from fifty to sixty years—after the great Cardinal's death. But such as it is, and for what it is worth, here is the curious note:

It was set down by her as a known matter (presumably in the royal family) that the Cardinal had occasional fits of such madness that he believed himself to be a horse, and under this delusion would run round his room, neighing and kicking out in hippic fashion, landing stable assaults with hoofs upon his serving men. When such fits struck him, he was seized, bound, set into a bed to sweat them off in a violent heat. When he awakened from the coma which followed, he remembered nothing of it all.

The very extravagance of this startling passage helps to condemn it. It may also seem to have against it that so enormous a trouble could hardly have been kept a secret. But we have in its favour the knowledge that the most intimate things about the great hardly ever get told to the outer world, and that this is exactly the sort of ludicrous story which would be kept within a very narrow circle, handed down through one family—the royal family of France, whom Richelieu served most intimately.

He may even on one occasion have suffered for some few days from general and prolonged illusions. As in so many points of this life so curiously over-documented on some things and under-documented on others, we have here again to trust to rumour. But the rumour is too strong to be neglected. For instance, there is one very persistent tradition that on hearing of his having obtained the Hat, he fell from the intensity of his emotion into a brief fit of madness.

We may conclude at least, I think, that Richelieu occasionally, but rarely and in private, appeared to contemporaries as a man with nerves at breaking point— and that, I repeat, is pretty well true of any man of great achievement. But in public there was no sign of it, rather did he found a legend of fixed impassivity and maintain that legend unbroken.

Now all this weakness and even peril he subdued by that unique instrument of will, in the use of which he stands super-eminent in all the story of Europe. There is no creative figure in history (though all founders in history are but exponents of will) whose will was of such uniformity throughout forty years and of more than mortal strength. Nor was it in the least relaxed by the coming of death itself; the phrase on his last breath, hardly heard, was an example of it. This will had about the quality we find in the operations of the physical world, their unchanging sequence, their inevitability, their invariable results. Strength is almost too weak a word to use. We need to present the will of Richelieu by some new word which shall have no connotation of effort and rhythm, or of nourishment or of limitation. It was absolute.

But here note the triple element in his soul of which will was but one component. For that will of his was put to the service of ambition, but, because ambition meant for him, in its turn, the service of a particular office and man—his ministry and the national monarchy —therefore did it breed very early in its exercise the third component, devotion. It was this colour of devotion, which so many have missed, that explains him and his unceasing purpose.

Ambition, the mixed desire for fame and power, appears in him at the outset of manhood. You see it in his persistent attainment of the episcopate before his twenty-first year was ended, in his rule of his diocese, in his thrusting himself into the light of Paris and the Court, in all the conduct of his first years and in the maxims which he has left us as his confession of conduct. To ambition he owed the base necessities of his original advance. For while those who would attain power abroad

RICHELIEU IN 1635
BY PHILIPPE DE CHAMPAIGNE
IN MUSÉE CONDÉ, CHANTILLY

over the rivals or enemies of the State *may* do so nobly
if they are born to high place or are summoned by authority, those who would attain political position of
themselves must—without hope of escape—stoop to base-
ness in their beginnings; and it is the strongest argument for hereditary rule in any aristocracy or crown that
it *may* provide the commonwealth with rulers who have
not suffered from the taint of intrigue and subservience.
Those not acting with hereditary right cannot avoid that
taint. Having risen, they may release their souls and
subserve the good of their fellows and the state with
dignity; but they will always bear within themselves
the reproach and memory of unworthiness in the past.

It was so with Richelieu. He has himself told us his
rules for "arriving." To speak little, to listen much, to
feign interest in the dullness of superiors, to flatter and
to frighten. He might have added (but he is silent on
this) to swallow insult, to postpone revenge, to watch
unceasingly all those around who are using every hour
the same talents and vices to advance themselves, who
will therefore obstruct him in his progress and attempt
to supplant him when he shall have reached his goal.
Richelieu in youth—until his fortieth year—feigned
friendship, he stooped to fraud. He accepted patronage
from those whom he later destroyed.

To blackmail, the common weapon of the politician
and the courtier, he never descended in any matter of
which we have heard; but he fawned upon the Queen
Mother in the days of her power, he watched every
opportunity for advertisement and impression, he

moulded his early sermons with an eye to promotion,
he trained a not insignificant talent for oratory in assemblies to the same end. He allowed himself to complain loudly and with exaggeration of poverty and unjust neglect. One may say that never, till past thirty,
did he do or say anything in connection with the government that was not directed to entering it at last, by
whatever means; nor, till close on forty, that did not
aim at recovering and consolidating his power. In this
he had for an excuse to himself that he was conscious
of supreme aptitudes and of a genius for the highest
affairs. With that unction to salve his honour he wounded
it without scruple, till he could afford independence—
but he did not reach such freedom till he entered the
Council for good and mastered it, in 1624, and by that
time he was already close upon his fortieth year.

Only by so devious an approach and by such play to
its conclusion could he become the ruler, and establish
himself in that place.

But once so established there arrived for him, and
grew, that quality of devotion which henceforward illuminated his life.

It is a great error to see, in his management of Louis
XIII, the mere tricking or amusing of an inferior mind
by a superior, a still greater error to conceive that his
attitude to his King was at heart contemptuous.

What that strange man, the monarch of Richelieu's
day, was in his contradictory qualities, we shall appreciate on a later page. But whatever estimate is made
of him, we must take it for a fixed point in the history

of the time that Richelieu's reverence for the throne was constant and exalted: and with it there went, as an emotion identical with it, a profound attachment to the King as king and to the nation incarnate in the Prince.

Of devotion we have plenty in the annals of human achievement. It is a creative power constantly present, whether attached to a religion, or a family, or a state. The life of every saint is an example of it, and the lives, in so far as they are true and not legendary, of the various national heroes. But the particular note which distinguishes it in the rare men of Richelieu's type is that they direct their effort to one human object rather than to a general idea, and that human object not themselves.

A high power of intrigue, a fierce determination to arrive at power and maintain it, these things are of their nature at conflict with devotion, and a combination of them with devotion is exceptional indeed. But when you do get that combination the effect is tremendous, and the monument it leaves is lasting. This was the strength of Bismarck—that he was concerned with the family of Hohenzollern and his own particular monarch and the aggrandisement thereof; and this was the strength of Richelieu, that he was concerned with the French royal family and with the glory and strength of the particular prince to whom he was born a subject.

The distinction between devotion to an idea or cause and devotion to a personality or restricted conception, such as that of a dynasty, is not hair-splitting. It must be emphasised, for it is very real. A man can serve politically a general idea, notably that of patriotism, or that of a religion, and yet retain full personal ambition and make his own advancement take the first place while he pursues that general aim; for there is no jealousy between the individual and such a general idea; the one does not compete with the other. But when one individual must serve another the case is different. the selfishness of ambition may rend and ruin that relation. With Richelieu it never did so. Nor let it be said that he only served Louis because on Louis depended his position. Mere ambition would have led him to intrigue with the brother and heir of a childless king. He never did so. He unswervingly held to a master often on the point of death, well knowing that, should he die, ruin and exile must follow.

His supreme gifts in administration, diplomacy and internal government were set in a frame of military talent. We are made not only by our heredity and our use of it, but largely by the vivid impression of the moment when youth is ending, the training of the formative years just before maturity, and in those years Richelieu was at the Academy, learning war. It was only by a family accident, the details of which we shall follow, that he took Orders. He was destined for his father's profession and that of all his caste who did not take livings, the profession of arms. This military training, the studies and the life were things which—though he was under their direct influence for so short a time— affected him throughout his life. He would have excelled in war—and that, we must remember, was a strong bond between himself and the King.

You find the decision of the great soldier perpetually appearing in the career of this sickly indomitable man: the decision, the appreciation of detail, the choice of lieutenants, the judgment of a map, the seizing of opportunity and surprise, and, in the use of country, what the French call "the eye." You see it in the Rhé campaign, before La Rochelle, at Casale, in the rally of the year of Corbie, in his grasp of the German situation when he called Gustavus Adolphus into the war.

We have not, unfortunately, the elements with which to test (save in the studies of quite early youth) Richelieu's rapidity of assimilation; but every probability is in favour of its being exceptional, as it is in great captains. For Richelieu's action time and again was so parallel to rapid and immediate military decisions, that we may presume the same quality in him as in the chief soldiers of history, mastering a situation in a moment.

Hence we see him using without hesitation men of his own cloth for successful commands by land and sea, and hence we see him depicted in armour. His favourite portrait of himself shows him more like a Marshal than a Cardinal, riding in command.

We have to regret one effigy of him, also probably military, which might have been of a special value, and comparable to the famous bust of Cromwell, formerly the property of the first Lord Revelstoke and now standing in the House of Commons; for like that bust, it was almost certainly of contemporary Italian workmanship. This was the stone effigy of Richelieu standing above the back gate of the Château of Meilleraie in Poitou, near Parthenay. It was smashed at the Revolution. The torso and certain fragments are now in the Departmental Museum, having been collected by the Statistical Society of the Deux-Sèvres. The head was discovered in a Roman shop by the French School of Art many years ago, but I believe that the authorship of the statue is unknown, only fragments of the name remain.

With this military character in him went not only a sure judgment of men—it never failed him, whether in choosing an agent, tracking a domestic enemy, or dealing with a foreign rival—but, what is not often found in conjunction with such judgment, a readiness to take advice. Napoleon was his equal or superior in the first, gravely his inferior in the second. Until the death of Father Joseph he followed that counsellor carefully, and in what was perhaps the chief political decision of his life—I mean the determination not to occupy the Rhineland—he deliberately subordinated his own view to that of the older man whose decisions he so trusted.

His judgment of politics as a whole, of the nature of society, is admirably expressed in that "Testament" the authenticity of which, foolishly challenged by Voltaire, is sufficiently established. It is practical, full of reality, taking the hierarchy of society as he found it, and men in their common moods. He is therefore lacking in that disturbing appetite for justice which may imperil the society, and which may even consume or overset great states. In this neglect of justice he stands apart from the main current of French enthusiasm as it has run from the Middle Ages down to our own, for, in defence of justice, in contempt of order, the French approached anarchy a score of times.

And here we must note in the man one very striking characteristic, which was twofold. Intensely national as he was, he excelled in a faculty which his fellow-countrymen as a rule lack, *and he knew that he excelled in it;* he appreciated the singularity of his talent.

This quality was that of persistence, which must not be confused with tenacity.

Richelieu himself said in his "Testament" that seeing what qualities the French have of daring, lucidity and the rest, they would have mastered all rivals long ago and stood alone (he had, perhaps, the Roman Empire in his mind) were it not that they are easily deflected from one interest to another, or that, after they have pursued a particular policy or a new invention, or what not, to the point where they are already the superiors of their competitors, they will turn aside to some other thing, especially to civil war, or at the least to quarrels within the State and to the fury of party.

I repeat, this is not to say that the French lack tenacity, to which they are, if anything, exaggeratedly attached. Having determined upon a thing, the French character tends to exceed in its pursuit, and, while fighting for it, to hold out to the death. But it can be distracted from one conflict by another. The appeal of a new interest withdraws the French from the prosecution of the old. A particular and enormous case of this we have before our eyes in the preliminaries and even conduct of the Great War. Their religious quarrel weakened and blinded them, and has, so far, thrown away the fruits of the struggle.

I say that Richelieu's appreciating his own difference from his fellow-countrymen in this respect—his standing outside himself, so to speak, and watching the premium on his own action given him by an exceptional persistence—is a very rare example of observation. It is as though an Englishman were to be not only famous for fervid and continual rhetoric, but for achieving a quantity of practical results in politics by such rhetoric, and were in his reminiscences to dwell upon the absence of this quality (and of any ordinary respect for it) in English life.

On religion Richelieu threw the same actual, prosaic, uninspired regard which he turned upon temporal matters. For in religion there are three things to be said about this great cleric, which are not self-contradictory (each forms part of a united and consistent character) but which sound oddly associated in modern ears:—

First, he was a strong believer: he never doubted at all. He argued well in defence of the faith, and wrote clearly and most sincerely in support of it. He was full of Catholic practice,[1] industrious in reforming his diocese, exact in his clerical duties.

Next, he was almost devoid of priestly character. He took his priesthood as a lay profession; his episcopacy

[1] Witness the touching story of his *Novena* of masses to be said if his prayers for relief from headache should be answered, and his devotion to our Lady of Ardillers, to whom he brought the King and Queen to give thanks after Rochelle.

as an apprenticeship in government, his cardinalate as a means of power. No scruple would have restrained him in the matter of celibacy, or rather of his vow of chastity. Most of the gallant stories about him, or hinted of him, are false. The myth that he was the lover of Anne of Austria is ridiculous, and it may securely be denied that he was the lover of Marie de Médicis. He showed, in public at least, no lack of restraint, nor even any inclination towards women. But *had* he had occasion to judge that an amour would benefit his career or the State, he would have undertaken it as a task. In point of fact I can see no sufficient evidence that such an occasion ever arose, but the divorce of a cleric from the priestly office is as well seen in his case as in the most worldly of the eighteenth-century ecclesiastics.

Lastly, he had no zeal, such as had so many men of his time, for the triumph of Catholicism; he did not consider Europe as a battlefield between tradition and revolution in doctrine and philosophy. He considered the conflict between them mainly as one by the right manipulation of which the interests of the French monarchy might be advanced. It is probable that he hardly understood, he certainly never yielded to, the instinctive feeling all around him—that unless French policy were whole-heartedly Catholic in that critical moment of 1620-40, Europe would never be re-united. He presumably thought the ultimate re-union of Europe, or the ultimate triumph of Catholicism certain, and would not, to accelerate it, sacrifice one detail of his policy for the consolidation and aggrandisement of the nation he governed. Hence toleration at home and alliance with Protestantism abroad against the Catholic Powers. Hence his nickname of "the Cardinal of the Huguenots." Hence the worship of his achievement by those who accept the new religion of Nationalism and have forgotten, or think impossible, the idea of Christendom.

So much for the main lines of his genius, around which stood a host of lesser qualities, notably a great love of order in his surroundings, an exact care for his carriage and dress, a strict ordering of his hours.

What of his defects? Was he cruel?

That is a question to be asked at the outset of any man who achieves this or that against the will of many of his fellow-creatures. For cruelty is not only the worst accusation that can be brought against a man, defiling the whole character, but it also loosens the character, like a false string in a musical instrument which makes all playing on it intolerable. One might say with justice that there never yet was a great man who was cruel, and that anyone who admires cruelty or condones it in any other man, is incapable of seizing what greatness is.

It is a question we must answer with particular care in Richelieu's case, because to see him as cruel is the commonest of all the errors into which men fall to-day in their judgment of him.

The contemporary enemies of Richelieu also accused him of cruelty. All his victims, their friends, their relatives, called cruelty his chief mark and him a monster of it.

But the accusation cannot be maintained. It is due to

a confusion between things similar in effect but wholly distinct in motive. In order to appreciate how that confusion arose, and what there was in Richelieu's character which gave rise to that accusation, we must define carefully a capital point in the matter of human intention.

Cruelty is the love of giving pain for its own sake. We do not call a man cruel who is violent in revenge, who gives pain in passion, by accident, or for a further purpose unconnected with suffering in itself. We call a man cruel who takes pleasure in the suffering of others and inflicts it with that object.

Now we observe in the career of Richelieu a quality which is inhuman, and since cruelty also is inhuman, the two may be—but should not be—confounded.

That quality in Richelieu which is inhuman is his detachment from human emotions for the service of the State and (what was in his mind inseparable from the State) the Crown. "My only enemies were the enemies of the State"; and, Heaven knows, he made as many enemies as a man could: angry, implacable, tortured, but always disappointed enemies.

It was inhuman in Richelieu to be thus detached, as it is always inhuman to be above the general balance of mankind, and to sacrifice the proportion of the whole to a particular part. But the inhumanity was not the inhumanity of cruelty. There was nothing in it of disease. It was ruthless as war or the forces of nature are ruthless.

It has been remarked as something special about his public action that no one of the many plots laid against him during the eighteen years of his supreme power was exposed and ruined without the sacrifice of a human victim. Each one has an execution attached to it. A single example of this inflexible rule you may find in the execution of the Marshal de Marillac. His elder brother was the "Keeper of the Seals"—a post which we cannot in the early seventeenth century translate by the English term "chancellor," to which it no longer corresponds, but which was among the higher offices of the State. This elder brother had conspired against Richelieu in the effort of the King's brother and the King's mother to oust the Cardinal, which will be described. The Marshal himself, the brother, remember, not the chief conspirator, was with the army in Italy. He was arrested in the midst of the camp, tried, not for conspiracy at all, but for malversation of funds, and executed. It was grossly unjust. It was murder. But it had a clear political object: to make an example. I shall later return to it.

That is only one of many instances, but it is striking enough. Clearly Richelieu was determined to strike terror into a powerful family which had nearly succeeded in destroying his supremacy. Clearly, in order to strike such terror, being unable to make an example of the principal royal offenders, he acted against the chief subject family involved by putting to death a member of it. The accusation, which was only one of peculation, may have been well founded; but it is suspicious that the charge of malversation could nearly always be brought against almost anyone highly placed in the armies of those days, because there nearly always passed through their hands large sums for provisioning and pay and the rest, which sums were only loosely checked, and it was always possible to query monies unaccounted for.

But there was no excess of, nor any delight in, severity. Richelieu identified himself with the nation which he was directing; he was convinced that his fall—especially early in his administration—meant the renewed disturbance of the nation. It was the task of his life, and his sole interest in life, to leave the nation united, and the most powerful families powerless before the Crown. He attained that object, and he would not have attained it without such severity.

The same judgment applies, I think, to the other exceptional case of de Thou. Certainly to spare the brother of Marillac would have been justice, and without a doubt to make the brother of Marillac a victim for the plot of his senior was an injustice; but not a cruelty. In the same way to put de Thou to death shocked opinion, and rightly shocked it; for de Thou was not a conspirator, but a confidant. He was what the mechanical phrase of the lawyers (which has no regard to justice or honour) calls an "accessory before the act." Legally the execution of de Thou was justified, because he knew of the conspiracy and did not divulge it. Morally his execution was monstrous. De Thou had to choose between honour to a friend and service, not indeed to the State as he conceived it, but to an all-powerful minister. He preferred honour.

Nevertheless there was not in the execution of de Thou any element of cruelty, nor even of vengeance.

What was present was implacability. Not delight in suffering, but indifference to suffering so that a public need might be attained: and that was Richelieu to the marrow.

I myself would find, perhaps a little oddly, a recognition of this in the story about de Thou's surviving sister.

It is said that when the burial of the Cardinal was being prepared in the Chapel of his own choosing at the Sorbonne, de Thou's sister offered very large sums to the Fellows of the Sorbonne to be allowed to put a modest inscription in the neighbourhood of that coffin, upon the side of the vault where none would see it: the text from St. John, when Martha speaks to our Lord before the resurrection of Lazarus: *"Si fuisses hic frater meus non fuit mortiuus."* "Hadst thou been here, my brother would not have died." [1] It was refused, of course, but in the solemn irony of such an awful double jest there is no accusation of cruelty, but rather of that inhuman character of fatal, inexorable power.

Two lesser accusations stand against him, and each is well founded. He was avaricious—though his avarice was tempered with a noble love of magnificence—and he was vain.

As in the fault of early intrigue, Richelieu could salve his conscience in the point of avarice with the example of the great celibate churchmen before and after, who all would plead that the mass of their accumulation

[1] "Hadst thou been *here*" (in the tomb in the Sorbonne)—that is, had Richelieu died in time, de Thou would not have died.

would revert to public purposes. But he was prompted by avarice to unscrupulous action. He compelled or tricked men into selling their land to him below its value. He would obtain a promise of concession before offering a sum, and then have the property assessed by his own valuers and paid what they subserviently made out. He even bullied a citizen into giving up his home by the threat of a special tax. He loaded himself with pluralities. Before he died he had an income of over a million pounds a year. He left by far the largest fortune of his time. He did all this while the nation—and especially its poorer half—was being taxed on a scale hitherto unknown. It was this anomaly which earned him an universal hatred—to which he was indifferent.

And he was vain. That, and his plotting intrigues in youth are the two derogations from his greatness. I did not count in that vanity his passion for emphasising his noble birth, for after all the old grandmother who ruled the house of his childhood was a Rochechouart, and a noble house whose fortune has diminished has a right to parade its descent. It was not this, but his vanity in lesser things, that was a blemish.

His contemporaries and his own actions leave no doubt of this foible. Popular reports and even the judgment of courtiers close to government, would exaggerate the weak sides of such a powerful master. But the universal evidence of his readiness to take offence on the grounds of wounded vanity is too strong to be neglected.

For instance, when it was heard that the Bishop of Lodève had written a Latin epigram on the Cardinal and was secretly showing it to an acquaintance, men concluded at once that he was ruined. It is a less striking instance of this failing, but an instance none the less, that he should have taken such pride in the title of "Grand Master of the Fleet." The title of Admiral had been suppressed since 1622. Richelieu had taken the equivalent place so far as the political administration of maritime commerce and of the fleet was concerned: but it was an exaggerated thing to put the prows of a ship as the decorations of the vaults of his palace, as though he were a great sea-captain. Again: we shall see him later showing a strange jealousy of Corneille, and indeed his vanity ran to that literary sort which is too often comic. He wrote well, clearly and strongly. His memoranda, his judgments, his letters, are those of a good composer. But he wanted more. He could have wished for the magic of words—and in this he was absurd; for the Muse is not to be commanded.

There then is Richelieu; in the mixture of whose capacities and lackings is as much unity as in most men, and, for the one purpose of his life, political genius quite transcendent: genius such as arises but once or twice in the whole history of a nation.

VI

THE SURROUNDING FIGURES

MEN of ambition, whose weakness, and therefore passion, is for the exercise of real power, must both manœuvre and attack in the world surrounding them. They must deal very rarely as agents, nearly always as rivals, and often as mortal enemies with the characters which oppose or lie in flank of their progress.

Men whose much lesser ambition, whose weakness, and therefore whose passion is for publicity, decorations, a post (with its salary and opportunities for peculation) and the sham façade of ruling, the simulacrum of power, they also must shuffle and conceal, outwit and trip up their fellows, but all this they do in a fashion too petty to be called manœuvre and attack: and in this sham battle they must at heart treat every political rival as a colleague.

Between the first and the second type there is all the difference that appears between the pike and the eel: between the soldier and the actor.

To-day we are familiar with the second sort: Parliamentarians are of that kind. With the first sort—Cæsar, Napoleon, Bismarck, Wallenstein—we have lost acquaintance for so long that we have difficulty in understanding its mode of action. We have forgotten it because for now a century and more in the commercial countries, for a lifetime in the rest, real power over the community has lain more and more with the immensely wealthy controllers of production and exchange, and recently with the monopolists (for such they now are) of metals, fuel, transport, information, food and finance. The privileges of these, their organisation, above all, their secrecy of action, have come to be admitted without question. No one can control *them* who control us all. Those who still have attached to them the old labels of rule are, at their best, men of intelligence chafing at the poor part they are condemned to play, at their worst, maleficent and corrupt mountebanks, while the general run are nonentities whose pride it is to carry an official label: "Secretary of State for this," "Chancellor of that," "Président du Conseil," and all the rest of it.

But the great monopolists who are now the true depositories of power have not the attainment of power for their motive. Their motive is the acquisition of wealth, and power arrives to them accidentally and late in their careers, as an adjunct only of their gold. Often they neglect it. They never sought it for its own sake; and even those who, having swept up vast fortunes, become attracted by the novel opportunity for using wealth as an instrument of rule, do so clumsily.

The ambition of these new masters of ours, their weakness, and therefore their passion, being not for power but for brute money, what the struggle for mere power must be, we of to-day can hardly seize, for we have no examples of it before us. The men who did in past time (and shortly will again—for it is in the nature of man) aim continuously and fiercely at real power, and power alone, work upon major lines. They serve, with ardent care, whatever will bestow power, they act intensely against whatever may intercept it; they destroy competing careers utterly; they strike hard at the precise moment; they command; they kill.

Of this sort was Richelieu, and because he was of this sort, it is essential to our comprehension of his action that we should know the principal characters among which that action took place. They are very numerous, and in such a study as this I must confine myself to a few: the Queen, Anne of Austria; the Queen Mother in whose service he first rose; her younger son, Gaston Duke of Orleans—during nearly all the active part of the reign the heir apparent to a childless brother and ready to supplant that brother; (François) Joseph du Tremblay, that Capuchin upon whom Richelieu all his life relied; the true chiefs of Huguenot rebellion, the Duke of Bouillon, Rohan, the Huguenot leader in arms; and, before all others, the King, Louis XIII.

With the King must we begin, for upon Richelieu's relations with the King all turned. France lived by monarchy. Even in the worst of the perpetual rebellions and civil wars which are the very history of the nation, the idea of monarchy overshadowed all.

The King, then, was really king. It depended upon his will whether or no any man should be his minister, or exercise any *legitimate* power whatsoever of administration, justice or public force in the State.

The original condition of Richelieu's effect upon Europe, though that effect proceeded from the Cardinal's own genius, was the King's approval. On one occasion

after another when Louis was within an ace of eliminat-
ing that supreme servant, he came down, not without
hesitation, upon the side of retaining him; on the chief
occasion of all, "The Day of Dupes," that decision affected all future history.

What kind of man was this upon whose wise but not
necessary choice the presence of Richelieu in European
affairs depended? What was the nature of the will which
thus decided in favour of maintaining Richelieu's energy at work in the affairs of Christendom?

The character of Louis XIII is difficult to seize, for
it comprised qualities hardly ever combined in one man;
it suffered from most unusual gaps and voids. Yet it is
essential to appreciate its main lines in approaching the
great historical problem of Richelieu.

The commonest, because the easiest, error to make
about Louis XIII is to despise him; yet it was his choice
—not his necessity—that Richelieu's mind, which has
given its shape to all the story of the West, should continue at work; and the first thing we have to understand
about the man is that he was not dominated. He was not
a man to be overawed, still less to be frightened. He was
born too late in the life of a father, Henry IV, in whom
wars and debauch had exhausted a vigorous Southern
stock. From his first childhood he lived by the aid of
physicians who, though they have been blamed for excess in the methods of their day (bleeding and purging
ceaselessly) were successful in preserving his unstable
body. His nerves began wretchedly. He saw ghosts as a
child, and so feared the dark that he must have attend-

ants about him to watch his tardy sleep. He was always
ailing. He died young (at forty-two). But he was not
weak. So far from feeling in Richelieu a superior power
which he could not withstand, he was of the sort that
resented any attempt at mastery. You have but to look
through the various episodes of his life to see that he
reacted with exceptional promptitude—much more rapidly than do most men—to the challenge of another will.
At sixteen he alone, amid hesitating older friends, decided the sudden overthrow and death of his mother's
favourite who was usurping power. He rated protesting
judges of his with fine authority. He withstood conspiracy after conspiracy, and always with success.

He was brought up with the severity, but not with
more than the severity, common to the age; yet he was
brought up badly—as might be expected of such a
mother. For indeed she half neglected and half bullied
him, having a sort of favouritism—not very warm either
—for Gaston. He was not sufficiently grounded in the
classics nor in his own language and literature, but even
had he been well trained in them he would not have
maintained culture after his boyhood, for books were
abhorrent to him.

Richelieu's own rooted conviction that ignorance, *in
the right place,* is of advantage to the State (he admired
it particularly in the populace and in all that takes no
active direction of affairs) must have been confirmed by
the solidity of that negative advantage in his young
master. (The Cardinal was sixteen years older than the
King.)

Louis XIII's distaste for learning was, even in boyhood, something more than a lad's aversion from lessons. There was something furious about it and something original. It was abnormal, but it was a piece of true energy in one who, here and there again, in one department after another, seemed to be incapable of energy. Indeed that is the very essence of our problem in appreciating Louis, that every quality he possessed, he possessed in fragments. He decided sharply and well—but only on a quarter of the occasions when decision was necessary; in the rest he simply avoided decision altogether, not with hesitation but completely.

He made hot favourites for brief periods—for long periods had none. In four things alone was he continuous and of a piece: in his sincere religion (he dedicated France to Our Lady of his own motion, and never failed in practice); in his attachment to all military things; in his manual aptitude—odd excellence, but the complement of his illiteracy—(he could carpenter well, garden excellently, shoot, ride, and work in metal; he could shave others—surely a rare acquisition in kings or subjects—he could shoe a horse with any blacksmith); and lastly in his maintenance of Richelieu in office.

His ill-education, coupled with his natural disposition, made him secretive. His mind turned inwards. He might have been, but was not, capable of cruelty: yet he took a sort of sullen pleasure in making others suffer those inconveniences which he himself boasted to bear. For instance, he would keep men about him in the coldest weather when he went ferreting; he was observed to note their suffering from the frozen air, on his indifference to which he prided himself. He took the same ill-conditioned pleasure in noting the fatigue of those whom he wearied on horseback in his long hunting rides, and longer rides in war.

Such a disposition is offensive, but it is not feeble.

But the most intimate abnormality about him, the most illuminating, is that of his closer human relations. His development was perhaps arrested—he had no beard for the barber till well on in his twenties. His indifference to women was extraordinary. It would not be extraordinary if he had been wholly or partially incapable —but the perplexing point is that he was not. It is true that his marriage was the common boy-and-girl marriage of royalty, but even at nineteen his mentor and guide, de Luynes, had to push him, recalcitrant, shirt-clad, protesting, into his young wife's bedroom, insisting on his duty to the dynasty: a duty for which he was perfectly competent but which he had no inclination to perform.

When he was disappointed in his first child by her miscarriage, he associated with her no more for thirteen years; and this although it was of such moment to the monarchy, for which he had so profound a feeling, that an heir should be given it. During all these years men took it for granted that no heir would come, and the ground was open for perpetual threat of rebellion and usurpation by his brother. We shall see how his next effort—at the age of thirty-seven—resulted at its first experiment in the child who was to be Louis XIV, and in his few years of life remaining children continued to be borne to him by his wife as naturally as to any other father.

It is common-sense to look, in such a case, for mistresses. There were none. He was strongly attracted, once and again, to some lady of the court—usually a pious one; but the attraction remained platonic: utterly so.

It is obvious to conclude that perversion alone could account for such a neglect of natural things. But of perversion there is no trace. A superficial acquaintance with no more than the few main external and apparent facts would lead at once to the conclusion that he was vicious. A detailed knowledge of his intimate life, a full acquaintance with all that those who knew best and would least hesitate to write or speak, makes it quite certain that he was nothing of the kind. He was as virtuous as he was cold. He had friendships, one after another, so violent as to be often ludicrous; such intense friendships with men, now brief, now prolonged, are a feature of his whole life. They were each and all without a shadow of offence. The nastiness of the last Valois had no place whatsoever in this Bourbon.

Then (one may ask) being so empty of manliness with women, so given to over-sensitive affection in friendships—and many such—was he not effeminate? He was the very opposite: loving rough jests and gestures and taking especial satisfaction in the exercise of his body; never more determined (and he was a man of determination at intervals) than when he was at the full use of his muscles and hands and eyes, in sport or on campaign. Then (you would suggest) he was a good companion? Far from it: morose, stubborn, silent—and often jealous. Then there was nothing to be predicated of him in general: he was but a bundle of incongruities, most of them unattractive, and, in combination, futile? No, for he had those steadfast, unifying things about him on which I have insisted. He steadfastly served, and gloried in, kingship. He well understood that fine French phrase *"Métier de roi,"* "The trade of being a king." He had physical aptitude and used it continually, he had sound religion all his life, was all his life the soldier.

There you may see him with his pale long hollow face set in long black hair, firm yet open mouth with its too thick lower lip, his slight occasional stammer, his half Italian liquid dark eyes, not downcast yet not daring, his careful dignity in carriage, his most unhumorous and neutral gaze.

Now it must be particularly noted that this strange man disliked the Cardinal. There was none of that active repulsion which legend has credited him with, but there was an unceasing strain and distance. For he could not but feel that *such* a figure, however respectful, however devoted, was a sort of master.

In early youth, when he was less silent than in his later habit, he had expressed the feeling openly, and to the very end, though he was grateful as king, (as an individual he hardly knew what gratitude was) yet he continued to feel the air created by that imposing intelligence repugnant to him.

Why then did he maintain Richelieu at the helm? Not because his own judgment of European affairs was sound, but because, with all his unhealthy streaks in mind as in body, he had solid sense in a thing vital to authority: the appreciation of his own limitations. Also because—a thing still more important—he had solid judgment upon actions which came immediately under his eye.

Louis could not have told you whether it was better that the Catholic League in Germany could be played as a trump against Austria, or whether it was wise to turn to Gustavus Adolphus. He could not of himself have decided the degree of toleration advisable, in the interests of the monarchy, after La Rochelle. He certainly could not have devised a policy for the Valtelline or a combination against Spain. But he did note that in everything Richelieu undertook things happened as Richelieu had intended they should happen, and he saw that the things which happened increasingly strengthened the Royal Office which was sacred to him, the Crown he had inherited and must transmit. Richelieu strengthened it until he had enlarged its power out of all knowledge and the process was apparent to Louis. It was this direct, simple, sufficient appreciation of a prime reality which did all the work.

Had Louis XIII been more vivacious, or especially intelligent (he was not unintelligent though uninstructed), he might well have broken with the Cardinal in moments of conflicting decisions. Instead of that, he carried on.

To complete our understanding of why this diseasedly reserved man, and this easily offended man, acted so steadfastly on the one main line of his reign, there is another point of importance to be grasped; the more important to our understanding of the time because it has been so much neglected.

I have said that Louis was military: from the childhood when he ranged little toy silver regiments and harnessed toy guns to dogs, to the last great day before Perpignan. I have said that Richelieu was essentially a commander. Well, the two men having this one capital national quality in common, though very differently exercised in each, were linked by it. They were both, at heart, soldiers

Louis XIII would never have made a good general officer; Richelieu would not only have made one of the best general officers in history, but did in practice act as a general officer of the highest talent: and if he had been called Emperor instead of Cardinal, the whole world would see it.

Louis XIII could never have swept over a mass of detail with his eye, choosing the exact instant in which to plant the blow, to fall on the defensive, or to retire, organise, and triumph through organisation. He could not even have handled great numbers of men.

Richelieu had all those qualities. But both men differing so vastly in the degree of their military talent, were military to the core, and therein is found the true point of contact between them.

The King being vain or jealous, the superiority of another in his own field would have been a sufficient cause for rupture. On the contrary, it was his very devotion to arms which made him understand what a great man-at-arms stood disguised in the insufficient figure, too-pointed subtle face, and clerical robes of the personality for ever at his side.

Two royal women, both by the accident of a state marriage, each without capacity, stood prominent in aid or obstruction of Richelieu's principal and original efforts: Anne of Austria, the King's wife, Marie de Médicis, the King's mother. The first was of little or no effect upon the development of Louis XIII, the second of great and evil effect: both play a large part in his minister's career, Anne of Austria as a nuisance and later a plotter, the Queen Mother as, at first, a patroness, next a drag, at last an enemy.

Anne of Austria, sister to the King's contemporary Philip IV of Spain, was, as a young woman, a character remarkable in nothing but her misfortune. Her misfortune was that of being Louis XIII's wife. We have seen how she was treated. Such treatment coming on a rather silly soul, with no strength and not a little sentiment, bred no real scandals—she defended herself even against Buckingham—but it bred an uneasy boredom. Her mother-in-law did all in her power to put her wrong with the King—a task too easy. Because Richelieu rose through her mother-in-law, she treated him as her enemy of set purpose in the beginning of his power, when he had himself caused the ruin of that mother-in-law she still intrigued and conspired against him to the end. She was nobody as yet in 1624, but she was the Queen; and her opposition was, by the effect of her position, appreciable though not formidable to the Cardinal. He met her futile resistance with some contempt and, when it came later to plotting against the policy of the State and aiding her Spanish brother, with severity.

It was very different with the Queen Mother: by her influence, under her regency in the first year of the reign, Richelieu rose. With her he would have desired to remain associated, had she not taken the initiative in bad temper at his growing power, in envy of his incomparable talent for affairs (she had none and yet claimed to exercise it), in jealousy of his influence with her son. To the last (a just judgment must decide) he would have kept her friendship if he could, nor did he ever—when it was in his power—treat her with disrespect, but rather with an excessive deference. One thing only he came to forbid her, which was a foolish attempt at continuing her dangerous and foolish interference in the policy—especially the foreign policy—of the Crown. Not even his reinstatement in her despite during the sixth year of his power would have been her ruin, nor caused her exile, had she not, in his right judgment, endangered the State.

He has been accused of ingratitude towards her, and of pursuing the common course of kicking down the ladder by which he rose. I repeat that the accusation is

unjust. Not that Richelieu would have hesitated to do
anything which might confirm his power, and rid him
of a person who could only be a hindrance to strong government, but he did feel real gratitude to the woman
who had patronised his early ambition: he showed deference to her long after it had ceased to be necessary to
his career.

The attack came wholly from her side, and was due
not only to the jealousies and envies I have noted, but
also to a plethoric vanity somewhat coloured by disappointed coquetry—though it sounds comic to use the
word "coquetry" in connection with such a face and
form.

Marie de Médicis, this mother of the King, was perhaps the worst possible choice fortune, or Providence,
could have made for the position she filled. The French
monarchy was patriarchal. Opinion demanded respect
and submission of the child to the parent. She was unworthy of it. Indeed, the French monarchy suffered successively from two female regencies, and the two women
—Marie de Médicis and her daughter-in-law Anne—
both of them incapable of ruling in their different sorts
of incapacity, both of them managed to keep the country
in weakness abroad and civil war at home while they
held power; yet by a compensating stroke of fortune,
each was the instrument for putting a powerful organising brain at the head of the State—Marie de Médicis
launched Richelieu, Anne of Austria supported Mazarin. Each had some personal affection for the man thus
patronised—an affection disappointed in the case of the

elder, but ending almost certainly in marriage in the case of the younger.

Marie de Médicis was a big, heavy, dull woman, enjoying none of those political virtues (such as inflexibility of purpose or horse-sense in negotiation) commonly attached to heaviness and dulness. So far from letting herself be managed, she had an exasperating ambition equal to her incompetence. She loved to rule because she could not do so. Her private vanity was always on the alert, and always suffering irritation. Her choice of men (if choice it could be called, for they rather imposed themselves) was blind. Yet she performed this great service involuntarily to the Crown, that she it was who provided the opportunity whereby Richelieu climbed into power.

Her unwisdom was apparent in every act of her life. One odd example of it we have at the inception of the reign, or rather just before its inception. The facts are certain. The reader must decide upon their character of coincidence or something more.

Henry IV had been warned by a soothsayer that on the day after his wife's coronation he would be killed. This prophecy, of which we have record, was of profound effect over the King's mind.

The coronation of the Queen Consort was a normal thing; she had the right to insist on it. But a wise woman, seeing the condition of her husband's mind, would have spared him the anxiety, however much she might have ridiculed his superstition. She did the opposite—she fussed and insisted, until at last he gave way.

He allowed the coronation of his wife to take place on the 13th of May, 1610. On the 14th he was stabbed to death in the streets of Paris.

Her unwisdom was permanent, and of the worst and most permanent effect in the favouritism she showed towards her younger son.

Gaston (of Anjou by title at first, then Orleans) was not the altogether worthless fellow which conventional history makes him. I will discuss his character in a moment.

He, at any rate, was the heir-apparent for the twenty-three years during which the King had no son, and the apparently certain successor to that unhealthy brother for the thirteen years during which Louis XIII abandoned relations with his wife. He was therefore necessarily the centre of intrigues framed against the royal power and directed towards the disruption of the State.

That did not prevent his mother from showing him every favour, from supporting him even in conspiracy—and that only out of personal pique—until at last she caused his own ruin and exile to follow upon her own.

She was particularly unwise in the successive experiments she made as regent, or which were made for her as regent, in the placing of one insufficient man after another at the head of affairs.

She was disastrously unwise in the bringing up of her eldest son.

What Louis had of fitness for a king he drew from himself or from that dead father whose memory he so ardently worshipped. Much of his unsuitability he owed to physical circumstance, but more to the neglect and folly of his mother. It was in great measure her disdain (to keep him from government she spread rumours of his mental deficiency) which made him morose and stubborn in his relations with authority in boyhood and colleagues in manhood. She was in great part to blame if he was slow to learn, and while resenting injury, deeply hid his resentment.

We have seen from his character as a whole that it would have made his upbringing a work of sufficient delicacy for the most careful watcher. In the hands of his mother it was disastrous. She met his stubbornness in childhood with orders for a discipline—vicariously imposed by others—unaccompanied by that sympathy without which discipline is worse than useless; she herself left him in the main to subordinates, and such attention as she did pay to him was not directed to the reformation of what was ill, but only to the suppression of whatever for the moment exasperated her.

She made no effort to prevent his exaggerated partiality for one associate after another. On the contrary, she welcomed such distractions as useful for keeping him from any idea of entering the Council in his early youth. When he sat there he was allowed no voice, and on one occasion she turned him out of the door by the elbows, though he was past his childhood.

She was wholly hostile to canalising such energies as he had towards the business of ruling. She never fostered his singular attraction to arms; she hardly understood it, or even noticed it.

But her capital absurdity, and the proof of Richelieu's wisdom in ultimately denying political power to such a woman, was her infatuation for the adventuress (and her subservience to the husband of that adventuress) who brought about her first exile from the Court.

We shall find her falling into the hands of a servant—a fellow-countrywoman, an Italian (for the Queen Mother was Italian to the end, in speech, accent, thought). She gave to that servant's worthless, uncertain and intensely unpopular husband (himself an Italian) all that could be given, loading him with wealth, and making him a Marshal of France. The populace were enraged. The nobles in the capital for the most part indignant. She showed no faculty for testing or respecting the vague but intense force of public opinion. And when the crash came, the two favourites doomed (one by murder, the other by law) she was taken wholly by surprise.

In the interval between that first exile and final catastrophe which drove her from the country—an interval of thirteen years—she did nothing but exert the influence she had to the hurt of the State, and, even so, had no set plan behind what she did.

Her public actions in exile were made up of private jealousies, dislikes, and partialities. Had she been a trifle more intelligent one might credit her with some appreciation of the Catholic standpoint in the great quarrel of the time, for her name was always used in connection with the full Catholic programme, which would have supported Spain, spared the Austrian monarchy, and destroyed the Huguenots at home.

But her motive in all that had nothing about it European or religious. She did not even act as an Italian; she acted (or was used) partly as a member of her own family with a purely domestic reason for supporting the Papal policy, much more as an angered woman in late middle age[1] taking her revenge upon a statesman by whose power she was exasperated, and whose earlier lack of docility to her attraction or commands inflamed her vanity.

Not the least of Richelieu's claims to our admiration is that he was able to deal with that most dangerous of situations: the presence of official power in hands unable to use it. He would have spoilt all by acting too violently, or too early against the clumsy interference of the Queen Mother.

He was patient, he was even loyal; and when he had determined that the thing was to end once and for all, good fortune (but also the weight of his past services) enabled him to drive the woman away at the right and the last moment. He did so before his great European plans had been set in action, but while they were preparing, in the months before he called Gustavus Adolphus into the field as a subsidised ally. Had he delayed, and had the remaining influence of the Queen Mother

[1] She was close on thirty when Louis was born, a woman of forty-three when the first quarrel arose, of fifty-six, when she was finally exiled, and close on seventy when she died—within a few months of her son.

disturbed the foreign policy of 1630-1635, his work might have been ruined.

Gaston, Duke of Orleans, Marie de Médicis' younger son, is a far simpler character to appreciate than his brother the King. He was good-looking, lively, not unattractive in temper and without a head: easily influenced to plot, or rather to lend his name and authority to the conjurations of others; still more easily frightened out of the perilous positions into which he had allowed himself to be led; eager to succeed Louis and even to supplant him—an accident from which the State was saved. From first to last he is the direct enemy of Richelieu. His accuser, the figurehead of coalitions against him, on one occasion (in which his courage failed, as usual) directly planned his assassination. So rooted became at last this habit of attack and opposition, that even after his brother's son was born and there was an heir to France—three years after—Gaston is still proposing to lead armies from his exile. In himself he counted very little: but his birth made him the peril he was; his birth also saved him from the full penalties of his repeated treasons. Though he was the Cardinal's most persistent opponent out of so many, there was perhaps none of whose personal value he need take less heed.

To these Court figures we must add the great Huguenot nobles, still almost independent, who were at the heart of the rebellions and whom it was Richelieu's business in life to wear down and reduce to the obedience of subjects, powerless before the King.

Without doubt the strongest personal force in that

field of action was the Duke of Bouillon; and it is an interesting speculation what would have happened if these two intelligences, each absorbed in the network of public action, and these two wills, each so intense, had come into direct conflict as protagonists: if, for instance, Henry de Bouillon had by accident been thrust to the very captaincy of the Huguenot forces in the great crisis of the year of La Rochelle. As it was, this master of a separate principate on the extreme north-eastern frontier and of the Sedan stronghold thereon, never came openly into the active battle. He remained the adviser, supporter and chief of the powerful Protestant faction which so nearly dismembered France.

He stood between the two great societies, French and German, which have the Rhineland for their boundary, as a link, or makeweight, or buffer, and in the religious quarrel he was the chief of those opposed to the unity of Europe.

Let me describe the man. He was of the great House of La Tour d'Auvergne; he brought to the Germanies and the Empire, wherein his action was of most effect, the French diversity of mind and strength of intention, as well as the French lucidity; but he brought none of the French racial feeling, however distantly. He had wholly detached himself, in that age of rising nationalism, from the nation whence he drew his race.

This man, with the sanest and the most energetic face of all his contemporaries, eyes strong though cunning, firm mouth hardly hidden by the pointed beard, short crisp hair, muscular body and readiness of gesture;

a man singularly successful in leading others by suggestion, and even by command; a man who dominated,
one might say, wherever he went, and, as he was the
most balanced of his time, so also was the least moral
—working wholly for himself—had married the heiress
of that great House which is at the fountain-head of
the Crusades, the House of Bouillon; the House whose
fortress still stands, though half in ruins, on its long
lonely rock-ridge of the Ardennes, with the river sweep-
ing round it and solemn forests on the hills. She, after
two years of marriage with this Count of Turenne, (for
such was his title) died, and left him by will the principality of Sedan. New Sedan was the stronghold which
could aid or bar invasion over the north-eastern frontier
of France; and note that at this moment it was not held
of the French King. Henri, Duke of Bouillon was,
though a French noble, something like a petty independent sovereign as well.

Henry IV had been half afraid of him, half his master.
He had in a manner curbed Bouillon's power; but he
tolerated it, and he hesitated to challenge it.

Bouillon was not one of those Huguenots who drew
their religious profession from the first sincere zeal of
the Reformers, nor even, as did Henry IV himself, from
the political Protestantism of the great nobles, drawn
into the conflict by a hope of sharing in the loot of the
Church. He was, in the proper sense of the word, a
renegade, for he had grown into manhood on the Catholic side, and he had abjured his religion wholly for the
prospect of gain and power, because, by such abjura-

tion, he could better play the part of independent pivot between the Protestant Germanic states including Holland on the one hand, and the Court of Paris on the other. Moreover, his Protestantism was Calvinist; a point of importance at that moment when the cleavage between Lutheran and Calvinist was still deep—so deep that German politics largely turned upon it.

After his first wife's death he married a princess of the House of Orange, that is, of Holland, and thus became the uncle by marriage of the young Count Palatine, who in his castle at Heidelburg stood as the centre of German Calvinism, weak and foolish though he was. This was the lad who had married the daughter of James I of England, and whose own mother also was of the House of Orange. Of that young Count Palatine the Duke of Bouillon had been left the guardian.

Now things stood thus at the moment when Germany was about to break into that profound and destructive tumult called the Thirty Years' War. The Duke of Bouillon held this position of guardian to the young Prince Palatine, and of chief personality among the Calvinist leaders, just when the House of Austria was about to make its main bid for recovering all Germany to Catholicism and establishing throughout Germany the complete monarchy of the Hapsburgs—a plan, opposition to which is the main concern under Richelieu's rule.

The Duke of Bouillon, Count of Turenne and Prince of Sedan, perpetually held his hand. Of how he affected the German problem I have spoken. His chief interest to Richelieu lay in his attitude towards the French. He was one of those men who appreciate the value of perpetual and vivacious talking on the condition of never saying anything they choose not to say. King Louis XIII of France was such another: a spate of words which not only masked the mind as effectually as a cascade will mask the space behind it, but also persuaded, impressed, directed lesser men. This garrulous reserve of his, Richelieu knew well to be his strength, and so, still loquacious, he held his hand.

Standing there between the Germanies and France, Bouillon took almost as great an interest in the latter as in the former, proving that that word "Sedan" has a recurrent meaning in French history. He was the acknowledged chief of the French Protestant movement, and therefore of the attack upon the Crown, yet never was himself at issue or in peril: he was the man whom all consulted upon that side, to whom all turned, by whom perhaps not a few were subsidised, and yet the man who never risked in that quarrel the goal at which he aimed.

And what was that goal?

I make no doubt that it was the resurrection of the old idea of Burgundy: of an independent Rhenish state between Germany and France.

He failed to attain it. He came nowhere near it. Therefore the supposition may seem extravagant. Yet that, I take it, is what such a man at such a time would have in mind: the building up again of that central state of the Rhine, a revived Lotharingia; the western part of the Rhine Valley, with the lower valleys of its western tributaries, Meuse and Moselle. Such a state had Burgundy precariously been under its great dukes, descendants of the kings of France 200 years before, a state which linked the Alps with the North Sea; and could play perpetually upon the rivalries of French kings and German emperors and princes: a state the lack of which (in some form) renders crude the racial quarrels of modern Europe.

That is what this astute, voluble, secretive, intelligent, not combative and yet especially courageous man had at the back of his head for an ambition. It is odd that with such vast schemes in hand and with such a character, his own title of Turenne is best remembered through the military talents of his younger son.

Lesser in weight, nobler in morals, "paying with his body," as his compatriots say, was another Henry, Henri de Rohan, first Duke, who with his younger brother Soubise held the captaincy of the Huguenots and created the last rebellion which led to the fall of La Rochelle.

The family was very ancient, a cadet of those dukes (or princes) of Brittany who to the end of the Middle Ages were independent sovereigns under but a vague bond of nominal vassalage to the French kings. Hence was he treated as half royal even by his royal master and enemy in the field. Hence also the ducal title which Henry IV had given him twenty years and more before the last Protestant civil war which Richelieu ended.

But what gave him most position was not his long descent from the lords of Rohan in the Morbihan country, it was rather his father's marriage. For his mother was of the House of Parthenay—of Poitou like Richelieu's—and the House of Parthenay was a branch of those great Lusignans who stand out so highly in the mediæval story, with King John of England and the Barons' wars, and all the business of that attempt at a union of France and England under one throne which began with the Crusades and ended at Formigny after a struggle of three and a half hundred years.

This woman, the Parthenay wife of the elder Rohan and mother of Henri and Soubise, was of iron, as were so many of those Huguenot rebel women of the seventeenth century. She was as much a warrior as her son, and we shall see her in La Rochelle eating rats with the rest of them in old age, refusing to surrender. That son was trusted by the Protestant masses of the southern and western towns beyond his peers. He was a good leader, full of endurance as well, not much intelligence in his thick red head, but enough to carry on a campaign in those times of loose order, and certain not to betray. That was his chief point in days when most men, especially the great, fought each for his own hand, and when at the appearance of defeat captains would change sides. He had married Sully's daughter, much younger than himself, and she made a fool of him on all sides.

The other great nobles of the Huguenot cause were —with justice—less trusted by the towns of the South and their middle-class Presbyterian groups, by the consistories and the ministers of the Calvinists. But in him they felt secure. And because he was also a strong soldier, he may be taken as a representative of what Richelieu had to count with in the field of civil war.

Now to all those we have passed in review, from the King to Rohan, we may say that Richelieu at the height of his power was distasteful. Some had always been, and remained his constant opponents, some grew to be so, some supported; but *all* were inimical. If ever there were a man who had to live spiritually alone it was he. He loved perhaps one being, his niece, whom he made Duchess of Aiguillon. But when he looked about him to find who might feel some affection for himself, he found none—or one only.

It was the price he paid for a combination within his soul of three things: an exalted superiority to other men in decision and understanding; exercising that superiority in the forcible reduction of all to order; absence of sympathy with human hearts through an exclusive interest in problems and political ideals.

That isolation weighed upon him heavily; but he was too strong to attempt escape.

To the King whom he served so triumphantly, his very power of achievement was an irritant—for though Louis accepted such an advantage by his reason, to his emotions the sense of mastery was odious. To the Queen Mother he was a potential lover who had been cold and a servitor who had taken her place; to the Queen-wife a persecutor; to Gaston an upstart usurping the dues of royalty; to Bouillon a direct enemy in policy, and to Rohan an enemy armed. To the hosts of dependants and spies an exact taskmaster; to the lawyers a man curbing them; to the millions of the peasant populace and to the artisans and merchants of the towns, a rapacious taxgatherer who robbed them outrageously and himself accumulated millions.

But one being had followed with interest which immediately turned into sympathy, the first steps of that career, had stood beside it constantly as agent and still more as prompter, increased in personal affection throughout its progress, and rejoiced, on the approach of death, to find his leader and confidant secure in victory. This man was François le Clerc du Tremblay, of sound birth, of talent quite unordinary, of passion for the Faith more exceptional still, a Capuchin.

The Capuchin order of Friars was a reformed branch of the Franciscans. It had arisen, as had the Jesuits, under the necessities of the Reformation. Founded just after the outbreak, its object became the recovery of Christendom and the re-establishment of the Catholic faith throughout Europe. To this one end were its energies directed, and with that end in view did its recruits join the new body. Joseph du Tremblay, not without possessions—a large château in Poitou and a good house in Paris—of a legal family which had established itself on landed property, decided in youth, after some experience of travel and diplomacy, to enrol himself among these missionaries and to join their effort at restoring unity and order.

But Joseph du Tremblay—the "Père Joseph" of French history (his name in religion was Joseph)—differed from the mass of his fellow Capuchins in this: that he conceived of the task as Gallic: hence his enthusiasm for a Crusade against the Mohammedan which his contemporaries thought extravagant and moderns irrational: hence (what is more to our purpose in this book) his fixed conviction that the recovery of civilisation was not to be effected through the Empire but through France.

The Papacy, and the regiment of Capuchins serving it, read the restoration of Europe in terms of Germany. Spain was saved, Poland was saved, Italy and the Southern Netherlands also. In France the victory had already been won, at least officially, by popular pressure and the conversion of Henry IV. If religious anarchy survived in part, the government could in time eliminate it. The great bulk of our Europe (they said) was secure— but the Germanic world, still most opulent and populous (for the Thirty Years' War had not yet ruined it) was still cruelly subject to insecurity. In the German-speaking cantons of Switzerland, denial of the Faith prevailed and the endowments of religion had been largely lost. In the Empire there was present everywhere, on the Danube towns as at Donauverth, on the Rhine towns as at Strasbourg, at the gates of Vienna itself, in the Slav land of Bohemia, in the Magyar of Hungary, in the virtually independent principate and cities of the centre and north, the same state of dissent and quarrel in religion, of looted religious income. Let the Emperor turn his nominal sovereignty into a real central and autocratic power, subjecting every rebel city and noble, let him restore the material support of the Faith where it had been stolen, and the Continent would be itself again; over Holland and Denmark that influence must prevail. The detached and numerically small communities beyond the sea, Britain and Scandinavia, might remain innocuous or feel in their turn the general impulse. Europe would be Europe once more and Christendom Christendom, when the one great unstable area of the Germanies was pacified and re-edified in the Faith.

Therefore, upon the Germanies and the effort there begun by the Empire to create a homogeneous Catholic State, let the Capuchins concentrate. Such was the apparent objective, and to this policy the Capuchin mind assented.

Not so Joseph du Tremblay: he stood out alone—but how powerful an opponent! In his judgment such a solution would end in creating a new Europe Catholic perhaps, but also, especially (or more) Hapsburg. Austria meant Spain as well; and Austria and Spain in combined hegemony left the French Crown and people dependants on one side as would be Poland on the other. The restored Empire, its Spanish cousin, would, even at the outset of such a victory, hold all the Iberian Peninsula, all the New World, all the central mass from the Baltic to the Alps; all the Islands (save Corsica), all Italy (save the decaying city States and Piedmont divided from them by the Spanish Milanese). At the conclusion of the victory the Papal States, enclosed in that universal sea of Hapsburg might, would lie under its protectorate with the Pope a Hapsburg chaplain.

Such an issue seemed to this active and illuminated mind intolerable. The Catholic Church must prosper by the French energy and with the French Crown at least strong and independent; better yet, predominant. The old and well-worn phrase of the first Crusade, the motto of the Middle Ages, *"Gesta Dei per Francos,"* was not for him an antiquarian motto, but a living expression of Providence. Let the Capuchins re-evangelise everywhere, let a Capuchin be the first to preach a Catholic sermon in Béarn after a blight and silence of fifty years,[1] let Caupuchins reform institutions, create special "works" and found religious houses for the restoration of religion —but in the political field he would be no party to the Austrian policy: on the contrary, he would actively oppose it. To the attempt at a complete imperial rule he would oppose all its enemics. He would even support the Protestant rebels and Protestant foreign foes of the Hapsburg Empire, and with his vigorous diplomatic industry, his ceaseless voyaging in his rough habit from Court to Court and all his business of negotiation and counsel, he would aim at securing the strength of his own prince and people, Louis XIII and the French.

It is evident how such a temper matched with that

[1] The South of France was the focus of French Protestantism, but the flame was at its hottest in Béarn, that is, the district at the foot of the Western Pyrenees, including Pau, Tarbes, Orthez, Lourdes. Its ruler, Jeanne d'Albret, boasted that she had exterminated the Faith by massacre and confiscation, and that no child born in her reign would so much as know in manhood what the Mass was. For fifty years no Catholic doctrine could be heard.

of Richelieu. The two men were of one heart; and the elder (the Monk was born eight years before the Cardinal) was knitted with his junior in one arduous and at last successful labour over all the useful years of life. The two men so contrasted in person and demeanour—Father Joseph was short, bullet-headed, of a vivacious Socratean ugliness, with prominent strong eyes under bushy russet brows in a cowled russet head, nourishing a great straggling russet beard—made one force.

The doubt, long debated, as to which was the originator and guide in foreign affairs, Father Joseph or Richelieu, is a question irresolvable because there was no rivalry, nor perhaps, save upon rare occasions, any conscious clash of wills—though often a divergence on pace [1] and on the expediency of immediate action. Richelieu was clearly the commanding figure, but Père Joseph was much more than a mentor; he supplied decisions—the capital decision of all, the abandonment of the Rhine, was his. He supplemented all Richelieu's thought.

But indeed the two men were one.[2] One Province had bred them, Lower Poitou of the meadows and sea-marshes: more or less one rank—the lesser nobles and the

[1] We have echoes of it in reported phrases now familiar to all: *Richelieu's*, "Not so fast, Father Joseph!" *Joseph's* (to Richelieu) that he approached a particular difficulty "like a wet hen."

[2] I leave aside Michelet's thesis that the Capuchin was the Cardinal's rival and intrigued to supplant him. It is fantastic, and due to that which warps all the work of that great historian, from the trial of Joan of Arc to the misconception of the civil constitution of the Clergy. His domestic misfortunes had turned him eccentric in the matter of the Priest, and when he saw a cleric he saw red.

risen lawyer bourgeoisie turned squires. They had met in that same province when the younger was in his early twenties, not yet eminent, the elder in his middle thirtieth years. From that first meeting they had found each other's souls and were of a single mind.

SECOND PART

THE PROCESS OF THE ACHIEVEMENT

THE APPROACH

IT IS a main factor in Richelieu's historical position, in the sort of fabric he wrought and its close texture (whereby it survived) that he was condemned to a long and slow apprenticeship. It is as though Napoleon had passed ten years with no more than a regiment to command and another eight before he became a general officer. The young man was determined on public life from at least his coming of age, or earlier; he was over thirty before he entered the Council. He was present in it but a few months. He went into neglect, fell suddenly from employment, was in a sort of exile and struggled for eight years to recover his place: apparently without fruit. He was just on forty when he reappeared, somewhat suddenly, and not without the aid of accident, as head of the ministry—and, following closely on that, as supreme director of the nation till his death eighteen years later.

But it is characteristic of him that this apprenticeship was of his own choosing. He was not launched into a career by stress. He aimed from the first (and of himself) at what he desired, and reached after a lengthy course perpetually baffled, never discouraged. His advance towards it might be compared to a man's tortuous progress through a difficult country of dense woods and fens, all of which he succeeds at last in turning or breaking through. But the obstacles detained him nearly twenty years. He was in full maturity when his first brief chance appeared: he lost it: he was on the verge of middle age when he emerged at last with the way open before him.

The family whence Richelieu sprang was of more distinction than is generally appreciated. Richelieu rose, like most men who have played great parts in history, with considerable social advantage behind him.

The completeness of his power, especially towards the end of his life, and the way in which he triumphed over a host of men of higher blood, has led in his case, as in that of Cromwell, to an exaggeration of the contrast between what he reached and what he started from. For though Richelieu owed nothing, as Cromwell did, to connection with an immense family fortune—on the contrary, his family was embarrassed—yet it had a very long descent and the simple coat (three chevrons on a plain field) which often accompanies ancient lineage. Moreover it had, in the immediate past, risen to some eminence. This position was largely due to a great marriage. The grandfather of the Cardinal, Louis du Plessis, had married a Rochechouart, just before the outbreak of the religious wars. It was a lucky accident. The lady, Françoise by name, was no longer young nor of good temper. She annexed him in the country house of her cousin, Anne de Polignac—a family greater still.

But though this marriage raised the husband, he had an amply sufficient status of his own. In origin the du Plessis were manorial lords of the lesser sort; what the French call "the lesser nobility" and what are called in

England "the squires." The hamlet and few fields which gave them their name is one of the innumerable French "Plessis" [1]—in this case Plessis near Néons, in the valley of the Creuse; but there were many other manors accumulated in their hands through the course of the Middle Ages, and though, since the sixteenth century, manorial dues had lost much of their old value, the clan was wealthy enough.

The descent of this Louis, the Cardinal's grandfather, was from the younger branch which had come by a marriage into possession of the manor of Richelieu in the Angevin march of Touraine, but on the very edge of that province, and in air and character of soil and landscape attaching rather to Poitou, so that its lords counted themselves Poitevin. They had got it at the end of the Middle Ages about a hundred years before the Cardinal was born. This also was a manor house of no great pretensions, roughly fortified, representing of its own estate but a modest revenue, though its owners received rents from many others.

The son of this Louis, the Cardinal's father, of whom brief mention has already been made, had been specially prominent at a very critical moment in the history of his time. Although he lost, by speculation, much of the fortune he possessed, he had the advantage of great courage in a time of ceaseless fighting, and also the advantage of a useful virtue; loyalty to a master.

[1] The place named comes from the Latin "praxillus"—an interwoven hedge or palisade; a term which came to mean an enclosure, and so later, a manor house or small castle.

His first master, Henry III, put him at the head of the royal household as early as 1578; seven years later he made him Grand Provost, and gave him the highest rank in the Order of the Holy Ghost.

An accident, coupled with his promptitude and sincerity, brought him suddenly forward. That accident was the assassination of his master, the King, by Clément. He, in person, arrested Clément immediately after the murder. He was of great weight in securing, on the spot, the recognition of Henry IV, though he had nothing of the Huguenot about him. He was instinctively loyal to the legal heir, "The Head of the House of France"; he followed the new King's fortunes faithfully; he fought at Arques and at Ivry, and died in harness at the siege of Essone of a camp fever.

Such services made a deep impression on the memory of Henry IV, the best side of whose not very exalted character was good comradeship in arms. The future Cardinal, who was a child but five years old when his father died, had that tradition in his favour. The name of the dead soldier was not forgotten, and when his boy was old enough to receive advancement, the King was ready to favour him with the rest of the family.

The Cardinal's middle-class mother (who had the making of his character in childhood, and from whom he must have inherited that long and judicious patience which was not in his father's blood) unceasingly kept the name of the family before the Court from the early years of her widowhood until the youngest of the boys was grown up. It was she in particular who saw to it that the King should reserve the little bishopric of Luçon as a family living for them.

She was a very good manager of her encumbered income, and appears to have restored the fortunes of the Manor sufficiently to rid it of debt. More than that she could not attain. Though it would have been a just action on Henry IV's part to have granted a pension, it was never granted.

Yet it is an error (perpetuated in a whole shelfful of monographs on Richelieu) to call her embarrassed family *poor*. The widow was worried about money because her dead husband had gambled, because her eldest son, Henry du Plessis, lived among the smartest of the Court and was spendthrift, because the many buildings dependent on the various estates were dilapidated through age and far more through the ravages of the Huguenots after fifty years of civil war (nowhere was that chaos worse than in Poitou). But the total income would have been a good revenue for a family living on its land remote from affairs, and was sufficient, with careful management and saving, to restore the Richelieu position in a few years. Its exact amount we cannot determine; but we know that one item of it in ecclesiastical endowment, worth, gross, several thousand English pounds a year, was but an appendage of the whole. She husbanded it as it had never been husbanded before. Her quiet industrious life was spent in that task, under what was perhaps the irksome, certainly the severe presence of her Rochechouart mother-in-law who survived interminably.

Armand-Jean, her third son and fourth child, was born on the ninth of September, 1585. Of that date we are sure from a contemporary official document. But it is strange that of a man so eminent, in such a generation of manifold records, we should still be uncertain of his birthplace. Coming of a family so mixed with the Court, and being himself so strongly attached to lineage and domestic tradition, one would have thought that he would have left a written statement. Yet to this day the thing is disputed and will perhaps always be disputed. For the most extensive research has failed, so far as I know, (there may be something in the mass of MSS. at New York, which I have not been able to examine, but, if so, I believe the present holders of the title know nothing of it) to discover conclusive evidence.

Jal found in the baptismal registers of St. Eustache in the old Paris Hôtel de Ville the note of his baptism, which took place (eight months after his birth) [1] on the fifth of May, 1586. The date of his birth is there given also; *but no record of where it took place.* On the margin of this entry was written, later and in a different hand, the fact that his parents lived in the Rue de Jouy. Mademoiselle de Montpensier says that she had seen in the country house of the Richelieus the room in which the Cardinal had been born; for though he splendidly re-

---

[1] By a French custom the ceremonial baptism may, and commonly does, take place some time after a child's birth. The sacramental baptism is administered immediately after birth and privately. In this case the long interval was due to the delicacy of the child, perhaps also to his mother's ill-health. For she nearly died in bringing him forth, and they *may* have waited till she could travel to Paris.

built the old fortified manor house of his ancestors, he
deliberately preserved this room: why should he do so
save as his birth chamber? Now she was as nearly contemporary to Richelieu's career as the older readers of
this book are to Mr. Gladstone's. La Fontaine bears the
same witness. It is further to be remarked that the tradition in his household, going back to old family servants
who remembered him, was constant and certain that he
was born at Richelieu. Sellier, in his monograph on the
Pharmacie Centrale (which occupies the site of the old
Hôtel d'Aumont) says that Richelieu was born there.
Certainly his elder brother married into the family
which owned the Hôtel d'Aumont, but beyond that
Sellier gives no proof. Hanotaux, who has taken such
pains with the details of Richelieu's early life, discusses
the point very thoroughly and decides for Paris. In
favour of which there is the detailed life by Pure, (which
is not indeed contemporary but which was written in
close intimacy with the family after Richelieu's death),
and three phrases from the Cardinal himself (in 1628,
1633 and 1641, two in speeches, one in a letter) in which
he calls himself "Parisian." But this last evidence is not
of great weight. A public man flattering an audience
or a correspondent is no sure guide, and the terms used
are vague.

We can only conclude that the matter remains doubtful and will perhaps always so remain.

His childhood on that remote country estate was
well schooled under a prior from Saumur. At twelve
years old (in 1597) he was sent up to the University

of Paris, quite in the manner of a well founded family but without any very great state. He was served by two lackeys from home and accompanied by a private tutor to the College of Navarre, with the title of "Marquis de Chillou" taken from one of the Richelieu lands. He got there a grounding in the humanities that served him all his life and moulded his spirit. It was one of the deepest of his concerns when he came to govern that the State should nourish letters, and in his respect for them there was something much more than convention. He understood what they do to the Commonwealth. He could not have accepted—had it been given in his time— Dr. Johnson's extreme (and prejudiced) judgment that the greatness of a nation depends on its writers. But he thought and said that without a sufficient literature no nation could be great or even permanently strong. Now this mood of his towards the Word was planted in his teens on the hill of the Latin Quarter.

It has historical importance. For though, when his own rule over France began there was already behind it a whole century of crowded genius, from Rabelais to Ronsard (and I would include Malherbe), yet the nation did not yet breathe an atmosphere of literature, nor was there a sufficient audience for it. The wealthier and middle classes upon which such an air depends, were absorbed, the nobles in their civil wars, the bourgeoisie in their law, their commerce and their fierce religious dispute. It is with the seventeenth century, and especially after the first third of it, that things change—and Richelieu stands at the fountain of that change, himself of some original effect upon it.

Greek he knew a little, Latin thoroughly. He uses it even in his private correspondence at times, writing it rapidly and familiarly, not with scholarly style but with a straightforward intimacy as of a daily instrument: and in the course of his life he grew to speak and write with perfect ease the Italian and Spanish necessary for his information abroad.

When the main studies were over—after his eighteenth year (he had ended them in the Collège de Lisieux, or perhaps of Calvi under the renowned Henneguin)—he passed from the classics to the second and more vivid impression of his formative years; for in that moment of adolescence when it merges into manhood and when experience is of its deepest effect, the moment which, for most of us, determines the character of our lives, he entered with delight into military training at the Pluvinel's "Academy": a training place for the army. There did he learn that trained horsemanship which all remarked in his maturity when he would ride on parade before La Rochelle or in the Passes of Savoy; there did he grow skilled in sword-play with the youth of his rank, and there did he begin those studies in the history of war which he always retained. He had found his vocation; and though he might not follow it, it coloured his whole life.

That he did not pass on to a commission and "the career" was due to a chance which deflected his future into Orders. It happened thus:—

Already in 1600, when the boy was still at College and only fifteen years old, Henry IV, who never lost sight of his comrade's children and widow, offered Madame de Richelieu a lady-in-waitingship to the Queen—Marie de Médicis. She hesitated upon the honour, almost accepted it, but at last refused. She feared the expenses of the Court and the life of Paris and the Palace. She was still occupied in restoring the estates and fortunes of the family. The King understood her motive. He sent her £10,000 as a private gift, he took her eldest son, Henry, (who had been a page at Court) into his service as gentleman of the Chamber with a pension of £2,000 a year to support the position; he gave to the second son Alphonse the bishopric of Luçon. But in 1605, Armand "de Chillou," being then twenty and about to be given his commission, Alphonse abandoned the episcopate (he had never been consecrated, nor did he reside) and determined on monastic life. He left for the Grande Chartreuse, and Madame de Richelieu proposed to her youngest son that lest the endowment should leave the family, he should give up his hopes of soldiering, take Orders and succeed to the See.

He obeyed: it may be with a sharp intuition of opportunity, at any rate promptly and without argument. From that day you see Armand du Plessis engaged without intermission upon his one business of advance. He is started, his ambition is awake, his will has awakened fully to its service, and he goes forward by every effort of subterfuge and calculation at first, of unwearied

PRESENTATION OF RICHELIEU TO HENRI IV

FROM THE PAINTING BY GIUSEPPE AURELI

industry throughout, upon his conquering business of nearly forty years.

I say, "it may be with a sharp intuition of opportunity." There is no document nor any confession of his own upon the matter—and he was very young. But when we see how he handled immediately his new chances, and when we remember what Orders meant in that day for a young noble, as a gate into public life, the conjecture comes near certitude. By appetite he would have preferred the sword; by reason, serving his fixed determination to "arrive," he accepted the gown, and turned it to the account we know.

The bishopric of Luçon was of no great antiquity. It was a little See carved out of the great historic diocese of Poitiers by John XXII at the beginning of the Avignon Papacy—presumably to favour some French family by provision of a revenue for them. The date was 1317.

It is an error often repeated that the See was hereditary in the Richelieu family: far from it. James, brother to that Louis (the Cardinal's grandfather) who made the Rochechouart marriage was the first one of his blood to become its Bishop, and that but twenty-one years before, in 1584. Only from that year was it regarded as an appanage of the House.

He did not reside, any more than did later his grand-nephew Alphonse; and when Armand was proposed to succeed to this last, the work of the bishopric was deputed to the domestic chaplain of the Richelieus, a certain Hyver, who held it after the fashion of those days as a "warming-pan" to keep it going until that one of the family who might be nominated to it should care to take his place. Meanwhile this "locum tenens" of the See was bound by a formal contract, enforceable at law, to retain but a portion of the ecclesiastical revenue for his maintenance or as a consideration, to hand over the remainder to his patron, and to resign the whole if or when that patron should elect to come into residence. It was flat simony—and universally practised.

What the attachment of Luçon meant in revenue to the family I will attempt to estimate in a moment. Let me first remark that, as an honour, it was not very desirable, and, as a residence, not tempting. It is important to appreciate this in connection with Richelieu's later actions. The town is remote; access to it was, in those days, to be had only by rough earth roads. It is small and stands on the edge of the sea-fens of Poitou, much as Ely does to the sea-fens of East Anglia; but closer to the coast. In the seventeenth century it suffered from such a neighbourhood more than it does to-day. The fens over the vast flat of which it looks, towards La Rochelle on the southern horizon [1] were drained, but not so thoroughly as they are to-day. The somewhat malarial atmosphere had affected all its past history, and helped, when he took up his residence, to increase the physical weakness which Richelieu had inherited.

But here a warning is needed. His continual com-

[1] If you look for it aright La Rochelle lies twenty miles south of Luçon over dead flat land and tidal sands. From the higher windows of Luçon in clear weather you can make out the spires and towers of La Rochelle on the extreme horizon.

plaints of the distresses of Luçon, "the dirtiest See in France," his reiteration of its unhealthy character (reminding one of Swift's "the worst air in all Ireland"), his grievances upon its furniture and peopling—all these must be taken with reserve and at a discount. It was the policy of the young man, as of the mother who had trained him, to advance the family by this perpetual contrast between what they had and what they claimed as the least that in decency they should be granted. We have seen that though the father had left his inheritance encumbered and the estates embarrassed, and though it needed Madame de Richelieu's housewifery to restore them, the manors were many, and a woman who gets royal presents on the scale of £10,000, while one son, hardly of age, gets a royal salary of £2,000 a year, another goes to the University with servants and a private tutor, another receives a See, is not in penury. They were sincere in saying that the sons and widow of the man who had saved two kings [1] deserved even more of the Throne; they were not affluent for their rank, if we count that rank by the Grand Provostship and the Rochechouart marriage, but they were of the rich.

In this connection let us consider the revenues of Luçon. The gross income of the See was 18,000 *livres* a year, or £9,000 of our English money (1929). For the *livre* (or franc, the ancestor of the modern French franc) had, during the first campaigns of Richelieu a purchas-

[1] Two kings. For the Cardinal's father had been with Henry III in the Barricades, and had secured his flight from Paris—when he would have been murdered; while, by his immediate recognition of Henry IV, he, more perhaps than any man, saved that throne also.

ing power of some sixty to seventy francs of this present
year (1929), ten shillings English, two dollars and fifty
cents,[1] and in 1605, the year of Armand du Plessis' acceptation of Luçon, it was worth more. The purchasing
value of money was falling all the time.

This £9,000 a year had to pay the upkeep of cathedral,
palace, gardens, canonries and close and cloisters, expenses of visitation throughout the diocese, and some
part of the residential expenses of the Chapter.

What remained as net revenue, after all outgoings, to
swell the private income of a non-resident titular bishop?
We have no precise documents to guide us, but certainly
not five thousand, and perhaps only three—certainly
more than two.

It was no gigantic addition to the fortune of a Poitevin noble, but it was appreciable; and it was as *income*
that Madame de Richelieu regarded it. Her famous son
made of it something greatly more.

The King's letters-patent granting him the bishopric
were issued in 1605. He entered Luçon to reside there
at the very end of 1608—the feast of St. Thomas of
Canterbury (Dec. 27th). The manner in which he em-

[1] This equivalent, 1 livre = ½ a modern English Pound which I use
throughout this study when I quote sums of money in modern terms, is
much higher than will commonly be found in the text-books. You will
generally hear it at something more like a 1/4 or a 1/5 of a modern
English Pound or even 1/6. But then the academic authors of our text-
books copy in this, as in most things, from earlier text-books, and those
from earlier ones again, and so on, in a chain. We can estimate the
livres of, say, 1627-1635 pretty accurately from the detailed accounts of
military expenditure. For instance, 60 are needed *per* mount, to horse a
troop. Well, £30 is not too much for a trooper's horse.

ployed those three and a half years has been explained on
a dozen different motives. There is only one to make his
actions consistent: he was laying a foundation.

I do not mean that this man, more than any other
destined to very great fortunes, could foresee them, nor
even that he had as yet a clear conception of his actual
end. No one could so foresee or exactly plan, and he
was but a lad of twenty. I mean rather that he saw as
did no other young noble of his day, among so many
who were given bishoprics for revenue, that if he took
his new trade seriously he could build on that experience
and pass on from it to great things in the service of the
State.

He plunged into theology. It was a singular effort of
concentration; his first exercise of self-mastery and his
first test of self-control. All the year 1606, during which
he came of age, he was working as though the subject
was to be the chief occupation of his life, having for master perhaps the great Caspéan, more certainly—and it is
of interest—the Englishman, Richard Smith, the famous
Vicar Apostolic during the persecution under James I.

Meanwhile, during all that year the King was pressing for the necessary confirmation to the bishopric—not
for the young fellow's consecration as yet, he was four
years below the canonical age, but for the Pope's acceptation of the royal choice; a necessary point.

Paul V, new to the Throne, (he had been elected but
a few months) full of preoccupation in the tangle of the
diplomacy he had inherited and of the Venetian quarrel,

sent no reply. By the end of the year the lad took Henry
IV's advice and went himself to Rome.

There he had a great and instant success: his memory,
his eloquence in thesis and address, far more the sense
of power which so young a candidate gave forth, aston-
ished them sufficiently for considerable record of it to
remain. Bellarmine put him high. They said of him—
the report, if not contemporary, is well founded—that
there was that about him which promised to rule not
only a diocese but a world.

But the young Richelieu was not in Rome for successes. He had come with a definite object. To return,
in spite of his youth, with the Papal confirmation to his
See. He took action. He swore to a false age and almost
certainly confirmed the oath with a forgery: the substi-
tution of his own name for that of his elder brother
on an abstract from the baptismal registers.

There is no doubt that this trickery took place. The
thing has been debated, as any historical point may be
debated, and we are not as certain of it (of course) as
we should be were there material proof, such as the document itself, which might be submitted to microscopic
examination and any erasure and substituted name so
discovered. But though Hanotaux, the best-known critic,
hesitates, La Croix, the most careful and detailed historian of this part of Richelieu's life, accepts the accusation,
and that after so full an examination of the evidence as
is convincing.

The main argument against what was so universally
received and has all tradition behind it, is the fact that

exemptions from the canonical rule were not infrequently granted, and that there would have been, therefore, no need for the young man to substitute his brother's altered birth-certificate for his own.

But there is one very convincing text which so strongly supports the tradition that it seems conclusive. This is the sentence in the Papal Brief signed in December, 1606: *"licet ipse sicut accepimus in vigesimo tertio aetatis anno. . . ."* Now here is the Pope saying "this young man can be made a bishop though he is only in his twenty-third year." In other words, he is exempted from the ordinary rule of waiting till he is twenty-*five;* but the Pope sets him down as twenty-*three.* It is hardly credible that this would have been done without some document having been presented to the Secretariat of the Holy See, and that document representing Richelieu as being twenty-three years of age in December, 1606. He was, as a fact, only three months past his twenty-first birthday.

Cardinal de Givry consecrated him on the seventeenth of April, 1607. He returned to Paris, he had new successes in debate in that summer, and was received as a Fellow of the Sorbonne by the autumn—on the thirty-first of October. He continued to design his advancement, preached before his friend and patron, the King, in the Lent that followed, twice fell ill—grievously the second time—but with the winter determined to break with precedent, to abandon the Court for the moment and to go into residence at Luçon.

It was not what young nobles with benefices generally

did! They stayed at Court. His retirement to duty had all the appearance of turning his back on opportunity—but it was wisdom at long range. He took the long journey to the west in bitter weather, travelling in the huge unglazed coach of the day by shocking ways, and reached the main market of the district, Fontenay-le-Comte, on the twenty-first of December. There he rested. Six days later he entered his cathedral and was enthroned—he was but entering his twenty-fourth year.

To see what the young man does in his bishopric during the next six years—till 1614—one would discover his character and decide that his episcopal task was sufficient to it and to all his energies; for he fills all his time with a surprising mass of labour. His lucidity and energy inform that labour and bring it to fruit everywhere, so that one would add: "This youth in his twenties will rise, perhaps, and probably, to be the re-maker of things ecclesiastical after the whirlwind of the religious wars: he will die in some one of the great Archbishoprics, the chief figure in the French Church."

But to discover (as contemporaries could not) what other industry, equally extensive, more personal and still more arduous, he was pursuing in the cause of ambition, is to get a vision of genius quite other; greater than seemed possible to his station, of less virtue than inspires his local action, divorced from, and transcending, his apparent absorption in the duties of his office. At the sight of it one would pause as at the unexpected prospect of something on a new scale, difficult to grasp, and one might say, forgetting his years: "This man will be either ruined in a mighty adventure or will rise in it to be the master of all others."

It is as though, while watching a man successfully building up at the beginning of life a good retail business in grocery and promising to end as the controller of a great provision company with many branches, one were to come unexpectedly upon proof that, all the while, he was making plans to enter the highest finance and to capture the banking of the country. It is as though one were to come, among the papers of an able young regimental officer, upon notes and documents which showed that he intended foreign conquest at the head of great armies and gave proof he could lead them to such victories.

In his diocesan work this prelate (a bishop twenty-four years old!) set out on these lines: to reconstruct the ruins: for the sake of reconstruction to impose and practise order: for the sake of order not only to proclaim but to achieve what is called "toleration."

In a few months he restores his half-ruined episcopal palace—living meanwhile in a private house. In a few more he has rebuilt the vaults of the cathedral and that heap of stones which was all remaining, at his advent, of the second church in Luçon. He cleans out and sets free the choked drains through the marshes, and particularly that "canal of Luçon" upon which the rest depended. He brings back regular service in every church of the district, especially in his own.

All the ornaments of the altars, most of the altars themselves, nearly all the plate and vestments, had gone in fifty years of religious war. He replaced them. He rebuilt the west front of the cathedral. It had been highly decorated. The Huguenots had smashed every object of beauty they could reach, and the steeple also had fallen. The present façade (most of it later still) shows how utterly mediæval art had been lost and with what this age replaced it. He went about the diocese seeing to the setting up of religion in the despoiled villages, and of the material fabrics. Among other details men noted the decent re-enclosure of the cemeteries with good walls where these had been overthrown by their use for defence in the ceaseless partisan fighting. He fought for and obtained a subsidy for mason-work from the province and its governor. He contributed throughout of his own, and watched the placing of the stones. He was the first to found in France one of those new *seminaries* which the Council of Trent had ordained. For until that belated reform of the Church the priesthood was formed haphazard without regular systematic training, and the first necessity for the revival of hierarchy was a full educational organisation. There was none such yet in any other French bishop's town when Richelieu made his in 1612 at Luçon. He re-evangelised by the vigorous use of the new orders. He brought into his little city the Oratorians and the Capuchins.

All those years of his till his thirtieth are filled with activities of this kind, and if the details and accounts of the work were lost in the sack of the place during the Huguenot revolt in 1622, the monuments remain.

In re-establishing order, his first care was to settle

the standing quarrel between the See and the Chapter; his next to fix the limits and character of the Protestant opposition.

For twenty-five years—since his great uncle James du Plessis had been made nominal bishop, a year before Armand's birth—the residue of the yearly revenue had been paid away in form to the absentee titular, in effect to Madame de Richelieu in her château eighty miles away. Of what amount that residue should be, how much of the nine thousand pounds a year should be kept for upkeep and provision, for the livelihood of the canons, services, education, the stipend of the "locum tenens," and the rest, was in perpetual dispute. The Chapter kept what they could, and as many of the rents were under their own hands, (the bishopric was lord of the town) they could keep much. On the other hand, the titular absentee bishop, the lady who was in turn the first bishop's niece by marriage, the second bishop's (Alphonse's) mother, had her steward also collecting dues; and he was more powerful than the Chapter in the country places. She ever claimed more than she could receive: they, as constantly, called themselves robbed and defrauded.

The composition which this first resident bishop after so long an interval successfully confirmed, brought the dispute to an end. No one thought it could be done. It was done by that singular handling of negotiation which marked the man throughout his life and in which he here passed his apprenticeship.

The Protestants who knew what his policy of toleration was to be, were encouraged to certain excess. He did not himself exceed in setting bounds to it. When they tried to raise a conventicle under the shadow of the cathedral, he forbade it—but for fear of street rioting between the congregations, not on the plea of consecrated land—and he provided from his own purse the sum sufficient to buy another site.

He insisted on the payment of tithes—including the local parson's due of "bushelry" [1] by Catholic and Huguenot alike. He also forbade the invasion of the Catholic cemeteries for the burial of the Huguenot gentry. One such invasion had already led to violent fighting; and he was determined to end such disturbance, but they could not claim the thing as a right, and his decision was accepted. That his firmness or sense of proportion had such successes seems the more remarkable when we remember that of the three bishops' palaces in the Sees of Poitou (Poitiers, Maillerais and Luçon) one, Maillerais, only twenty-three miles off, was in Huguenot hands and held as a fortress.

With all this he saw to moral order within his own jurisdiction; he called a synod in the year after his entry and another in the next, sitting there enthroned, a young solemnity among the greybeards. He issued orders fixing the feasts and holidays, and emphatically condemning the superstitions that had arisen during the anarchy in the countryside. He issued long letters-general to the parish priests. He enjoined their use of named books

---

[1] A Poitevin custom. So much to the parish priest on every bushel of rye, oats, barley and wheat.

and studies. It is striking to read these emphatic documents with their careful phrasing, exact commands and amplified details, page after page, and to appreciate that the hand which wrote them in their entirety and signed, was that of one whose contemporaries in age were at tennis or subalterns in the Guard.

But for the comprehension of the whole man and his life's effort—what it grew to be so many years on— it is the policy of toleration, first emphatically announced within the narrow circle of that distant See and in that little town, which chiefly arrests us.

The meaning of the word "toleration" as it is used to-day bears little relation to its meaning in the mouth of Richelieu and his contemporaries. To grasp the profound effect of the policy of which he was principally the author and which ran through all his public action, we must read it for what it meant in that time and place, in the France of 1608.

The plain and necessary definition of toleration in all times and places is, a political agreement that the expression of certain ideas and the action of certain practices, even those to which most of us may be hostile, shall be of free exercise, as shall be ours, to which others may be hostile: practices and ideas connected with transcendental religion—that is, with opinions or even convictions not referable to positive proof by the evidence of the senses. Thus fox-hunting, though repugnant to some, is tolerated in Great Britain, as is the Mass, though detested by the greater number. But cock-fighting and Mormon polygamy are not tolerated. Degrees of por-

nography are tolerated in France which would not be
tolerated in Ireland. The expression of atheism is tolerated in the United States, but not the transport or
sale of wine—and so forth.

In all ages and everywhere certain practices and the
expression of certain ideas have been forbidden, and always will be. Others, though detestable to great numbers, or even a large majority, are tolerated—*i.e.* "borne
with."

The general term "toleration" is therefore without
political meaning save in a particular application. If a
man say "I favour toleration," the words are void of
sense unless he intend to be understood by his hearers
(as he always does) the toleration of some special and
definable act or the expression of some particular and
definable idea.

To-day the things thus to be understood as tolerated
are usually opinions or convictions connected with transcendental religion—that is, with opinions or convictions
which are not susceptible of positive proof such as must
convince all, but deal with things either beyond the
common appreciation of our senses or having no real
existence. We are asked to tolerate such things because
they are thought indifferent compared with greater interests, such as public order, the pursuit of wealth, the
physical well-being of the community; and also because
they are not regarded as the cause of evils not tolerated.

In the France of Richelieu's day, and indeed throughout Europe, the application of the word was other.

It signified a special policy: to wit, the permission

under a Catholic monarchy and amid its subjects mainly Catholic, of Calvinist expression and ritual, although none doubted that such a philosophy would produce effects generally regarded as evil, and although the sect was strongly hostile to its fellow-citizens. This policy of toleration had a definite basis and two clear doctrines, to wit: (1) the doctrine that national unity was of supreme importance, (2) the doctrine that it was better served by such permission than by the use of public force to suppress the dissidents. That national unity was of supreme importance most men would have agreed. Few remained in that day who remembered that the unity of Christendom might be more important still. For Richelieu there could be no question but that national unity was of supreme importance: it gave all its meaning to his life. But would that unity be better served by the toleration or the destruction of the minority? His unvisionary mind, fixed on the things within its range and seeing all clear-cut, decided: "By the toleration—not the destruction of the minority."

The corresponding policy of the English Government (ever since it had fallen into the hands of the new fortunes built on the ruins of religion, that is, ever since 1559, during all the reign of the Cecils—1612—and on until its task concluded in 1688) was the contrary.

In England national unity was achieved by the gradual extirpation of the Catholic faith from the people—a process half achieved when Richelieu came to Luçon—and by its final destruction piecemeal in the following eighty years; so that the country entered the eighteenth century as one Protestant block—which it has since remained.

But the conditions of France were very different. The policy of toleration had much to recommend it. Moral unity and its corresponding national strength might better have been achieved by the persecution of the seventeenth century Calvinists until they should be all exiled or wiped out—but the arguments for toleration were at least equally strong. Richelieu accepted them from the first days of his episcopate, and acted on them to the end of his life.

After the religious wars which filled all the last half of the previous century, the Calvinists had boasted a drawn battle. It was their leader, Henry of Navarre, who had become king, as Henry IV; and who, though accepting Catholicism as a necessary condition for holding a Catholic throne, remained, in memory, the young and brilliant soldier of the Huguenot armies. It was, when Richelieu came to Luçon, not ten years since the Calvinists, boasting that drawn battle, not defeated, had received from that king a most solemn and perpetual engagement (the Edict of Nantes) giving them not only equality with the Catholic majority in the professions and in posts of government, (the governor of Richelieu's own Poitou, from whom we saw him soliciting subsidies for the rebuilding, was a Huguenot) but for at least eight years strongholds to be maintained at the general expense and the right to elect and convene a

Consistory to rule their body. They formed a state within
the State. They were armed; they had a full organisation for renewed war; they were led by half the nobility and more than half the magnates of the country.
They were, though a minority, in a far more formidable
position than had been the Catholic majority in England
under Elizabeth, for in England the national leaders
of armed revolt had taken the wealth of the Church and
the masses had no one to fight for them. So much for the
positive side: the reasons for dreading Huguenot power.
On the negative side there was nothing like the incentive
for ruthless and prolonged suppression of Protestantism
in France that existed in England for the suppression
of Catholicism, where the governing class being now
based upon Church plunder, the possible loss of it by a
Catholic restoration was a nightmare to it. In England
the toleration of the old National religion would have
meant its complete recovery—and with that the new
landowners would be in peril. In France the Huguenot minority was unpopular and unlikely to increase.

Again, France had only just emerged from an almost
continuous lifetime of religious war in which many a
village, and even a town or two, had disappeared, and
others had been sacked and burnt by scores, in which
hundreds of thousands had been killed by war, massacre and famine, in which innumerable national glories
in Art had already perished; while great monuments
by the hundred—such as the Cathedral of Orleans, the
magnificent tomb of William the Conqueror—had been
destroyed. The end of toleration meant the renewal of

all that. In the long run the powerful armed minority might be turned out or crushed; but what would remain except ruins?

Richelieu, then, was fixed for toleration: on a cool calculation he decided first. But remark that, so far, all that appeared on the surface was a Christian mansuetude: the repetition of well known phrases such as "more is done by persuasion than by force"; "Our duty to the civil power is in the civil order: our religious feelings are in another order and do not concern that power." Richelieu's pronouncements from the day of his enthronement when he appealed for support, "from those whom I know must differ from me," to his first entry into power eight years later, were all upon that tone, with hardly a hint of political motive for the line he took. It is all the old story of conversion by appeal, of respect for the rights of sincere conviction and the rest; and perhaps the most typical passage out of the many which mark these early years is this, which I quote from his speech in 1615, when he had the weight of responsibility on him, when he was close on thirty years of age, and when he was spokesman for the clergy. "As for those of the Protestants who live peaceably and obey the King, we should attempt their conversion by example, instruction or prayer. With no other arms should we desire to approach them."

No one in 1608, no one in 1614 at the States General, no one two years later, when he came to his first Secretaryship of State, no one who had previously heard him since his first declarations as bishop of his diocese, would have made anything of his gentleness to the faction save the expression of a sincere and charitable mind.

It would be doing Richelieu an injustice to say that he spoke thus out of mere ruse and cunning. He believed what he said. The toleration he thus praised in the abstract was a rule of public conduct which would have filled his mind whether he had achieved power or no. But it was only half a statement. Behind it, or beyond it, unspoken, and only to appear in later records, was the mastering political sense which was his guide. He accepted toleration in order to buy internal peace at the least cost so as to have his hands free for external action in Europe.

For Richelieu in those early ecclesiastical days was, under the cover of such zeal and active work in his function, preparing his approach to much greater things: and to this preparation we must now turn.

He was determined to be seen sufficiently in Paris— and even moderately at Court. He was equally determined that the ambition which filled him could not be hampered by the common reputation of the young, noble, absentee bishop of the day. See how he manoeuvres.

At first he hardly leaves his palace, save for a villeggiatura in his favourite priory of Coussay—a personal heirloom from his father. Then, in the second year he makes ready his plans for the capital. His absences must be discreetly short, he must not have the air of eager and open seeking after aid from courtiers. He must be called; he must not seem to be pushing himself.

There exists, dating from the early part of 1610, a most illuminating document only discovered in our own day. It is the written memorandum which the young bishop drew up for his conduct on his first approaches to the Court. He tells himself never to appear anxious for favours, least of all from the run of men in high places. Never to fish for invitations, especially to dinners: dining out too often is a waste of time. He tells himself to talk to a company in any room so that his hearers may be interested, yet with nothing they can take away to his detriment, such as a harsh or witty pronouncement against others; to keep a proper regard for his cloth, "a neighbourhood to God's house as well as the King's"; "Never to leave to chance what can be achieved by calculations"; "Never to let an opportunity go by"; and—this should be retained—"so to answer queries as to avoid both the blame attaching to a (discovered) falsehood, and the perils of telling the truth. *In such occasions retreat with your troops still in good order and your baggage intact.*"

The characteristic thing is not that he should have thought about discreet and necessary lying—we all think of it. Nor even that he should have formulated it in his mind: many a man might turn it over within his private musings until they had taken the clear form of rules. It is rather that he should methodically have set them down —like a plan of a campaign—when he was still months short of twenty-five!

To him so planning came the news of Henry IV's assassination. It may have reached Luçon by the eighteenth

of May, 1610, on the morning of the fourth day after
its happening. That would have meant special posting at
nearly eighty miles a day. It is more likely to have
reached so remote and small a town on the fifth day, or
even the sixth—the nineteenth or twentieth. Note how
that "opportunity" is seized.

Richelieu was genuinely shocked. He revered Henry
IV with a family devotion and with gratitude. He held
to him not only through the traditions of his own father,
but through the King's kindness to him, and his half
ironic trick of calling the boy whom he had nominated
so early, "My bishop." He remembered the sermons
preached before the King and the praise of them. Be-
sides this personal feeling was the public concern of a
mind which understood better than most the gravity of
the moment: the popular ruler stabbed by a Catholic
madman: the great Huguenot nobles let loose without a
master to hold them.

Yet his immediate, almost hasty, act is to write a very
long, very adulatory letter to be given to the King's
widow, the new Regent, Marie de Médicis. He writes
down for her every flattering phrase he can think of.
The long epistle, in all its exaggeration, veiled as an official condolence, is completed and sent off by the twenty-
second!

He despatched it to the head of the family, the brilliant Henri, the dead man's gentleman-in-waiting, one
of "the 17" who dazzled Paris with their extravagance.
The elder brother snubbed the younger and told him
that he had refused to deliver so crude and unusual an

address. Marie de Médicis never saw it—but Armand neither quarrelled with his senior nor wearied in the fixed course he had taken—he was determined to reach the ear and favour of the Queen Regent.

He watched the menace of the great Huguenot gathering at Saumur in the following year and Sully's retirement from it with great bags of public gold. Of that chief of the Calvinists, whom, as Governor of Poitou and distributor to Luçon itself of largesse, he had addressed in terms as flattering as those to the Queen Regent, he notes for his memoirs: "He came into public life with £3,000 a year. He left it with £25,000."

Well, Richelieu himself came in with nothing and went out with millions heaped on millions.

He is tireless in the pursuit of his aim. He preaches the Lenten sermon before the boy King, Louis XIII (then fifteen) and his mother. In those sermons he continues to fix her attention upon himself. No one could estimate better than he the gross insufficiency of the big woman. None the less does he pursue unswervingly the way that shall lead him to take advantage of her power. He stays in Paris to the end of the year.

So it continues. He has already so far succeeded that she uses him to give her private reports, receives him in Fontainebleau, when, in June, 1614, came the first main step. The Government from which he was still so far, had determined to summon the States General. The writ for it reached him in that month. In that last of the great National Councils he contrived by careful canvassing, using his deserved reputation as a public speaker, by the support of his patron the bishop of Poitiers, by the relations he had already made at Court—perhaps by some recommendation then proceeding—to be chosen a representative of the Clergy for Poitou, and in February, 1615, at the closing session, he was picked to make the famous speech which was his true entry into public life.

Though I am not concerned to chronicle the public acts contemporary with his life, nor even his own public acts, but rather to attempt an explanation of the man, yet that explanation demands a brief outline of what was passing before he comes into that official eminence from which the history of his time is under his survey and part of his own life. It is necessary to appreciate the general situation which young Richelieu, planted in Luçon, and in his country retreat at Coussay, was watching sideways from behind the ecclesiastical duties in which he appeared to be absorbed, the situation into which he penetrated by his private correspondence and already active intrigue. The situation of 1608-1614.

At the moment when he came into his episcopal city to be enthroned, Henri Quatre was at the inception of action in that great plan for checking the Hapsburg power in Europe—the combined mass of Spain and the Empire—by alliance against it of Catholic France and the small Protestant states. It was essentially the same policy as later Richelieu himself was to carry forward, and the minister who presided over that preparation was the Huguenot Sully.

So early in his life Richelieu himself was not concerned with such great affairs.

The whole situation, and the scheme which dominated it, crashed on that May morning in 1610 when Henri Quatre was stabbed in the streets of Paris.

Thenceforward all changes, and the four to five years between that moment and Richelieu's first great opportunity, the States General at the end of 1614, and his own triumph in the February of the following year, passed upon three main lines of development: the situation of the heir, the child who was now King; the foreign situation; and the domestic.

The child Louis whom Henri Quatre left upon the throne was not yet nine years old: he was to pass into his 'teens apparently less significant even than childhood could make him. He seemed to be marked by nothing more striking than violent fits of anger, for which he was whipped, and to have no occupation growing upon him but playing at soldiers. He was left on one side altogether. His gross and foolish mother was only too glad so to leave him, and you might almost say that the time was not only one of a royal Minority, but of a Minority in which men forgot that there was a king.

That state of affairs went on long past the years 1614 and 1615, many months after Richelieu's first public appearance. It went on up to and beyond Richelieu's first ministry at the end of 1616; it did not end till the sudden revolution of the following year when the boy was well advanced towards his seventeenth birthday, and so unexpectedly proved his ability to insist upon his right and to emerge with something approaching to royal power.

In the foreign field, the murder of the lad's father led to a complete reversal, a ruin of the edifice which he and Sully had raised—it was necessary that it should be so, disastrous as the contrast seemed to those who had looked forward to re-arranging Europe to the advantage of the French Crown by checking the allied powers of Austria and Spain. The business of Juliers,[1] which had been the pretext of Henry IV's projected war, was polished off according to plan—it was too far advanced to be stopped —and the Duchy was detached from the Empire. But after that, everything was put full steam astern.

The sudden change was necessary for this reason, that the crisis of the Minority made it imperative. The magnates had lost their master. The moral power over them of the lazy, ill-tempered, incompetent woman left as Regent was without weight. They and the inextricably allied force of Huguenotry were capable of, were preparing for, renewed civil war; and under that threat an advanced foreign policy was impossible.

But there was more than this negative factor; there was the positive inclination of the Queen Regent herself —half Hapsburg—and much more of the men surrounding her, for leaning towards that strong Catholic

[1] Succession to the Duchy of Juliers and Cleves, a Protestant minor German state on the lower Rhine, was in dispute. The Hapsburgs claimed the right of dealing with it as overlords. Henry seized on the pretext to support Protestant claimants and gathered a great army which was to attack—with allies—on the Rhine, in the Jura, and in Italy, the power of the Hapsburgs.

reaction which had already gathered so much power in Europe and which was about to determine all the coming years.

Within a year of her husband's murder the Queen Regent (or rather, her advisers) had designed the Spanish marriages. The boy king was to marry Anne, the sister of the young heir to the King of Spain, and his own sister, Elizabeth of France, was to marry that heir and be the future Spanish Queen.

As soon as she felt free to do so, Marie de Médicis announced the arrangement publicly. In the following year, in the month of August, 1612, the marriage contracts were drawn up and solemnly published.

It seemed from that date as though the new government of France, weak and vacillating though it was, had definitely joined the strong movement for restoring religious unity in Christendom, and that the Hapsburg might, controlling (on the map) three-quarters of Europe, would have a subservient French alliance wherewith to accomplish its task.

But the key to all this, what made it possible, was the unstable situation at home—the movements of the magnates. The ministers of Henri Quatre had remained in office, the three old men, Villeroi, Sillery, and Jeannin, whom they called "The Three Greybeards." With them the fourth, who had been far their superior, was Sully, himself bearded enough and bald, hated, shamefully avaricious, but also a close administrator of the public funds, quite out of tune with the new time on account of his obstinate Protestantism, as on account of a general unpopularity which, now that his master and old comrade was dead, left him open to his enemies.

The three others, and the Queen herself, made things impossible for Sully, who, fearing disaster, resigned. But immediately after the Huguenots called their great national assembly at Saumur, and threatened the crown with rebellion. When the Commissioners of the Crown ordered them to separate, they refused, saying they would not do so until their grievances were set right by the Queen Regent. Though they had all the Edict of Nantes and its privileges behind them, they still enjoyed the monstrous advantage of walled cities, garrisoned them at the public expense though the eight years of temporary arrangement were long past. They asked much more and proposed, on the top of the fortified cities which had been given up to them, of the dual system of government in which they were partners, of their admitted religious freedom, to organise new assemblies province by province.

They were already within an ace of renewed civil war when the Regent began that sole method which her weakness allowed, and which was to be renewed so fatally during the insignificance of the King: paying blackmail. She bought at an enormous price the two chief men of the threatening Huguenot faction, Sully with £150,000, the Duke of Bouillon, the chief of them all, with a less certain, not exactly known, but larger sum.

The assembly dispersed, the Queen Regent (Sully

now gone, given a provincial governorship and removed from the Treasury) was free to control that war-chest of £3,000,000, which had been accumulated by the late king for the proposed Spanish war, and which had now no employ, since his army in Champagne gathered for that purpose had been disbanded. (It was in this moment of freedom that Marie announced the proposed Spanish marriages, and later published the formal contract of them.)

But the paying of blackmail is an endless process, and the appetite of the recipients grows with what they can compel the victim to give.

In 1614, the thing began again. Condé, the first Prince of the Blood, began to stir against the "evils of the time" —the Queen Regent, in the hands of base favourites, the delays of justice. Moreover (what was really grotesque in its degree of cynicism) he, his pockets bulging with public money, loudly denounced the dissipation of the public treasure. He stood behind walls in Mezières with Bouillon and the rest, and they were all bought off once more, Condé himself with a quarter of a million pounds and the others with sums in proportion, apart from posts and pensions and governorships and all the rest of it.

The shameful market, known as the treaty of Ste.-Menehould, was concluded on the fifteenth of May of that year, 1614. But the great rebels were not wholly bought off. They kept a weapon in reserve. They demanded the summoning of the States General; for they thought to find in that body a support against the Queen.

They had used as a lever for their power the public indignation against the Queen's Italian favourites, the Concinis, the strong feeling of the lawyers and higher middle
classes against the Papal claim to depose a French king,
even heretic, the dislike of the new system of hereditary
judges, and the vague but strong discontent against what
seemed the weakness of foreign policy compared with
the national plan of the late king, whom the nation in
bulk had adored.

In their use of the States General the magnates were
disappointed. The Crown had worked the elections with
success, and the Assembly did not seriously oppose the
Queen Regent. She even found herself strong enough
to change the meeting place from Sens to Paris, and
when the great national consultation was inaugurated on
the twenty-sixth of November, 1640, by procession and
Mass at Notre-Dame, it allowed itself to be played upon
by the manœuvres of the Court. The nobility attacked
the heredity of bought magistracies, and demanded the
abolition of the Paulette. The Third Estate or Commons
(which meant in practice the great bulk of the lawyers)
replied by proposing a reduction of those lavish pensions
wherewith the Crown had bribed the magnates. The
Paulette, they said, brings in £800,000 of revenue to
the Crown a year. The Pensions cost 5½ millions—
sheer loss to the Crown.

Meanwhile in the triangular duel the Commons opposed the Clergy by proposing a solemn resolution that
the Crown of France was of divine right and therefore

subject to no foreign power in any degree, not even the spiritual power of the Pope.

It was in a national assembly thus rendered incapable of action that Richelieu rose, just before its dissolution, to make himself thenceforward famous by his speech for the clergy and his defence of the Throne.

II

FIND, CHECK, AND KILL

RATHER more than three years before the summoning of the States General, François le Clerc du Tremblay, the Capuchin—in religion Father Joseph—was preaching the Lenten sermons at the great convent of Fontevrault, in the Loire valley, to the north of Richelieu's country and within hail of the priory of Les Roches which, with that of Coussay, shared his leisure.

Fontevrault was one of the most important religious houses in Christendom. Its abbess was a Bourbon princess, the aunt of Henry IV. Its revenues were enormous. It had dependent on it a great number of other establishments, it governed a large retinue of servants and field workers, it was the lord of many manors who were familiar with its rule; it had the patronage of many livings throughout the West; it had fallen, in the long relaxation of the religious wars, to become a fashionable country house with all the good breeding and external habits of the great world and with nearly all its luxury and falseness.

The work of restoring religion after the fever of the Reformation, which was everywhere in Europe at its height, demanded the reform of a foundation which had not grown corrupt but very worldly, and the work of restoring religion being the main business of Capuchins, Père Joseph tackled Fontevrault and all the example which depended on it.

185

The aged abbess, too feeble for the task, died towards the end of that course of sermons. Père Joseph fixed at once upon her successor; anothe royalty, holy and ascetic in life, secluded, a widow, hating publicity and state, retired in a convent at Toulouse, "Madame d'Orléans." He could not persuade her to take on the burden. He was tenacious and set upon it. To aid him in procuring that appointment he bethought him of calling in the young bishop of Luçon, eight years his junior [1]—and there you have the origin of the career—from that appeal to the young man (whom he had never met) sprang the closer acquaintance with Marie de Médicis, the introduction to public life, the opportunity of 1614, and—two years later—the first brief Secretaryship of State.

Why did François le Clerc du Tremblay send for Armand-Jean du Plessis de Richelieu? For three reasons: similarity, neighbourhood and reputation. The older man had heard often and fully of the younger's gifts, especially his diplomatic gifts of handling the characters and interests of others. He had heard of the restoring and reformation of the bishopric—a work after his own heart and parallel to the effort at Fontevrault. He had heard all this and more through neighbourhood—for Père Joseph was Provincial—that is, head—of the Capuchins in Poitou. Further, Richelieu had done the things

[1] Père Joseph himself was only thirty-three, but Richelieu was nearly eight years his junior: the one born on November 4, 1577, the other, as we have seen, on September 9, 1585. Note, to understand his public position, what his parentage was. His father had been the President of the Parlement and Ambassador to Venice. His mother was a Lafayette; a near ancestor, Marshal of France.

du Tremblay had done, soldiering, preaching, an effort at letters, organising, restoring, and he was of much the same blood and rank: both men had (and used) intelligences far above their fellows.

All that was a bond. And perhaps their contrast was a bond: Père Joseph indifferent to his caste, planning a crusade, ugly, roughly dressed, intuitive and eager to act; Richelieu too boastful of rank, subordinating religion to civil policy, careful of carriage, expression and raiment, calculating all things. Later a third bond was to appear. Each discovered in the face of Europe, that a choice had to be made by France between Nationalism and Catholicism. Each instinctively attempted the same compromise—making France their main object, but believing or hoping that this would not hinder the Church. And in their compromise the two stood almost alone.

Therefore was it that Père Joseph, long prominent in the governing world and entering everywhere, sent for this aid from a man not hitherto "placed" and eager beyond everything to acquire just such a political and social entry as the other had easily reached and cared nothing for.

Since Madame d'Orléans was obdurate, Père Joseph got another string to his bow, Madame de Lavedan, another niece of the Bourbons; and, to decide between them, to get an order which should appoint one or the other, he proposed to visit the Queen Regent and to take Richelieu with him.

The Court was at Fontainebleau. Marie de Médicis issued the order for election and Madame de Lavedan was

chosen. Then Père Joseph talked at length of Richelieu
and of his aptitude for service and for rule. He talked
to one not capable of judging or choosing, but susceptible
of impressions; the effect of the conversation remained
and grew, and it was the foundation of what followed in
the relations between him and Marie de Médicis, Queen
Regent. Hence her reliance on him later in the year to
send her notes and reports of things passing in the west,
hence her attention to his preaching when he came again
to give a short course in Paris, and hence her predisposi-
tion for the occasion of which he took such full advantage—the occasion of the States General.

When on that twenty-third of February, 1615, Richelieu was chosen to be the mouthpiece of his Estate, and
to speak for the whole body of the Clergy, he would, had
he been any other ambitious man in his thirtieth year,
have directed all his skill to the fulfilment of his function as an *ecclesiastic*. He was speaking for ecclesiastics,
his promotion should normally be through his profession. Superiors in it were watching and judging his per-
formance. It was his chance for rising rapidly in the
hierarchy and for exchanging little Luçon, with its insufficient income, its smoky chimneys, bare walls, pewter
plate, for the ample revenues of the great Sees, and for
splendour at Court.

Now Richelieu did indeed sufficiently display his high
gifts as a speaker upon those lines. He gave the full
programme of his colleagues in exact terms and in excellent proportion. He pleaded for what later, in office, he

denied—the giving force of law in France by royal authority to the decrees of the Council of Trent; for the exemption from taxation of his Order, of whom it was the right of government to demand aid by their prayers rather than by their endowments [1]—another principle which, in power, he treated as negligible. He pleaded for the resumption by clerics of church revenues alienated into lay hands. But to all this he added two other matters which were his own. The first was a strong plea for that fixed policy of toleration. The second was a piece of exaggerated rhetoric designed solely to impress the Regent in his own favour.

As to the first we know his feelings in the matter and his deeper motives. It is the second which I would here emphasise, for it was in this that he was original, left the road another man would have followed, and aimed straight at power without scruple and by direct effect.

The boy King of fifteen, Louis XIII, still wholly subject to his mother's heavy and contemptuous dominion, sat upon his throne beside hers. Convention and, all

[1] I will not break this passage to discuss what sounds so odd an anomaly in modern ears. But I will ask the reader to remember two capital points which render that reasonable in the France of 1614 which would be absurd anywhere to-day: (1) The word "tax" meant still not what it means now, the basis of regular and necessary revenue, but an *exceptional* effort to meet a passing strain—commonly of war. This effort, in *theory,* demanded armed service from nobles, payment from the non-fighting commercial and agricultural classes, nothing from the Church, which was forbidden to take part in war and which was sacred. (2) Such an ideal, long out of touch with real conditions, was not attained nor attempted to be attained. In practice all paid—and paid heavily already: Clergy, Nobles and Commons.

would have thought, policy demanded that the chief references in the speech should be to him. Richelieu concentrated wholly on *her,* and that with an exuberance of phrasing by which one of more ability or critical sense than was possessed by what he was addressing, would rather have been repelled. But men of Richelieu's rare sort know humanity thoroughly by their thirtieth year, and this incompetent, large woman, crass in her middle age and still passionate, was not difficult to understand. So he spared no epithet. He made it crude and unmistakable—for it was hers to say "yes" or "no" to any post or office: to open or shut the gate of public life. And this is how he feeds her:—

"Happy the King to whom God had granted such a Mother! So filled with affection for his person, with zeal for his State, with experience in the conduct of affairs! . . . who has directed the ship of State through such storms and reefs as must attach to a minority!" (She had paid blackmail in terror to the magnates, had allowed the Huguenots to assume, impudently, privileges even greater than the Edict gave them; she had emptied the treasury, ruined foreign policy and rendered the very Crown odious—all within five years.) "Madam!" (he continued) "all France is compelled to proclaim its obligation! To bestow on you such honours as antiquity would grant to those who could preserve peace, and secure the repose of the people! Much as you have accomplished, halt not there: in the advance to glory and honour not to go forward is to fail. Persevere in this, the wisdom of your administration! Thus will you add to that glorious title, 'The Mother of the King,' yet another, 'The Mother of His Realm'!"

She was very pleased and she remembered him.

When the King proceeded South in great array that summer for his Spanish marriage, Richelieu is honoured at Poitiers. He is given the household of the Princess Elizabeth, later Queen of Spain; he is made secretary in one private department to the Queen Mother, who still ruled the land; and when he writes to her at the end of the year it is in such terms as these:—

"Since I cannot find words noble enough to offer up thanks for the unmerited honour you have deigned to bestow on me, I will dedicate all the actions of my life to that one end. I shall implore God to shorten my own days that He may add them to yours, and to overwhelm me with all manner of misfortunes (saving the loss of His Grace) if only at that price He will endow you with every species of prosperity. That is my desire indeed!— as being Your Majesty's very humble, very obedient, very faithful and most obliged subject and servant: Armand, Bishop of Luçon."

That is fairly strong. No one can put such language down to convention.

When the Court returned in the following year (1616) to Paris, it was with Richelieu as Almoner to the new young Spanish Queen, Anne of Austria, and, immediately after, with the title of State Councillor. In the summer the Queen Regent sends him to persuade Condé,

the first Prince of the Blood, to return to Court. He succeeded. Next, to reconcile her with the Duke of Nevers.[1]

In all this stooping and subservience to imbecility in
power, Richelieu had one excuse. It is excuse more easily admitted by modern men than by the generation of
Corneille, for to-day we take less account of honour. It
is the plea that conscious talent may use all means to
obtain its opportunity.

Here was a man possessing beyond all other men of
his time, and perhaps of centuries, three qualities—each
rare, in combination almost unknown: the gift of judging exactly the most complicated situation, in all its
details and in right proportion; the gift of persuasion
over individuals through a right choice of words and
tones and a profound divination of the individual character; the gift of directing a whole policy in its largest
outlines as well. Was he to leave such talents lying idle
(and that after chafing for eight years to employ them)
because of some scruple not even in morals but only in
the pundonor? When would genius ever rise if it indulged in such a luxury?

And indeed, not having indulged in that luxury, but,

---

[1] That worthy heir to Mantua, and though a French magnate, also
a Gonzaga of Italy, had written and published two letters in which he
said he was well aware of the deep respect he owed to the Mother of
his King; but that, after all, they of Gonzagas were princes before the
Médicis were so much as gentlemen. Richelieu could not persuade him
to withdraw. But he gives the reason in one illuminating phrase: "Il
n'en était pas capable." It reminds me of a man of our own day who
was blamed for not having succeeded in making clear an essential economic point to a professional politician of the Cabinet, and who answered: "Have you ever tried reading Theocritus to a cow?"

on the contrary, having bent double, he was now, in the September of 1616, upon the threshold of real power. . . . But to explain his grasp of it I must describe the situation.

Marie de Médicis at forty-three had been since her husband's death in the hands of a ferret faced, half daft, determined, lean, and swarthy servant, a maid, Italian like herself, and the daughter of her wet-nurse, in childhood, a life-companion, called Leonora Dori (or the Galigai). That maid had long been the manager of Marie as Queen to Henry: she had now become the complete mistress of the Regent—and later on, when she had to face her death for sorcery and was asked how, if not a witch, she from the gutter could rule a queen, she answered with accurate contempt: "By the power which a strong will exercises over a weak one." The base affair was not a mere piece of patronage. Leonora was raised to the highest ranks in the State. She had a husband of her own breeding and status, a gentleman, one Concino Concini, called by the French "Conchine." He (through her, whom he used to maltreat and coerce) was loaded with revenues, made Marshal of France, and given the title of Ancre.[1]

It was a grotesque position. These absurdities held all power: they dismissed ministries, they added to their fantastic fortune by every kind of commission and gift from the people they terrified. The great houses were on the point of rebellion, as we have just read, but the Con-

[1] From the town of Ancre in the Artois, known to us during the Great War as Albert.

cinis remained. The populace was wild against them, but, through the Queen Regent, they held on. The boy King no one heeded. He played at his games and his sport, having for bosom friend one Charles d'Albert, who bore the obscure squire's title of Luynes from some tiny parcel of land in Provence. This big, good-natured, handsome, rather poltroonish man, more than twenty years older than the lad, was held by him in deep affection, and the Queen Regent was delighted to find her boy occupied by that friendship and its accompaniment of hawking falconry, which kept him out of affairs. Meanwhile the two Concinis ruled: she at the Queen's elbow, he playing the master everywhere with his guards.

Well, Richelieu intrigued and manœuvred for the favour of the Concinis—as he had intrigued and manœuvred for that of the Regent whom the Concinis now controlled. He has himself recorded, with quiet indifference, his success in this tortuous aim. "I gained his *affection*" (he writes, years afterwards) "and indeed he showed some appreciation of me from the first time we spoke together." He said to his intimates "Here is a young man who can teach a lesson to *tutti i barboni*"— all the Old Beards of Henry IV's great tradition; for indeed he spoke Italian always and was not even as advanced in French as the Queen Mother.

He it was—and his wife the Galigai—by whom Richelieu passed the deep gulf between those who have not and those who have experienced power. There was talk of sending him as ambassador to Spain in that autumn of 1616. He refused the offer, for he saw greater things ahead.

Two Secretaries of State held office under the Crown, one for domestic, the other for foreign affairs. The latter, Barbin, a man of the Concinis, was made—through the Concinis—Keeper of the Seals (a more lucrative, less powerful post). Richelieu had ingratiated himself long before, with this man whom he knew to be an adviser, though a hanger-on, of the favourite. Through Barbin did Richelieu meet Concini; by Barbin was he now recommended for the vacant place.

But what decided the appointment was Père Joseph's advice. Even the Concinis knew that Père Joseph could judge both a man and foreign policy. He urged Richelieu's claim, and, on the thirtieth of November, 1616, there was sent round to the supposedly insignificant boy King a document which his mother bade him make regular and which he duly signed. It was the appointment of Richelieu to be Secretary of State for Foreign Affairs.

It seemed as though the end was attained. For though the Secretaryship had but recently been no more than a subordinate position and though it did not yet mean the full direction of foreign affairs, it was approaching its final importance.

Richelieu had passed into the inner circle. He was now of the Household of Government. He had crossed the boundary and had but to go forward to be supreme as soon as his talent could develop its full effect—and surely that would be in a brief delay! For all who met him— all, at least, with any judgment of men, even the ad-

venturers, far more the fixed observers—discovered at
once his eminence in action.

He might be the head of the active government in a
year—fortune made it eight; and that eight years' check
was partly of his own making. For it was Richelieu's
own attachment to calculable things, his own neglect
(and contempt for) instinctive guesses at long range,
which now tripped him up after his first entry, shut
him outside the doors, and kept him there till 1624. He
saw clearly—he had under his eyes and palpable to his
touch—the official power of the Queen Regent, the real
power of the Concinis. The approaching disaster he did
not see. It was, on a very small scale, a parallel to his
general attitude in Europe when he was all-powerful. He
saw—he had under his eyes and to his touch—the huge
threat of encircling Hapsburg power; he used it against
the Protestant princes. The ultimate siege of Catholic
culture, the growth of anti-Catholic things which continued for 200 years after his death, and to-day mainly
through his settlements, to threaten our very civilisation
—of all that he did not dream. Yet many a contemporary of his instinctively felt the menace.

The power he had worked so many years to attain,
he held less than five months. He had entered into office
on the last day of November, 1616, he fell from it disastrously and as by a thunder-stroke, on April 24th, 1617.

On that day Concini, Maréchal d'Ancre, passed in
afoot, as was his wont, through the low back door of the
Louvre, coming from his small private house in the

gardens, a crowd of his gentlemen about him. He was reading a letter. Nicholas de l'Hôpital, Captain of the Guard, pressed through his throng and arrested him. He had only time to cry in Italian "This to *me?*" and to feel for his rapier, when he fell, struck by three bullets.

Where all else had cowered, that neglected boy the King, but half way through his sixteenth year, brooding on disinheritance and the intolerable insolence of the intruder, had made his plan. He had secretly consulted with Luynes and those friends and officials about him whom the Queen Regent thought negligible. They had not dared: Luynes especially thought it best for the lad to fly and join a revolt of the magnates. But Louis was firm and had given orders of arrest to the Captain of the Guard. On death he said nothing, but Déageant spoke for him and said that if Concini resisted, he was to be killed. And so it fell out.

With the fall of that sinister mountebank his whole system crashed. The young King in some degree, his elder friends (and Luynes especially) in a greater degree, took over the helm. The Queen Mother, hearing the news, stood bewildered, her soul in a tumult, not understanding how a child, younger and less vigorous in her eyes even than in those of the Court about her, could have kept hidden within him, and now at last let loose in flame, that secret fire of revolt against management which, henceforward, through all his sense of insufficiency in affairs and need of counsel, was his smouldering passion. She refused herself to all, save

Richelieu. He alone was allowed to see her in these dreadful twenty-four hours.

He was at the Sorbonne when the thing happened, and was told. He set out at once for the Louvre. Even as he passed through the streets of Paris to the Palace, the mob was dragging the naked body of the dead Marshal with shouts of joy along the pavements.

When he reached the Council Chamber they asked him whether he came as one of the councillors only or as minister still. He said "As minister"—but as minister they would no longer receive him. He replied that he accepted no such decision, save from the King. He tells us in his memoirs that Luynes, now powerful in Concini's place, offered to keep him on. It is improbable; it is almost certainly false. Had he been able to continue, he would have done so, but he had been too much Concini's man.

However, he kept up not a few relations which he had, with forethought, provided himself with in Luynes' clique, and they spoke well of him to the young King. Moreover, his supreme abilities were now a commonplace with all men (indeed it was his rivals' knowledge of them that later retarded his return) and therefore he made the right negotiator between the fallen Queen Regent and her son.

He carried out that task with his customary perfection, and then, when Marie de Médicis was to leave for Blois, ten days after the murder, made a virtue of necessity, affirmed his nobility in refusing to desert a fallen benefactress, and followed her into her provincial exile.

I leave to a later page, as preface to Richelieu's absolute reign when again he returned to power, any outline of public affairs in the interval, and confine myself to that prolonged renewal of patient observation and manœuvre which restored him in the end.

He had in that ordeal of unique tenacity, which occupied what might have been the best years of his life (from his thirty-second to his thirty-ninth) one capital asset, one obvious handicap. The asset was his, now assured, reputation for a capacity out of all scale with any competitors, coupled with the fact that he had actually exercised power and given proof of those startling talents: his handicap was the association of his name in the boy King's mind with the odious régime of the Concinis and with their fall.

It was his task to eliminate from Louis' mind, as the boy grew into manhood, the prejudice that he, Richelieu, was not to be trusted, that he might prove ungrateful, that he might join the ever-ready enemies of the Crown and try to rise through them. At the same time he must, as a parallel task, keep before the King's mind the image of a counsellor, disgraced and kept apart, yet surely necessary. He must see to it that his unmatched judgment in domestic and foreign affairs should get round to Louis' ears, and to his attention, that with this reputation for unique political talent there should go a reputation for regular work in his own sphere and for solid ability in the narrow field of his clerical duty. He had refused, on taking office, to resign his bishopric —and his decision now proved right. He set out to prove the loyalty of his nature by devotion to the Queen who had advanced him, the stuff of which he was made by professional—and useful—labour; the necessity the Crown must be under, sooner or later, of recalling him, by a sufficient advertisement of his judgment on public questions. He would attach himself to the company and the correspondence of the Queen Mother, knowing that what he told her would reach her son, and calculating justly enough that this son would in time fall under her influence again, as also that the present set surrounding the throne and its immature occupant would pass.

The design was well ordered but not subtle. What was remarkable, rather, was the fixity of determination which maintained it unwearied during all those years filled with opportunity he might not use.

It is true that he was supported throughout the protracted trial by a certain force very difficult to define but of the strongest practical effect. I am afraid I must give it here, as I have given it elsewhere, a slang name, and call it the "one of us" feeling. It works more thoroughly in public life than in any other field of human effort.

Once a man has passed the hidden gulf which divides real power from its simulacrum, those who have shared in the experience, or who have seen him closely at his work of command, will never again regard him in the same light as they did before his advancement: and this is especially true of a man who, when possessed of real power, however briefly, shows that he can use it with mastery.

It was so with Napoleon. The reigning families might call him "General Buonaparte" as much as they liked and play at insulting him after his fall—but he had become one of their world for good and all, his titles were mixed with theirs, and, as against the non-royal, they were all in secret unconscious league to maintain his prestige after his death.

It is so with those great financial monopolists who alone hold the real powers in the modern world. They will fight one against the other. Now one will fall, but, as against the outer world, he remains "one of us" to the others. He is still bidden "think in millions," and ten to one, if he lives he will be restored.

So it was with Richelieu. He might be in disgrace and driven out, but he remained, from 1616 and his first ministry, "of the circle." Hence his gradual but large re-emergence.

For the first year or two it might seem impossible. He even has to leave Blois lest his being with the fallen Queen Mother should too much anger Louis—and the kingdom's new director Luynes. He is warned that he may be ordered away, and prevents the disgrace by going off himself to his rest-house of Coussaye, its quiet gardens and fountains—and he writes to the King once and again, to assure him that he desires nothing but a blind submission to his sacred will. He shows zeal in his diocese of Luçon. He goes below the surface.

When even that does not spare him, he is still resigned. The King, and the King's older advisers, send Richelieu off to Avignon, to live there in complete exile on land technically foreign (the Pope's) and as far removed as possible from effect in or on Paris. His elder brother Henri, on whose brilliance and power at Court Armand had always so much relied, is sent into exile with him. Richelieu does but the more humbly submit.

Though he had the Pope behind him, had he chosen to protest, he gauged the advantage of refusing such aid and wholly subjecting himself to the anger of the Crown. For the Pope, offended by such high-handed action against a prelate now of international renown, and alarmed at a precedent which both treated a bishop as no more than a layman and also ordered a residence at Avignon as peremptorily as might have been ordered one in Bordeaux, wrote strongly and urgently in protest, once and again. He saw to it that Richelieu should be treated in the papal city with special dignity by the Vice-Legate, and lodged now in the Palace, now in a fine house specially lent him. He gave every opportunity for the exile to play Rome against Paris. But the exile wisely refused. He employed his leisure in displaying sound zeal for religion and all his intelligence in that task, composing apologetics and in particular publishing with full advertisement his famous "Instruction for a Christian" written some years before. He counted steadily on time.

Relaxation was bound to come, and it came. He attached himself more intimately to the interest of the Queen Mother, he put before her continually what of herself she could not understand, the true situation, as it developed, in France and among the rivals of France.

Such knowledge percolated and made of what may be called Marie's "subsidiary court" a shadowy centre of policy more regarded than the substantial office under the King's eye. He remained constant to her in all her fortunes, and especially after he was allowed to reside with her at his choice. He did not abandon her even in her rebellions. After the absurd collapse of her "army" at the bridges of the Loire he appeared once again as the unavoidable pacificator reconciling her with her son. When she took up arms openly, he settled—or helped to settle—the peace.

She was grateful and—so much must be admitted in a character worth little—she was constant enough in retaining him; though, for that matter, she had the strongest practical motive in doing so, for there was no other strength that came within a mile of his. She conferred revenue upon him increasingly, and when his favourite niece was married, she not only gave her royal jewels, but the princely dower of £100,000.

He on her side played his part of supporter, councillor and friend with an assiduity sometimes comic. He even learned to play the lute that he might please her.

How I should like to have seen him, with legs crossed under his cassock, instrument on knee, eyes tenderly turned upwards and thin managing fingers on the strings!

These years were years of strong interior strain for Richelieu. In them his brother Henri, his chief support, whom the Queen Mother had made Governor of Angers, was killed in a duel there. It is the one occasion when violent grief, disturbing his faculties, appears in his correspondence. To see the great events of new rebellion, and rapidly changing foreign relations go past him unsubmitted to his brain which alone could discover and impose a solution, was intolerable. Hè suffered severely from the continued attacks upon his trustworthiness which he knew were reaching the King perpetually in his absence, as the lad grew up to manhood and was acquiring a character that would soon be fixed, and might be fixed to Richelieu's permanent bane. He had the shame of seeing his bishopric of Luçon sacked and all his papers burnt during the religious revolt of Soubise in 1622. He underwent all those things—but none of them deflected his purpose.

When the final reconciliation of mother and son after the death of Luynes was accomplished, the party he had consistently served was once in the saddle and his own way once more clear, he made a flank move of the first value. He proposed to himself to achieve what hitherto he had been promised in vain, the title of Cardinal. The Queen Mother had begged her son two years before to ask the Pope for that honour. He had very reluctantly said he would, but no one thought he would act. The Queen Mother pressed: Richelieu waited.

Now he thought the moment was ripe and he must have urged her—for she became importunate, and as she was now of the Council again, she was heard.

It was not an overweening pretension so late as 1622. Five years increase in fame and reputation, of themselves, even with men who have done little in them have effect. He had used them fully, though not in power. His name came first to all who considered the candidature. He had upon his side, apart from this indefinable but very essential factor of general opinion, the actual authority of the Queen Mother, now more than the coadjutor—once again the holder of her son. Yet the well-planned exaltation delayed. The Duke of Epernon's son was nominated first. Next Paul V died and the machinery had to be started all over again. The Nuncio put spokes in the wheels—he desired the Hat for himself.

But that mixture of good fortune and indefatigable tenacity which, with high aptitude is the making of such men in their personal as in their public designs, triumphed again. Just before his thirty-seventh birthday, on the fifth of September, 1622, he received the purple.[1]

To be Cardinal did not mean his return to power. It was not a direct advance. It was what I have called it, a flank move. It only gave him something on one side of his frontal reapproach to that Power which he had held for a moment and lost so suddenly all those years ago. But that something was very great. The Cardinalate gave presence. It made him a prince in a real sense among the magnates; and it gave him precedence before all others, and, on such a head, the red hat was a kind of crown.

There were still eighteen months to go. The aged and

[1] The fifth of September is the date of the act at Rome. It reached Avignon on the fourteenth. Thence it was sent to the Queen Mother who was on her way south and she told Richelieu who was with her at La Pecautère, a day's post off from Lyons: about 70 miles.

incompetent ministers, fearing the advancing shadow of such genius, did most to halt it. The King's memories and his dread of being controlled came next—but it had to be. Step by step the lost positions had been reconquered and the decisive moment was at hand.

On Monday morning, the twenty-ninth of April, 1624, the seventh anniversary of those days, apparently fatal to him, during which Richelieu had consoled Marie de Médicis for Concini's death and had prepared her for her fall and departure, Louis the King was alone with his mother in her bedroom, advising in affairs of State: being advised would be a truer phrase. It was decided that Richelieu should re-enter the Council.

He did so with the first days of May—the decisive letter, a secret one, making room for him by the removal of another, was written from the King's office on the ninth of May. Three months he remains subordinate in theory—no more than a member of the Privy Council— but rising above the others by the necessity of superior grasp and vision and manœuvre, like a diver rising through water by the necessity of physical laws.

On the thirteenth of August the nominal Prime Minister is deposed by Louis and Richelieu is at last installed in complete power.

He was to hold it to his death-bed, eighteen years on, and in the interval to fix the form of his country and of Europe for three centuries.

III

THE VALTELLINE

HITHERTO we have followed Richelieu manœu-
vring for power: at last imposed upon the King
and Council, partly by the strength of his claim, more
by the assiduity of his Patroness. And hitherto we have
followed him advising and judging of affairs. Now we
are to see him in action. But action is the test of men who
think and can advise well and clearly. For in action you
meet reality with its infinitude of detail and sudden,
incalculable, obstacles. If you can deal with it, your
intellectual power takes on flesh and fashions the external world: if you fail under the ordeal, you are, from
promise unfulfilled, less than if you had stood wholly
aside.

Therein lies the high interest of watching Richelieu's
first handling of affairs. We test his ability in practice
where hitherto we have only been able to test it moving
in the void—and the first exhibition is in the matter of
the Valtelline. He had advised action there which was,
doubtless, on the right lines. The vision and wisdom of
that advice, (which was not taken) contrasted strongly
with the vacillation and failure of those who, before he
held power, had dealt with the problem in action. Now
he has to deal with it. How will he prove himself their
superior in practice? The answer which the event provided is the first evidence of his eminence in active ordering of men and things.

The Valtelline is the valley of the river Adda, a stream which rises in the summits of the Alps on the Ortler, flows south a few miles by Bormio, and then, west for fifty, past Tirano and Sondrio, to fall into Lake Como; running through a lovely fertile valley about 2½ to 3 miles broad, walled in by mountains over which are passes into the Swiss Grison on the one side, and the Adige basin on the other: all ultimately leading to the Valley of the Inn and so to the Danube and all the German states.

It had been in 1624, for a quarter of a century, and was to be for fourteen years more, till the fall of Brisach, the most important geographical point in Europe. To-day it is of no account, as it had been of no account for centuries before the Reformation, in the political arrangements of Christendom. Its value in that one generation is a proof that history is not mainly a function of natural conditions, but rather of human will and morals; for it was solely the political ideas of the time, their effect upon frontiers and their conception of rights, which made the Valtelline what it was in the eyes of Richelieu and his contemporaries.

All the rivers which rise on the southern, Italian, side of the Alps, lead up their valleys to some sort of crossing over the range at their sources, but these saddles differ so much in facility that only a few have been used in practice by any considerable body of travellers. Most of them are too high, or ice and snow-covered or too precipitous on one side or the other, to allow the passage of armies. One which, of the practicable passes, is the

most difficult, is the *Stelvio,* and next to it the *Umbrail*
(or Wormser Joch). Now the Valtelline is that valley
which leads up to these two Passes.[1]

The Valtelline and the Passes of the Alps

Save for the artificial political arrangements of men,
no large column in arms or for commerce would use
those very high passages. Only forty odd miles to the east
of them runs the largest and by far the most convenient
corridor through the mountains, the Brenner Pass, broad,

[1] Neither leads directly into the Inn Valley, but both to upper Adige
only. From thence however a low, flat and easy road leads across the
watershed by the Rechsen.

not half the height of the Stelvio, and of so easy a gradient that a railway runs over it to-day with no need for a summit-tunnel. But the Stelvio is over 9,000 feet high (to the Brenner's 4,000 odd), therefore open for only a brief part of the year, and is very steep, especially on the northern side: the Umbrail is also covered with snow save in the height of summer. Yet were they both of capital importance in the year 1624, because they were the only direct gates between the Spanish Hapsburg territory of Milan and the Austrian Hapsburg territory of the Tyrol.

The Valtelline belonged to neither Spain nor Austria. It belonged to the Grisons. But it was the *only* road by which Spain and Austria could hold military communication, save by passing forcibly through neutral territory, a proceeding less agreeable to the morals of that time than to ours.

The Duchy of Milan, the Milanese, was in the legal possession of the Spanish Crown, under Philip IV. The upper Adige valley (which is the Italian or southern side of the Brenner) and the valley of the Inn and its tributaries across the range, were the possessions of his cousin the Emperor Ferdinand. If the right of passage through the Valtelline were accorded to the Spaniards, they could move troops by it from the Milanese to the Tyrol and thus succour their allies in the great task of re-Catholicising Europe under Hapsburg control. Not only could they get into touch directly over the Umbrail and the Stelvio, but also indirectly (and at the expense of a long détour of several days' extra marching) by a much lower pass between the Valtelline and the Trentino called the Tonale (six thousand feet); and in the Trentino they were in Imperial territory and on the road up to the Brenner.

A sketch will show the connecting value of the Valtelline. Here the Spanish Hapsburg territory of the Milanese is shaded with vertical lines, the Austrian Hapsburg with horizontal, and it will be seen how the Valtelline and the two passes lead from one to the other.

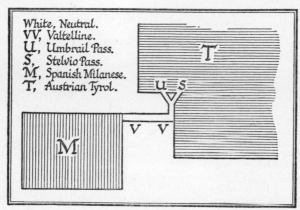

The Valtelline

But the Valtelline was neutral territory also, as much (in theory) as the Swiss Cantons to the north of the Milanese, the Venetian territory to the east of it, or the Savoyan to the west. Why then did it afford a special opportunity?

For the following reasons:

In the first place the Valtelline, though formally and legally dependant at this date upon the triple Swiss Canton of the *Grisons,* was not naturally a part of that territory. It was Italian in speech and culture and formed a natural part of the Milanese, running up as it does from the lake of Como on the north of the Duchy. It had thus been a portion of the Milanese since just before the Reformation, when the Duke of Milan, Maximilian Sforza, handed it over to be *vassal* to (not *annexed* to) the Grisons Cantons just over the mountains to the north of it. This union was never very solid, the natures of the territories were too different.

But a much deeper cleavage had recently appeared. The Grisons, looking northward, and under German influence, had become mainly Protestant. The Valtelline had remained Catholic. The initiative of zeal through Europe had been on the Protestant side and the Grisons were not backward in it. They could not resist the itch to interfere with the faith of their Catholic dependants and the strain was already heavy when the Spanish Governor of Milan built his fort of Fuentes on the extreme edge of his territory of Como, overlooking the mouth of the Valtelline, where the Adda forms a delta as it falls into the lake.

This was in 1603. The religious interference of the Zealot Grisons with the Valtelline continued: in the year 1620 there was an explosion. The exasperated people of the Valtelline fell on the Protestants and massacred them. The Grisons attempted a reconquest and were beaten: next, in a sort of Protestant crusade, Zurich, Berne and the Grisons combined to exterminate the Catholic Valtelline. This crusade was beaten in its turn —and then Spain intervened.

Feria, the Spanish Governor of Milan, had already got from the Grisons (in 1617) by force of a threatened blockade of their commerce with the Milanese, the right of passage through the Valtelline. He now (1620) marched his troops into the valley and occupied it in all its length with garrisons in every town, from Bormio at the top of the stream, just under the passes, down to Chiavenna, sixty miles away at its mouth near the Lake.

Thus on the eve of that critical year 1621, when the Hapsburg power was everywhere in the ascendant, when the Austrian Branch of it was going forward to its conquest of all Germany, when the Palatinate was tottering and, in France, the religious wars opening again in their fury, Spain held the Valtelline and the link between the two Hapsburgs, the military communication, was secured.

It was not so to remain.

There had been a strong bond between the French Crown and the Swiss cantons for centuries, as there had been between it and the Scots, and for the same reason: the lesser powers could be used against the greater rivals of the French Kings. There had been Swiss recruitment for the French armies since Louis XI, and active alliance with the Grisons in particular since Louis XII, more than a century past. Such an alliance seemed essential as against the power of Spain in Northern Italy, as against the House of Austria. But cutting across so simple an issue had come the passions of the Reformation and its wars.

What now should be the policy of the French in these

Swiss valleys with their hold on the passage-ways between Philip IV and Ferdinand the Emperor? We know how two divergent ways lay before the French Crown and nation: to aid the restoration of the Faith and culture of Europe as a whole—but at the price of suffering Hapsburg dominion, a united Germany, a dominant Spain: or to strengthen the nation at the risk of weakening the Faith and culture of Europe by permanent division.

We know that Richelieu accepted the second way—it is the whole meaning of his life—and we shall see him first swinging the helm round in this affair of the Valtelline.

It was the fault of the lesser men who had successively directed Louis XIII's affairs up to the moment of Richelieu's accession, *not* that they inclined for the first policy —for the saving of Europe and the Church, and accepting Austrian and Spanish preponderance—but that they were uncertain. Had they boldly and strongly decided for the full Catholic policy, they would have made history. They did not, for two reasons: first, that they could not see the wood for the trees; secondly, that Marie de Médicis, who had the ear of the King and was, in the last months, a member of the Council, was coached by Richelieu. Blundering though she was and personally favourable to the Hapsburgs, she could not, with such an adviser at her elbow, help the policy he opposed.

The results were pitiful. France appeared neither as a Catholic power, nor as a threat to Spain and Austria, but as a thing drifting.

After Richelieu had entered the Council, but before he had attained the leadership of it (in August, 1624) there is everywhere this "marking time." Richelieu himself exaggerates in his Memoirs the lack of decision in his colleague Vieuville, but it was bad enough and in no need of exaggeration, for, until the Cardinal himself became leader, French policy was torn between an apparent (and growing) political necessity to withstand the Catholic effort of Austria and Spain and in instinctive, racial, *not fully conscious* hesitation to support the Protestant advance and to the break up of our civilisation.

Hence the sending of a French envoy, Cœuvres, to support the Swiss, but to do nothing. Hence the acceptation of Papal garrisons in the Valtelline. Hence the failure to support the Protestant champion Mansfeld, hence the delays in negotiations with the Dutch.[1] Hence the halt in the matter of the English marriage. Every one of these actions had been begun, none properly followed up, because all were opposed to the Catholic side of Europe.

In the matter of the Valtelline, Spain, seeing the Huguenot trouble in France ended (for the moment) by the treaty of Montauban, offered a compromise. She had already in the treaty of Madrid promised to leave the Valtelline, but with such reservations that she could still hold on. She would now withdraw her troops from the Valtelline, but on condition that a neutral garrisoned it. She would hand over the towns to neutral *Papal* gar-

[1] They were promised loans on the sixth of July, six weeks before Richelieu attained full control on the thirteenth of August. But the support was not whole-hearted.

risons and only reserve the right of passage—which was the essential point at issue!

The French ministry had accepted that compromise prior to Richelieu's advent. On his attaining power, all changes.

First: on September 5th—only three weeks after Richelieu's accession to full power—Urban VIII was directly challenged. Louis XIII signed a letter demanding that the Treaty of Madrid be executed and the Spanish forts of the Valtelline in Papal hands be rased. The Pope refused.

Next, Cœuvres, in Switzerland, had orders to cease mere ambassadorial work and to levy men. He had a coach-load of gold. It was Richelieu's first use of money. With that he raised 3,000 of the Grisons, over 3,000 more from other cantons in Switzerland, and at a season when none could expect a campaign in those hills, on the twenty-fifth of November, he was on the march for the passes and the Valtelline with his half Calvinist army. It was Richelieu's first Protestant alliance.

That winter was spent in the reduction of the Papal garrisons—Venetian cannon from over the Bergamesque passes coming down from the south in aid of Cœuvres —and there, for the moment, was the end of Spanish passage through the Valtelline. Nothing remained of the Pope's neutral garrisons—which guaranteed that passage—but Chiavenna and Ripa down by the Lake, which were of no service for a march up the Adda. Bormio, Sondrio, Tirano, had gone.

By January, 1625, Cœuvres was attacking there also,

and besieging Ripa, so as to block the Spanish approach to the Grisons and the Splugen Pass; and meanwhile (*after* the reduction of the Papal forts had begun) another letter went off to the Pope saying that Louis XIII had no desire but to protect the oppressed and help his allies.

Meanwhile he worked on the Duke of Savoy's hesitation between supporting the Spanish power in North Italy as too strong to be thwarted, or opposing it as too strong to be left unassailed. There was no definite understanding of direct advantage to be gained—it is half the art of such things to convey an impression without compromising oneself. But Savoy thought it worth while to come down for the moment on Richelieu's side. Genoa was attacked, with French aid. Now, Genoa was not only the port whereby the Spaniards reached their Milanese territory, it was also the bank which financed their army. Therefore it was imperatively necessary for Spain to save it. It was saved, and the French forces and those of Savoy were hard pressed at one critical moment in the summer of 1625. But the diversion was of effect, it saved the position of the French in the Valtelline.

Richelieu, by a stroke wholly unwarranted in existing treaties, had cut the Austro-Spanish link and the road of reinforcement between them.

A simpler mind would have stopped there, and probably, in the reaction, lost the advantage as quickly as it had been gained. The Cardinal manœuvred at once. He claimed no conquest. He virtually disavowed his own general. He compromised on all *except* the power of

Spain to march at will up the valley—the only thing
that mattered, and even in this he so covered the essential achievement with surrender of more obvious points,
that he gave—as he intended to do—all the effect of
yielding and of establishing a just peace. Only after its
conclusion would the various opponents, rivals and allies
of France, discover that they had been tricked.

It was a long business—more than a year. The active
Valtelline business was done by the new year of 1625.
The Treaty of Monzon which—for the moment—regu-
lated the positions of France and Spain in the passes,
was not finally ratified till the second of May, 1626,
and during these sixteen months Richelieu, now for the
first time showing his full powers and giving example
of what was to come, handled at once five diplomatic
fronts (Spain, Savoy, the Pope, Holland, England) with
a skill that baffles our observation to-day—let alone its
contemporary victims; dealt sufficiently with a sixth
business, the support of Venice, and all the while was
fending off and settling armed rebellion at home.

That famous entry of his into the direction of French
affairs was not a final success. Most of its results were
upset shortly after by new civil war, and had to be recovered with the tenacity and continuity of action wherein
he excelled. But it gave proof of what he was and would
be in Europe, and, within its own limits, was a masterpiece.

Here are the factors. His main object is to check the
power of Spain and especially its armed junction with
Austria. But he is much weaker than Spain. He has as

yet no fleet—Spain has ships everywhere—and his armies
have not the value in personnel of the Spaniards, still less
any approach to their numbers. He must avoid open
war.

Now at this point we must grasp, and retain during
all our study of Richelieu's activities till 1635, an essential
principle peculiar to those times: a convention in which
they so differ from ours as to puzzle us. *To help allies
against a third party was not, under the ideas of the
seventeenth century, an act of war against that third
party.* Just as to-day financiers of A. will help B. against
C., without bringing A. and C. into conflict: just as
American munition makers could supply France and
England in the Great War while the United States still
remained neutral, so in 1624-1635 France could remain
neutral to Spain and Austria while subsidising and helping their enemies, her allies.

Those allies of Richelieu's—potential rather than
actual, and no one of them eager, each of them half
hostile—are the revolted Dutch Netherlands (still opposed by Spanish Power), England, Savoy.

How he handles Savoy we have seen.

England he attaches by completing the marriage of
its heir with the sister of the French King, and by emphasising the English quarrel with Spain which had
followed on the failure of Charles' Spanish marriage.

To Holland he gives, as a loan, that three-quarters
of a million pounds which had been promised but not
yet paid. But he prevents the army that Holland was
hiring from landing by way of a French port; he blocks

its offensive action so that Mansfeld is powerless. He
saves Spain from dangerous attack, which would have
provoked her to exert her full power. He plays upon
the fact that the two Kings are doubly brothers-in-law.
In a word, he manages *to prevent a direct issue from
arising,* and so preserves advantages which, in direct
combat following on such direct issue, he would have
lost.

Meanwhile he has to face at home two allied difficulties of another kind than the irritation of Spain at losing
the military communication with Austria. These allied
difficulties are the effect on opinion, in a Catholic country, of Protestant alliances against the main Catholic
powers, and the presence, in the Queen Mother and her
set, of a powerful social and political group, increasingly
favourable to the general Catholic crusade in Europe,
Austrian and Spanish, increasingly hostile to the balancing against Austria and Spain of the small Protestant
states. Add to this the beginnings—as yet slight but
already apparent, of disappointment in Marie de Médicis
with her old favourite and counsellor. He was not doing
what she wanted. He was acting alone.

Finally, there was the Huguenot rebellion, broken out
again at the opportunity offered by the drawing away of
the Government forces and money into Italy, and acting
from the sea where there was at first no Government
shipping to meet it. It is true that the rebellion was par-
tial only. It was a hot-headed enterprise of Soubise,
Rohan's brother, unsupported by some of the greatest
Huguenot houses: Lesdiguières, for instance, governing

the Dauphiné, commanding an almost independent army, yet using it loyally over the Alps on his frontier. But it was an armed movement most embarrassing at such a moment: embarrassing in three divergent ways. It roused the Catholic malcontents—notably Condé— to urge the neglect of all else, a complete concentration against the religious rebels and their destruction, which would have been fatal to Richelieu's foreign action by draining back into France all money and men then abroad. It made Richelieu's policy of toleration at home —a policy essential to his European plans—particularly difficult. The necessary suppression of a Protestant revolt in France was an irritant to the Protestant governments of Westminster and the Hague. They sent Richelieu ships to use against Soubise, as by treaty bound, having taken the money for them, but they saw to it that the crews should mutiny and that the succour should be baulked.

Now, in all this tangle, the Cardinal worked with the exact and manifold gestures of a conjurer. The English neutrality he maintained through the vanity of Buckingham and the fresh accomplishment of the Royal marriage. The Spaniards he held off by such advances to the Huguenots as seemed half alliance. The Huguenots he led to composition by a more pronounced leaning towards Spain. The Grisons, Savoy—and even Venice—having used, he thanked; but he left them unrewarded save that their fear of Spanish aggression from Milan was less.

Such a result was not arrived at by a mere recognition

of the complicated oppositions and cross-oppositions. It was not even to be arrived at by rightly estimating the strength of each factor. It could only be reached by an exact sense of proportion in dealing with each and an exact estimate of the relations each bore to the others in the confused pattern. How far could you insist on Catholic toleration in England—to meet the national feeling at home—and yet keep England off? How far could you hamper Spain without a rupture? How much could Savoy and Venice be persuaded to act by a vague prospect of negative advantages? These parts of problems and a score of others in the main problem, had each to be solved as by a delicate balance: if one effort upset the equilibrium by its excess, all broke down.

It may be said that all did indeed break down, for the see-saw level thus maintained during Richelieu's fortieth and forty-first year had disappeared by the summer of 1627. The treaty of Monzon had hardly been signed a year and a month when an English fleet set sail to make war on France. It had not been signed three years when Richelieu was again over the Alps in arms, coercing Savoy and facing Spain at Casale.

But the view that the opening years 1625-26 are a failure of Richelieu's plans is erroneous. Their immediate diplomatic effect was ephemeral: their indirect effect on the future permanent. Richelieu's original success in the Valtelline was the foundation on which was built the successful thrust on every side of 1626-30: the annihilation of religious rebellion at home, the continued safety from the side of England as from the side of the Pyrenees, and the origins of the great and finally triumphant intrigue against Austria. None of these would have been had not the Cardinal been able to make, as early as May 1620, the famous (private) boast that he had brought Spain into line from fear of the Protestants and the Protestants from fear of Spain.

In that "double cross" (to use the terms of modern political intrigue) the "mass of manœuvre," the "marching wing," the "mobile reserve" with which Richelieu first fixed and then outflanked his opponents and rivals, was the English marriage.

Charles, the heir to the Throne of England, had passed through France incognito with his father's favourite, Buckingham, in 1623. He had seen, in passing, Henrietta Maria, the young sister of Louis XIII, small, elegant, vivacious, dark, hardly more than a child as yet (she was not fourteen) with delicate fine hands and well made. An English Protestant gentleman, admiring her, grieved that so fine a creature had not true religion: but did not define whether this were Calvinist or Lutheran.

Charles had gone on with Buckingham to Madrid, in search of that Spanish marriage which stood in English policy thus:—

James I had married his daughter Elizabeth to Frederick, the young Elector Palatine, head of the German Calvinists and ward of Bouillon. He was a principal rebel against the Emperor Ferdinand and had lost his land. By the influence of the Spanish Hapsburgs with the Austrian he might recover it. Moreover a Span-

ish marriage was, at the moment, by far the greatest
thing a prince could hope for, especially the heir to a
minor state such as England then was. Charles himself—
in his twenty-third year—was willing enough. The difficulty was, of course, religion; but, then, religion was the
whole point of the alliance. It would give the English
Crown a foot in both camps.

The Spanish Hapsburgs were not enamoured of the
scheme. It offered them no great advantage, and though
Charles hinted (Buckingham perhaps prompting him)
that his later conversion to Rome was possible, and
though it was sincerely promised that the persecution of
Catholics in England should cease, the negotiations broke
down.

Buckingham came back home, angry and humiliated
—he was not a man of judgment and he allowed personal feeling to influence his action abroad. Charles
shared the emotion. James veered round and began negotiations for a French marriage in the place of the Spanish one.

In 1624, before Richelieu's accession to power, an English Embassy had asked for the hand of Henrietta Maria.
The negotiations were not going too well when the
Cardinal arrived at his place of control in time to make
them part of his vigorous but subtle new policy.

It was a Protestant alliance—the second of his advances
to that side of Europe. But to satisfy home opinion he
insisted on at least as much as had been promised Spain.
He obtained a solemn declaration from James and
Charles (and a Secretary of State for witness), that

Catholic prisoners should be released, their fines repaid and their private worship tolerated. It was not only as a move in his diplomatic game that the Cardinal insisted on and obtained these terms. It was also due to a genuine desire (on his part at least) to protect the Faith abroad, since he was directing his efforts against the political champions of Catholicism in Europe. We shall see him insisting on similar terms from Gustavus Adolphus, even as he was buying the services of that captain to throw him against the Catholic Emperor.

There was, however, on this side of his action, the negotiations with England, one thing which Richelieu did not grasp—for no one as yet saw it—and that was the rapid decline of real power in the English Throne and the equally rapid rise of the gentry who were the chief beneficiaries from the looting of Church wealth a lifetime before.

James perhaps intended to keep his word, Charles was compelled to break it or to risk conflict with that new strength of the gentry—expressed in Parliament, their committee for action—a conflict which was, sooner or later, inevitable and in which he was defeated at last and put to death, and the power of the Crown with him. He had to put off that peril as best he could, and his dread of it explained what Richelieu was puzzled at for years: the suddenly shifting attitude of the English Government in foreign policy.

Well, then, he used the English marriage to strengthen himself against Spain. He used the promise of toleration for Catholics in England to prevent Spain's direct action.

He used the poor chance of Catholic advance in England through the marriage to nullify the resentment felt by the papacy against the man who had seized the Valtelline. He used the open alliance with an anti-Catholic Power to prove to the Huguenots his readiness for peace with them. He used the alliance as a means for getting ships against the Huguenots. He used it as a threat against Austria in the matter of the Palatinate, though he had no intention of fighting to restore that principality to Charles' brother-in-law. And he even used that marriage as some slight asset in his effort to reassure the Queen Mother.

In all the ways wherein he used it he showed the mastery of his instrument, nowhere exceeding in pressure, threat or cajolement, and he attained the balance he demanded just in time to open his second great object after the Valtelline—the destruction of Huguenot political separatism coupled with the toleration of Huguenot religion. He did not secure the neutrality of England when the battle was joined: Charles and Buckingham made war in aid of La Rochelle in spite of the marriage. But—as in the matter of the Valtelline—Richelieu's scheme, shortlived in its first effect, gave a platform for his next action when he turned to put an end for ever to that "State within the State" which the Huguenots had formed, and to found the unity of the nation.

On March 25th, 1625, the Pope gave the dispensation for the English marriage. Two days later James died, and Charles, succeeding, ratified the marriage treaty as

King. On May 1st the marriage by proxy was solemnised
on a platform in front of Notre-Dame (the Duke of
Chevreuse, a Guise, and therefore cousin of the Stuarts
acting as substitute). In a week Buckingham had come
to France to take home the bride, and by mid-June the
sister of Louis XIII was in England as Queen.

Such was the criss-cross of weaving and counter-weav-
ing, a pattern of many threads, that showed, at the opening of his main action in foreign affairs, the calibre of the
new minister.

But we are not near to an understanding of Richelieu's genius unless we remember that during all this
settling of the Valtelline business and the pendant affair
of the English marriage, during all this management of
half-a-dozen diplomatic fronts and playing off of the
two half-hostile neighbours (Spain and England) one
against the other, he was at the same time resolving successive tangles of intrigue against himself and his policy
and the Crown in that narrow domestic world of the
court which was his field of action.

It is much the most remarkable thing about the man
that *before* he was secure and solidly in the saddle (he
was not that until 1631) and while he was at once changing the whole character of foreign politics and controlling them under conditions of such complexity, he was at
the same time determining, to his advantage, a series
of palace wars, and in one of these running his first risk
of assassination.

There are two main actions, the business of Bucking-

ham which filled 1625, especially in the earlier part of
that year; the business of the first great plot against the
Cardinal which fills 1626.

The trouble with Buckingham was this:—

Richelieu had measured his man. He had discovered
his virtues—courage, ardour, and patriotism. He had
also discovered his political fatuity and his silly weakness
of allowing personal emotions of pique or affection to
affect national policy. He judged rightly that the less
such a man had to do with the affairs of the French and
English courts, the better. On the other hand, he was
powerless to prevent Buckingham, who had the young
Charles in his hands, from being the principal actor on
the English side. Let us see how he dealt with that situation.

The Duke of Chevreuse, the elderly husband of an immensely promiscuous, active, and utterly unpolitical
young Rohan woman, had agreed with Lord Holland,
the handsome special Ambassador from England, that a
good way of cementing Anglo-French relationship
would be to get up a strong love affair between Buckingham and the young Queen, Anne of Austria. We have
seen what Anne of Austria's situation was. She had had a
miscarriage, her husband would no longer live with her;
she was romantic, she had a very strong and justified
grievance. Buckingham, on his side, was ready enough.
He was already inflamed; he was vain of conquest in any
case, and, in this particular case, really caught.

What babies these two intriguers, Chevreuse and Holland, were, to think that with a plan so simple they could

counter such an opponent as the Cardinal! It helps one
to understand the character of Chevreuse himself, that
all the while his young wife had Holland for her admitted lover.

Madame de Chevreuse took the journey to England
with Henrietta Maria, and therefore was present on the
French part of the journey as far as the coast.

When she got to England, by the way, she horrified
the French Ambassador by staying in Lord Holland's
house—"living under the same roof," as our ancestors
decently put it—and he reported on it as on an affair of
State. This irresponsible universal she-lover was already
a thorn in Richelieu's side.

At Amiens, on the way to the coast, the Chevreuse arranged that the Queen should be alone with Buckingham in the park by night. He took too sudden and
violent an advantage, Anne cried loudly for help, and
there the scandal ended.

Observe how Richelieu dealt with that opportunity.
He drew from it two immediate advantages, of long and
permanent effect.

(1) By making Louis thoroughly understand the pos-
ture in which he appeared, he dug very much deeper
down the gulf already separating the King from his
wife; and as that wife was, in her own shallow way, an
obstacle to all the minister intended to do, thus to alien-
ate her husband from her was a strong reinforcement of
his own position at the King's side, and a still stronger
reinforcement of his foreign policy, which Anne, with

her Spanish sympathies, opposed—in so far as she was
capable of public action at all, which was not much.

(2) By thus acting he made it impossible for Buckingham, with his conceit and instability and political incapacity, to mar his (Richelieu's) own position at Court.
Buckingham was not allowed to set foot on the mainland
of France again. The nearest he got to that was when
he landed as an enemy on a French island. There he
was defeated, as we shall see: a recurrent visitor to the
French Court, he would have been far more dangerous.

It is true that by this action against Buckingham the
Cardinal made a personal enemy of him, and that this
had a certain place among the causes which later led to
war. How great or how little I will later examine when
we come to the aid given by England to the Huguenot
revolt. But of the two evils, Richelieu, as usual, had
managed to fend off the greater.

The first main plot against the Cardinal in the following year was a much more serious affair. The King's
younger brother, now eighteen, the Duke of Anjou as
he was then called (afterwards Orléans), was thrust forward to be the figurehead of it, and the gay, debauched,
quite inconsequent lad was managed like a puppet. The
women knew what the relations were between the King
and the Queen. They took it for granted there would
never be an heir. The King was sickly, his young brother
might at any moment come to the throne. Those are the
factors of the position which remained perpetually present in one desperate intrigue after another for years, and
this was the first of those great intrigues.

The Chevreuse proposed to herself that this boy Anjou with his drinking bouts and his wandering by night
from pothouse to brothel, his swaggering by day about
the corridors of the palace, hands in pockets, whistling,
laughing—should be reserved for his sister-in-law the
Queen. The King would soon die anyhow; or, if Louis
were slow to fulfil that part of the programme, perhaps
they intended to get rid of him. They certainly meanwhile intended to get rid of the Cardinal. Not because
they thought him all-powerful: to say that, as many historians do, is to read into their minds a knowledge of the
future, which they had not got, and to give him in 1625-
26 that awful dominance which he had as yet not
reached. Richelieu was still in the eyes of all these shallow women of the Court, from the sparkling Chevreuse
to the lumpish Queen Mother, a new fellow rather out
of place (they called him "the Buffoon") who had too
much to say in affairs, whose influence with the Crown
offended them, but who was still easily to be disposed of.
They had not come near to taking his stature—for in
public life, or indeed in any form of human activity, contemporaries go by an average of the past, and there is
always a gap between their appreciation of a man's value
at any moment and his real weight.

With Louis dead, by nature or by art, young Gaston
married to Anne (the Papal dispensation would be a
matter of course) and exceedingly capable of giving the
Crown an heir, their plan would be accomplished.

Now the Queen Mother had other views. She wanted
her younger and favourite son to marry Mademoiselle

de Montpensier, the daughter of the Duchess of Guise by her first marriage, her reason being that Mlle. de Montpensier was, so to speak, a pullet in the hand, while Anne was still a hen in the bush. She wanted to make certain of an heir of her own blood while there was yet time, and not to let the Crown go to the Condés, who were next in succession. And Mlle. de Montpensier fitted exactly, because she had immense wealth, as well as a sound body. She was the richest heiress in the country.

Richelieu supported the plan of the Queen Mother. He had, as always, more than one reason for the policy he here favoured. In the first place he wanted to please Marie de Médicis. She had made him, and I think, in his very cold way, he was grateful; certainly with such an intelligence as his, and such a judgment of character, he saw that there was danger of trouble between him and her later on, and that he must do all he could to propitiate her. Next, he wanted to nail Gaston down, if I may so express myself. Once married to Mlle. de Montpensier, that amusing but tiresome youth would be pigeon-holed. He could marry nobody else, and the Montpensier marriage would not bring him into further intrigue. Lastly, Richelieu was determined to show that those who were intriguing against him should not have their own way. He was determined to show that he was master, even so early, even in that one point—and there his psychology of conquest was sound. For early success in battle often determines its issue.

Young, humming and whistling Gaston had an elderly and ugly Corsican for official mentor, or *tuteur,* to look after him, Ornano by name, to whom was given the title of Marshal. Is not that splendid title better associated with the *mesquin* world of the last hundred years, and especially of the Great War, than with some of its more absurd holders in the days when it sounded most grand? Are not Ney, Murat, Pétain and Foch worth something more than Ancre and Ornano?

This olive-faced personage was got hold of both by Madame de Chevreuse and by Madame de Condé. He urged the lad to refuse the Montpensier marriage. Meanwhile the conspirators roped into their scheme a whole network of the magnates. Nevers joined in the plot, Condé himself, Soissons; so did the King's two important bastard brothers, Vendôme the Grand Prior, and Vendôme Governor of Brittany. The Governments of Savoy, Spain and England were privy to what was toward. Gaston was to seize on some frontier stronghold —and, anyhow, Richelieu was to be killed.

But Richelieu's spies were already organised. On the fourth of May, 1626, Ornano was arrested and sent to the dungeon of Vincennes. He died there not long after; and men said he was poisoned—which he was not. Gaston, frightened and trying to see the King, was refused an audience. He got excited, and insulted the Cardinal, without effect.

The man who was principally used for the business of getting rid of Richelieu was yet another young fellow whom Madame de Chevreuse had lassoed, a noble of the Talleyrand family, Chalais. Long before the amateurs could get to work, the professional touched the

spring, and the whole intrigue collapsed. Richelieu took
the King off down the road to Brittany, to the Government of Vendôme; but not before he had full knowledge of the whole affair, and had compelled that terrified
boy, the King's brother, to swear loyalty and give details
of everything. That drama took place in the Palace in
Paris, and probably Louis never forgot it. The Cardinal
went through the ritual of offering to resign. Condé
hastened to make peace. The Vendômes were arrested
at Nantes. All had collapsed.

It must never be forgotten that Richelieu, of whose
absolute power we later speak (as yet such power as he
had was most precarious) held power even in his highest
moments only on sufferance of the King. What is more,
the minister was not master in 1626 of the lives of the
very great. At the end and summit of his career, fifteen
years on, there were few or none outside the Blood-
Royal whom he could not have had condemned to death
for treason, but he had not yet such power. When later,
in 1632, he put a Montmorency to death, it was a gam-
bler's stroke, very hazardous, which happened to make
good but might have failed. In this his second year of
office—indeed he had not passed quite two full years
at the head of affairs—he could only aim low; so his
shaft was set at Chalais. Madame de Chevreuse was left
at liberty, as were the others of the magnates. Though
their names were set down on the "Accusations" legally
and in due form, they remained free also. But Chalais
was to perish.

On the second of August the King signed an order for

the trial of that gallant, handsome young fellow, not by
the regular judges but by a commission. It was the first
ominous step in the path which the Cardinal was to
follow of irregular and arbitrary criminal jurisdiction for
sixteen years to come—right up to the end.

Three days later, on the fifth of August, the betrothal
of Anjou and Mlle. de Montpensier was ecclesiastically
announced, and on the morrow, the sixth—no great interval—Richelieu himself pronounced the nuptial bene-
diction over the happy couple. Less than a fortnight
later, on the eighteenth of August, Chalais was condemned to death, and on the nineteenth, clumsily beheaded (his friends had spirited away the regular execu-
tioner) in the market-place of Nantes.

Louis XIII was not impressionable, but this opening
revelation of his minister's implacability, this first awful
shedding of blood, affected him, and when he got back
to the capital, the third week after, he said in his hesi-
tant voice, and said it publicly, that what he had had to
do was not very consonant with his own desires. It was
a duty, and all that.

Richelieu had impressed his seal.

I think it true to say that from those hot August days
of 1626, and from the memory of the young man's death
(it was Richelieu's life against his) may be dated that
duel in the mind of the King which did not end for
more than four years, which was not really concluded
until the flight of Marie de Médicis and the confirmation
by Richelieu of his primacy after the Day of Dupes. I
mean a duel between the two emotions of repugnance

and duty. For that almost inexplicable character of Louis XIII resented throughout the careful, half-hidden mastery of his minister and the sense of dependence upon a far stronger brain, yet Richelieu was also preserved for the deep conviction that by this minister not only he himself, the King, (that was less than half the motive) but the Majestic tradition of the Gallic Crown and the inheritance of Charlemagne, was saved, secured, enhanced, made finally and permanently glorious.

Even before he had so reluctantly accepted the entry of this man into his councils, the elements of that duel had been present. Now that Richelieu had come into action—and with blood—those elements were in acute conflict. Fate willed it that the necessity for Richelieu's presence should out-weigh the King's repulsion. And the scale was turned by the presence of both men, side by side in arms, commanding soldiery; in which one point they secretly held ardent communion: La Rochelle, Susa, Casale.

IV

LA ROCHELLE

THE English marriage accomplished and a balance set between the many competitors and rivals upon every frontier, the next stone in the edifice which Richelieu had set out to build was the securing of a free hand within the country by the gradual suppression of rebellion.

Civil war had become a habit for over sixty years. It had come to seem natural. Henry IV had secured a peace of ten years which all looked back to with regret, but it was almost as much a peace of exhaustion as a peace of firm rule, and it was more of a compromise than either. The two warring elements, the King and the Catholic mass of the nation on one side, the great nobles and the Calvinist churches on the other, remained on their positions. The eternal civil war was potentially present in the minds of all. We have seen how, immediately after Henry IV's death, it menaced from the assembly at Saumur, with what difficulty the Queen Regent had averted it by heavy bribes. How Marie herself had begun it again at the Ponts-de Cé. Once more, even after Richelieu's accession, it had fired up in 1625, when Rohan's brother Soubise had taken advantage of the army's absence in Italy to seize ships on the Western coast and harry the coast. Montmorency (then Admiral of France) had defeated the rising, but it was a warning.

Now to put an end to Huguenot rebellion once and

for all, the essential act was a voluntary submission, or, failing that, an armed reduction, of La Rochelle, and that for two reasons. First because, on the material side, La Rochelle was thought impregnable by the Protestants who had made it their chief stronghold; secondly because, on the moral side, La Rochelle was the standing example and symbol of successful resistance to the Crown. The town was thought impregnable because it could always be succoured by sea, where the Protestant English Government could come in aid of it; because of its own pilots' knowledge of the difficult sea in front of it; and because the King of France had no fleet. Morally such a position made it the head and flag of the whole Huguenot body and its claims.

Therefore did the military instinct of Richelieu make straight for it as an objective, and the Churchman triumphed through two strokes of war which mark two turning points in his success: La Rochelle, the beginning of victory within, and Corbie, the beginning of victory without.

For in that prime issue between the survival or dismemberment of France, two main acts, two reductions of a fortress, were decisive: La Rochelle (1628) and Corbie (1636). They differ as much as sieges can in military character and still more in political circumstance. La Rochelle was of the first strength and size, Corbie quite secondary. La Rochelle was only taken after many months by an unequalled expenditure of money, energy, tenacity and skill, and might at many a moment in the long affair have been abandoned as impregnable. Corbie

was a foregone conclusion. In both cases a foreign invader had retreated before the operation was attempted.
But in the one case his invasion was of little consequence,
the unreduced fortress he had left behind was everything.
In the other the invasion was everything, and once the
invader had retired the fortress he had left behind was
but a relic of his attempt. La Rochelle will always stand
among the great military deeds of history. Corbie, as a
feat of arms, might almost pass unmentioned.

Nevertheless those two names mark the two turning
points in Richelieu's creation. After La Rochelle internal
rebellion based on the Protestant secession within the
State and foreign aid by sea, was doomed. It could never-
more destroy the nation single-handed. After Corbie the
hope of rebellion's doing so through foreign aid by land
was equally doomed.

The two are more than eight years apart. La Rochelle
is of 1627-1628, Corbie of 1636. To the second, therefore, I must turn in its own place which belongs to the
Imperial war, and here first describe that victory which
discloses in the Cardinal what posterity, even to day,
hardly perceives: a General.

La Rochelle and its merchant oligarchy had been for
a whole lifetime the heart of sedition and of national dismemberment, "the refuge of every malcontent, the support of every rebel." It had been in 1568 the capital of
that first Condé, the uncle of Henry IV, who had attempted to become the first Calvinist King of France and
who fell at Jarnac. In 1573 they had stood a first great
siege at the entry of the main religious wars. They had

compelled the King of France to withdraw his army of over 20,000 men from their walls. In the compromise (or truce, for it was no more) of the Edict of Nantes, twenty-six years later, they received Henry IV almost as an equal power: Sully sang his Calvinist canticles in their temples. They were the privileged self-governing port and citadel of the Protestant faction. They could pull down the old Catholic churches at will, without the King having power to stop them. They could forbid the presence of Catholic missionaries within their gates.

Hardly was Henry IV dead when they sent deputies to that national Protestant assembly of 1611 at Saumur which the Huguenots had sworn solemnly should never be convened, and which was openly opposed to the nation. In the next year, in September, 1612, La Rochelle had expelled an envoy from the court—to show its adherence to the rebellion against the Spanish marriage and its active part in "the hunting of the Roman Beast" as the Huguenot phrase went; the town sent out pirates against the coast on every side, cut off and appropriated the King's taxes. It levied toll on the shores. A group of its sea captains blockaded Bordeaux and were only dispersed after a prolonged and violent action by the insufficient royal fleet. La Rochelle disavowed the pirates and they were broken on the wheel—but the Huguenots loudly proclaimed them martyrs, and not very long after —in the autumn of 1620—La Rochelle was summoning an illegal assembly of her co-religionists, seeking the help of the Germans; next year capturing the King's vessels and whatever others they saw fit; the first year after fighting a first-rate naval battle against the national forces off the mouth of the Sèvre, it made—being blockaded by land—a moment's submission, but thirty-two of its ships came proudly in to the port, with the thousands of the Burgesses cheering on the quays as the chain was lowered, and Guiton their commander was the hero of the city.

There followed on this what has been called "the peace of 1622," for all the world as though La Rochelle were a sovereign state dealing as an equal with the King of France. It had been agreed in the truce that earthworks thrown up in the course of the fighting should be demolished. The King's forces saw to it, after the royal power had, for the moment, command of the sea, that the redoubts thrown up on the islands opposite La Rochelle by the rebels should be demolished; but they were so far from demolishing their own main redoubt outside the harbour, that they turned it bit by bit into a strong fort, the "Fort Louis." They said the King of France ruled of right and strongholds were his due. The merchants of La Rochelle replied that thus to overawe them was a breach of faith. The King's captains—notably Arnauld, that devoted soldier who died in 1623 from his labours at the Fort Louis—knew well that La Rochelle would rise at the first chance, and strengthened the work: Arnauld himself saying "only rebels could object."

To Arnauld succeeded Toiras—a favourite of the young King (as Luynes had been) because he was a sportsman keen on falconry: but he was also a good captain and Richelieu, who was not yet of the council, does not do him full justice in the "Memoirs." He may have peculated—he probably did, as most officials did in that chaos of Louis XIII's youth before the Cardinal's attainment of power—but he fought admirably and died under arms, a Marshal, years later in the Milanese.

Thus the town and port of La Rochelle were not only the chief centre of rebellion, they were also the chief type of the rebellion, and of much more than the rebellion—of all that the rebellion stood for, of the philosophy underlying it, the whole Huguenot movement in general, and the things which it half unconsciously aimed at; the results which would have followed had it obtained victory over the nation and the King.

For La Rochelle represented that principle of oligarchy, of government by a wealthy class, of the subjugation of the masses to the well-to-do, of the elimination of kingship—which incarnates the community and defends it against the rich.

La Rochelle stood for all this by its constitution and by its civic spirit. The mass of its citizens were content to be, and even proud to be, governed by such an oligarchy. It was a characteristic example of that tendency towards the destruction of Monarchy for the advantage of the wealthy, which tendency went, throughout the west, with the new Protestant spirit and was so signally to triumph in England and Holland.

La Rochelle was in the hands of a Senate rigidly composed of one hundred members—twenty-four chief officers of the town and seventy-six "Peers" (in the sense of equals), the whole forming the consultative and executive body which governed this wealthy City-state. Admission to the body was by co-option, so that it became largely hereditary.

It is true that the Constitution was much older than the new forces of the Reformation. It was a relic of one of those original mediæval town constitutions which sprang up in the great renaissance of our civilisation during the twelfth and thirteenth centuries. It went back in name and form at least to the Charter of Eleanor of Aquitaine, Dowager Queen of England, an Act dating from 1199. But the old democratic equality of the original senate had disappeared, and the common will of the citizens was agreeable to its disappearance.

La Rochelle, again, stood for something which the Protestant spirit had bred everywhere throughout the West, to wit, free-lance work at sea and the dependence upon sea power for political strength: because the old united Christendom was feudal, a land thing, with no organization by sea. The sailors of La Rochelle built better and sailed better than any other mariners in France, and they opposed the power of the French King as their predecessors and co-religionists, the Dutch sailors, had opposed the power of Philip II. Further, La Rochelle stood openly for the break-up of national unity, or, to put it roundly, for the destruction of France through the local sovereignty of those great merchants and nobles who were the driving force of the Huguenot party.

From time to time the monarchs had attempted to

change that constitution which was the essence of the town's rebellious isolation, and to set a perpetual chief at the head of the Senate, a chief nominated by the King. But the plan had always broken down, and the people of

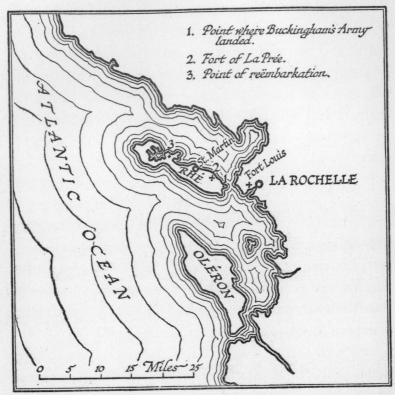

1. Point where Buckingham's Army landed.
2. Fort of La Prée.
3. Point of reëmbarkation.

Environs of La Rochelle

La Rochelle had recovered that ancient constitution to which they were so profoundly attached.

In order to understand the fighting on the coasts and islands of La Rochelle, the English descent on the island of Rhé and its defeat, the earlier adventures of Soubise, and the final siege itself, we must appreciate certain conditions which controlled all campaigns on the mid-western coast of France.

(1) The mainland was marshy and malarious. One of the principal resources of La Rochelle was the danger to any considerable concentration in front of its walls of ague and fever from the flooded meadows and sea marshes. This condition had ruined more than one expedition against the town. It did not affect the town itself, which was built on dry soil and well drained with a large main sewer, as well as having its harbour scoured out by the tides; but it gravely threatened any besieging force.

It is to the high credit of Richelieu himself, but perhaps still more to that of his adviser, Father Joseph, that this element of danger was kept in check during the famous siege. How it was done we do not exactly know; probably the strict discipline kept in the besieging army was the main element. But anyhow success on this most important of all points was assured, and the health of the besieging army remained reasonably good.

(2) The tide at this point of the coast is not exceptional in its rise and fall; only fourteen to fifteen feet at Springs. But it sets up strong currents. The gulf between the island of Rhé and the mainland, and that in front of La Rochelle itself between the island of Oléron and the mainland, are like great tanks which accumulate the tidal water as it rises, and discharge it with violence through the narrow channels at the entry of each.

Two consequences follow from this state of affairs.

(1) It is difficult for strangers to manœuvre in the

passages except at slack water. Thus a squadron of
enemy vessels attempting a course northwards inside
Oléron towards La Rochelle at the end of the ebb and
finding the flood suddenly making against them, would
be turned back and unable to make the passage, and the
converse is true of a course southwards between Rhé
and the mainland.

(2) All efforts at landing on the coasts of these two
natural basins must take account of their strong tidal
streams.

Everything depends in that peculiar formation of the
coast upon local knowledge. Therefore every advantage
was with the local pilots, most of whom were in sympathy with the Huguenot cause.

A force of vessels ordered from within the country by
the Cardinal and collected haphazard along distant
coasts, was heavily handicapped against another force
which could command through the sympathy of the
corps of pilots from La Rochelle.

(3) The difference between high and low tide at fall
and change of the moon, being about fourteen or fifteen
feet, at neap tides about ten to eleven, and wide shoals
extending upon either shore north and south of the harbour, approach to the shore in action, or for the purpose
of blockade, or of landing, or to relieve blockade, is restricted to a few hours of high water.

All this worked at first favourably for the Rochelleais
and their allies, unfavourably for the King and his ministers. The fighting round La Rochelle, from the first
adventure of Soubise up to the completion of Richelieu's

mole across the approach to the harbour, went against the Crown. But, after that, the conditions were reversed: what had made it difficult to attack the town from the sea, made it difficult to succour it from the sea, to the final reduction of the fortress.

(4) The harbour of La Rochelle itself was then tidal for all but quite small ships (to-day it almost dries out at low Springs). The fairway enters between big mud flats, which, at the lowest tides, are uncovered. The entry to the port is narrow, so that it could be closed in those days by a chain from the Towers. Only after half-flood was there draught for the vessels of those days to enter the port, and the opportunity for working in lasted but a short time, twice in the twenty-four hours. A vessel drawing twelve feet of water, for instance, might beat against an easterly wind towards the harbour during, say, three and a half hours at the most, from three-quarter flood to quarter ebb, but not longer, and in practice it would have less than three hours, since no one is going to risk throwing away his ship by gambling on the last ten minutes of the tide.

Such were the local conditions, which had favoured for years the independence of La Rochelle, but also caused the attempt of English peers to conquer the Island of Rhé, and their later attempts at relieving the siege of La Rochelle, to fail.

They also help us to understand how Richelieu was able to complete his great mole: the workmen had a shallow bottom on which to build. They also help us to understand what interruptions the people of La Rochelle suffered, even before the siege was completed, in their efforts to communicate with friends outside.

(5) Lastly, let us note the point which I shall especially emphasise and repeat, that, strategically, the holding of La Rochelle depends on the two islands off its harbour, Rhé and Oléron. If either of these be in hands favourable to the Rochelle cause, the town and harbour are secure of communication by sea.

It was on the twelfth of June, 1625, that the sister of Louis XIII landed at Dover as Queen of England. On Sunday August seventh, King Charles—or to speak more truly, Buckingham—decided to break the promise of toleration by which the French marriage had been obtained. Quick work!

The French government was startled. Personal pledges passed between kings were grave matters, and it seemed impossible that so solemn an engagement as that which the late King of England and his son had made with a Secretary of State to witness it, an engagement the fruit of which had been taken and which had, at first, been acted upon with such display of sincerity, should be torn up and thrown in the face of the other party to it in less than a year. It was but the Christmas before that the English courts had been ordered by the Crown to admit no further prosecutions of English and Scotch Catholics for the exercise of their religion, that the crowd of Catholics shut up in prison had been released and that the English Treasury had actually repaid the fines levied on the big landowners who refused to

worship publicly in the Protestant churches. It was taken
for granted that toleration had been established for good;
and behold, before the end of the summer, all the fun
of the fair—the priest-hunting, mutilation and death for
saying Mass, imprisonment for adherence to ancient
doctrine, and ruinous fines for lords and squires who
kept away from their parish churches—was set going
again as merrily as ever!

At first the Cardinal could make nothing of this be-
wildering breach of contract, but events were to en-
lighten him, though but partially.

Against the rebellion of Soubise—which was maritime
—and against that use of the sea which was the support
of La Rochelle and the Huguenot rebellion, he had no
ships. Montmorency, as admiral, had nothing to work
with until vessels hired from abroad in Dutch and English ports could be provided, and when Richelieu himself purchased the office of High Admiral (and abol-
ished the title,[1] calling himself only "Superintendent"
of Naval affairs) it was with the object of creating a
navy.

That force of which he was later the founder (the
organised Royal Navy of the French Crown may be said
to date from the Decree of 1634, as that of England does

[1] The title of Admiral in the sixteenth and earlier seventeenth centuries
meant in France and England "Commander-in-Chief of the naval forces
of the Crown." It was the office which that violent anti-Catholic Howard of Effingham held under Elizabeth, and Coligny under the Valois.
After Richelieu's day it was never revived in France. It was highly lucrative, including in its perquisites the right to wreckage flotsam and
jetsam.

from the contemporary levy of ship-money) had its
origin in his mind from this sharp experience of impotence by sea which so impressed him in the days of La
Rochelle. But it had another result of some consequence
to his general information and useful to him as he
watched over a period of fifteen years the gradual weakening of one rival among the many he had to meet in his
twin task, first of saving the French monarchy within,
next of making it predominant in Europe without.

One effect of this lack of ships was to give Richelieu
his first warning of what real forces were at work in
one of the many factors with which he was dealing: the
factor of England. On arranging to hire English ships
for the royal service, he was met by singular hidden obstacles and delays which might in part be explained by
the double-dealing natural to all diplomacy, but which
could not wholly be so explained. Something else was at
work, and that Something Else was soon to become apparent: it was the new Governing Class with the House
of Commons as its organ.

This new force the impoverished King of England
feared and must truckle to. This new force, with which
Mazarin, Richelieu's successor, was to deal, had taken
form.

The strange consequences following Richelieu's hiring
of English ships in 1625 did not fully instruct him—
far from that. Not even at the very end of his life did
Richelieu grasp the degree in which English monarchy
had declined and the wealthier classes—the squires and
merchants and their lawyers—had taken its place. Not

till long after his death did any man in England itself fully appreciate the extent of that Revolution. But at any rate the incident was a danger signal and prefaced the acts of war which were so soon to follow.

That the ships should be temporarily provided at a high rental for Louis' use, since Louis had not enough ships and needed them, seemed natural. The two Crowns were just allied by marriage; of the vessels all but one were private, open to anyone's hire. But their use abroad against Calvinist rebels gave a handle to the increasingly powerful English gentry in their struggle with the King. That embarrassed man was fain to propitiate the gentry, especially as he was about to meet his first Parliament, the embodiment of these Gentry.[1] In the Commons the Gentry and their lawyers could give organised and corporate expression to their opposition, using the ships for a pretext, connecting their grievance, at the least toleration of their excluded Catholic colleagues, with the duty of supporting Protestant rebellion against a Catholic Government. But let there be no error. Had not the religious pretext been present, any other would have served. The battle was already open between them and the monarchy.

Charles and Buckingham must, I say, propitiate such increasingly powerful enemies. Hence the startling and cynical repudiation of the most solemn pledges in the

[1] A large proportion of the English Gentry and populace (less of the merchants) were of Catholic sympathies in 1625; probably about a fifth or a quarter. But they were excluded from public life by the value of supremacy and were badly divided among themselves.

matter of religion, and hence the policy adopted in the earlier matter of these few ships.

It was the sly Coke who suggested the subterfuge. A letter was procured by him from the owners of the merchantmen to say that their humbler employees would rather die than fight Protestants—indeed, these mariners and longshoremen longed for martyrdom. The ships were sent over, immediately after Henrietta Maria's arrival, but every obstacle was put in the way of their being used. Their commanders were to object to taking French soldiers aboard, were to refer back for new orders, and did in fact re-cross the Channel. Then, by way of conclusion Coke suggested, and Nicholas arranged for a sham mutiny on the King's ship, so that Charles could plead the impossibility of carrying out the full contract. Richelieu got the empty ship at last—after nearly two months of double-dealing. But Parliament had already met at Oxford, and that Committee of the class whose fortunes were founded on the loot of religion and which was soon to be the master of England, could only be soothed by a show of bold doings against Papistry.

What Richelieu himself called "the extravagances" of the King of England went on apace side by side with the increasing menace from his Parliament. He was annoyed by his vivacious little child-wife (she was still growing!) and her devotion. He allowed to spread, and perhaps believed, a cock-and-bull story about her making pilgrimage to Tyburn to adore the place of Catholic martyrdom. He dismissed the Queen's French household with ignominy [1] and with language lacking in restraint, ordering them to be put out like so many "wild beasts" and calling them Mousers, which was his term for what were later called Mossoos. He allowed her to retain no more than half-a-dozen ladies, and, of these, four must be Huguenot. The treaty of Monzon in 1626, settling for the moment the differences between France and Spain, was not calculated to calm him. English ships, England being at war with Spain, were ordered to seize as prizes any French ship carrying Spanish goods or trading to or from Spanish possessions; failing proof of this they were to seize all French craft on suspicion. French shipping was almost swept off the seas from Calais to Bordeaux, and the captured merchantmen were sold.

When Richelieu's efforts at religious peace in France had failed, and since Rochelle was preparing for a renewed civil war, the English Crown stepped in as supporter and defender of Huguenot rebellion—and that was a move even more serious than the doubtful but arguable capture of neutral shipping for the sake of blockade. It was formally asserted that the British Government, having helped to negotiate the late religious truce in France, was the natural protector of the French Protestants in their new quarrel with their own Government; and even such a detail as the dismantling of Fort Louis outside La Rochelle, which the Huguenots maintained

[1] As they were embarking from the river steps at Westminster, a man in the crowd threw a stone at one of the Queen's ladies; but there were differences in popular opinion on the matter, for a second man, standing by, whipped out his sword and ran the first through the body.

was a breach of faith with them (Louis and Richelieu denied it) was brought into discussion as an English interest.[1]

But there was no act of open war. In the summer of 1627 a large and well-manned fleet was collected off Portsmouth under the command of Buckingham. Its avowed object was attack upon the Algerine pirates. Secretly it had been decided to use it against France in armed support of the Protestant cause. Such a policy was not personally distasteful to Charles—he had always been more Protestant in personal religion than his father, and the feeling had been intensified by the irritation he felt against his vivacious little wife and her foreigners.

Buckingham, indifferent to religion, with a Catholic mother, a sister married to a Catholic, and Catholics in most intimate relations with him, was not so moved. But he welcomed the opportunity of humbling French Cardinal and King. His personal hatred of Richelieu and Louis, since his attempted amour with Anne, combined with his desire to retrieve his military reputation (which he had lost in a failure before Cadiz). But what urged him to action much more strongly was his personal peril. He had been impeached. The new Governing Class of England, still hesitating to attack the sanctity of

[1] When Richelieu was dealing with the Huguenot rebellion of 1625 he began building among other works, a fort just outside the walls of La Rochelle to seaward: where the Sports-Ground is to-day, beyond the Park. It was called "Fort Louis." When the truce came, the King (that is Richelieu) gave a verbal and conditional undertaking to demolish it if circumstances permitted. It was not dismantled, and its permanence was the chief point at issue between La Rochelle and the Crown during the succeeding months.

the Monarch directly, attacked it through its chief agent. Hence the fury against Buckingham. He was the marked victim of the Parliament. A great national victory won by him at this moment as champion of Protestantism across the Channel would save him.

But the personal elements in this grave decision, strong as they were in those days, were not the principal. The principal one by far was the necessity, not only for Buckingham and the King as individuals, but for the very life of the Monarchs, to appease Parliament; for it was beginning to look as though, without some sop to that beast, the Crown itself might be devoured. Therefore it was that on June 27th, 1627, a fleet of over 100 sail, carrying 6,000 foot and a small body of cavalry, the whole excellently appointed and munitioned, set out down Channel from Stoke's Bay, by Gesport.

How much depended upon that armada! Had it returned triumphant, the English monarchy might yet have been saved. Almost certainly it would have left behind it in France a renewed civil war, in which the strength of the French Crown would at last have failed it, and perhaps the nation itself would have fallen to pieces. All the story of Richelieu's final achievement would have gone untold and Europe would have come down to us a different thing!

Buckingham and his fleet arrived within sight of La Rochelle after an unusually long passage of a fortnight. He did not propose to throw his force within its walls. He wisely decided on that better strategic plan of immediately attacking the island of Rhé, the situation of which I have described.

The campaign thus initiated by Buckingham for the capture of the island of Rhé was the first act in the drama of La Rochelle, and by far the most important, for upon its success or failure depended the fate of the port and all the disruptive forces in France for which that port stood.

Had the operation succeeded the strategical results would have been very great. With the island of Rhé in the hands of the English acting as ally of the Huguenot rebellion, that coast would have been barred to any fleet the French King could—much later—have raised. The English commanded the sea, and further expeditionary forces sent from the island over on to the mainland could have attacked the besiegers. La Rochelle would never have fallen, and perhaps the siege would never have been undertaken.

But the ultimate consequences would have been greater still, for the successful seizure of the island would have led to a general rebellion throughout all the South from Nîmes to the Atlantic—all the Huguenot lords and walled towns—a rebellion growing in volume and enthusiasm. The French Crown would hardly have held against it.

With English defeat on Rhé and the defences of Rhé permanently in the hands of the French Royal forces, the destruction of La Rochelle was only a question of time: blockade would inevitably reduce the city. For by so much as Richelieu lacked power at sea, by so much did he enjoy it by land. The sea was La Rochelle's salvation; with the sea approaches lost, her doom was certain.

On this account I shall make of the Rhé business the chief point in a military explanation of the result. The actual siege and capitulation of the port is but a pendant to it. The failure in Rhé is to the subsequent fall of La Rochelle what the blunder of Erlon near Quatre Bras is to the subsequent battle of Waterloo. It explains the issue.

It is an ill judgment to ridicule Buckingham's choice of that objective simply because he failed. The expedition was well planned; it was conducted with energy; it had all the merit of a surprise, and if it failed, it failed solely because there was opposed to the respective military talent of Buckingham the surpassing genius of Richelieu.

That genius showed itself now for the first time in the combination of manifold detail with exactitude, the combination of both with the utmost rapidity of action, and the conduct of the whole with untiring industry, which, associated in action with a wide, immediate grasp of all conditions, is the mark of military excellence.

Buckingham's expedition failed because the garrison of the island was relieved just in the nick of time, and it was only so relieved because Richelieu had, against very heavy odds, foreseen and planned everything.

The odds, as I say, were those of surprise. There was no declaration of war, and when the 120 sail, large and small, were observed passing the Breton coast making southward, nothing was ready. The moment the news reached Paris, Richelieu, detained there by the King's

illness, set everything in movement. Before that surprise
he had believed that he had ample time before him in
which to develop the French naval power, and already
three months before, he had given the first orders for
the preparation of the arsenals. But as yet there was no
one to send.

His first act was to call into the Council men experienced in sea warfare, and at the same time to send down
to the Basque Provinces, ordering the immediate equipment of the pinnaces peculiar to that coast, famous for
the rapidity of their manœuvre whether by sail or by oar.
He collected supplies from all sides. He sent a vigorous
military governor down to the opposing shore. He examined all the local conditions in so far as they could
be reported to him. The fragile ecclesiastical figure working from the bedside of a king stricken down in one of
his recurrent illnesses, behaved as all great captains have
behaved in such crises.

Buckingham had the start. The garrison of the only
fortified place on the island, St. Martin, commanded by
Toiras, consisted of no more than 1,000 foot and 200
horse.

There was also perhaps a company of 100 men in the
fort of La Prée, some three or four miles down the coast.
That was all.

That such works existed at all, or were garrisoned was
due to Richelieu's foresight.

On the twelfth of July, 1627, the British Fleet an-
chored in the roads between the southern extremity of
the island and the mainland, with their largest vessels

close in shore and their guns trained upon the spit of sandy land, about 1,000 yards long, which forms the southern extremity of the island. There Buckingham landed, not without difficulty (for some of his men were so reluctant that they hesitated, "though beaten with cudgels") and not without losses from the charges of the few French horse (soon halved in numbers by the firing from the Fleet) against the head of his landing party.

Toiras fell back behind the walls of St. Martin, and three days later the siege was opened. Attempts at carrying the place by storm failed—for though the fortifications were not fully finished, they were already too strong for such an attempt.

By the first days of August Buckingham understood that his task must be one of blockade, but this task appeared to be fairly well in hand. There was a very bad water supply in the little place, and insufficient provision. On paper, Toiras had enough food to hold out for two months, but in practice, by the end of one month— that is, towards the end of August—the rationing was severe, and it was formed, for the most part, of biscuit and water.

It was not until mid-August that the expedition of light vessels from the Basque coast was ready to sail. No serious effort at relief had yet been made. A couple of very small efforts to throw in a few men under the cover of darkness across the bay, and another to send in some small provision, had failed.

To render the blockade more effective, Buckingham,

to whose standard the local Huguenot gentry had flocked, drove the Catholic inhabitants of the island into the fortifications. There was one case of a woman killed with a child at the breast; she became a legend of the place. The wind blowing persistently from the north, the Basque pinnaces made the coast above the island no earlier than the twenty-seventh of August, and on the same date Toiras reported that he had but six days of biscuit ration left.

Richelieu went on pressing his orders to every neighbouring harbour, however small, offering high rewards for the first captain who should pierce the blockading line of British vessels, but it was impassable.

To the 8,000 men originally landed by Buckingham were added reinforcements—one of 1,200, and later one of 2,000. Dutch ships had been hired to provision the besieging force, and the great part of the crews from the ships were landed to augment its strength.

Meanwhile, though La Rochelle, closely watched by a royal army, had not yet fired a gun, 800 of the Huguenot rebellion had landed in the island and pillaged its population.

That race between rival opportunities which appears in the crisis of every conflict, was growing keen indeed. In a very few days Toiras must surrender to hunger. The fortification of St. Martin would be in Buckingham's hands. The whole island would become a base for further English action and security for the succour and provisioning of the port on the mainland.

Fate and his own energies, the fruition of labour,

came at last to the support of the Cardinal in that first week of September: even then they nearly missed fire.

The crews of the pinnaces, being southern from Navarre, were largely Huguenot, and many refused to sail to the relief of the island. The rebellion grew to such proportions that of 240 men (which was all that Balin, the Commander of the force, disposed of) all but a score had left him, and even these he held rather as hostages than as reliable combatants. He re-equipped the pinnaces with Catholic squires from the neighbourhood, volunteers, and soldiers from the regiment of Champagne.

With the flood tide six o'clock on the evening of Wednesday, the fifth of September, while it was still light, and the moon at her first quarter, Balin set sail. It was thick weather, rather calm, and the little body of pinnaces were dispersed, but he got them all together again during the night, or at least a dozen of them, and with the morning of Thursday, the sixth of September, came suddenly in the fog upon the mass of English vessels blockading St. Martin.

The opposing forces were not a hundred yards apart when they first made each other out through the *brume*, and it is to this that the successes then achieved must be set down. La Rochelle, like Wattignies, turned upon the luck of a mist. The move had been well timed—a difficult thing to do in that light wind—and the passage through the English line took place just at the height of the tide. It was made in those small boats because, along the shore, a stockade had been set which only vessels of a very light draft could pass, and these only at the very height of the water.[1]

Though the wind was so light, there had been very heavy weather twenty-four hours before, and that was another piece of luck for the relievers; it had opened breaches in the stockade. The provisions were landed, rations were raised to a quarter of a pound of bread a day, beans were added, and the garrison, which had already eaten its horses, was now able to hold out a few more days.

The relief was not a very great one, but it was decisive; and it was due at its origin to the foresight and energy of the Cardinal. The critical moment was now passed, and from that day La Rochelle was doomed. Balin's pinnaces got away again with the wounded and the women and children.

Five days later, and for the first time, the Council of La Rochelle, misunderstanding the situation, convinced that St. Martin must soon fall, fired their first shot against the royal army that sat camped before their walls.

There was a second slight reinforcement of St. Martin, following a week after the first. Buckingham, growing anxious, launched a second assault, though the first had failed at the beginning of the siege six weeks before, and success was now more difficult.

With the first days of October, a second, and far more successful piercing of the English blockade by sea took place. In the early morning of Friday the eighth, no

[1] It would have been less risky, therefore, to have waited for the spring tides of a week later, but they could not afford to wait.

less than twenty-nine relieving vessels of various sizes got in under the fortifications of the town.

By this time the expedition had obviously failed, and Richelieu, coming with the King, on October 12th, to the army before the city, was—perhaps he knew it— master of the game. The reduction of La Rochelle would be a very long affair, for they had determined not to attempt a storm: but it was certain.

Buckingham now made the one military error—the only one [1]—in his long effort. He should have retired at once. His fleet was intact, his men in condition. Immediate retirement in mid-October would have lost nothing of remaining military value, for the issue was already decided. He himself would have suffered less in reputation had he evacuated Rhé without loss. He hung on. A sufficient French force could at last be spared from the mainland to attack him. He attempted, too late, to reembark his men on the eighth of November and got badly mauled in operation. Out of the 8,000 Englishmen who had been under his command, less than 3,000 got home. He landed in England a beaten man and with violently increased hatreds to face as the consequence of his failure.

Now was Richelieu free to complete his work. The chronicle of the long remaining operation is of no purpose to such an examination of the man as this study

[1] Part of the undeserved blame which his name as a soldier has suffered, is due to one very unjust French contemporary criticism which said: "As a soldier he could neither come on nor go away." It was quite false. But this delay gave some colour to the second half of the phrase. As for courage, he was the first of his time in that virtue.

attempts; the siege of La Rochelle is pertinent to it only as an example of his power and judgment in military command.

He proposed to cut off the harbour from the outer sea by a mole. As the workers had to be out of cannon-shot from the walls of the town, and from the high battlements of the towers at the harbour mouth, he had to design it on a line where the distance from shore to shore was not far short of a mile—1,500 yards. It was built out from either shore simultaneously for the sake of speed. The task was nothing out of the ordinary (save in scale), for it was very shallow water except just in the few yards of the fairway in the middle, which were left open, both to let the tide pass and because they were too deep to build in easily. This gap was closed by a boom of boats chained together and great logs. He paid his men well and by piecework—a reasonably active man could earn ten shillings a day in the unskilled part of the labour—half as much again as the current wage.

Round the walls seven miles of trenches made a complete circumvallation from shore to shore, and twelve forts supported it. The army was admirable, and was, one may say, of his very creation: regularly and well paid, well fed, well shod, well clothed—as it needed to be for an operation covering two winters—and the Cardinal's business was to maintain its excellent discipline through the mortal weariness of siege work stretching on for over thirteen months. It was housed in stout huts, its provisions not commandeered but paid for, and its fire practice continued. Before that host Richelieu would ride accoutred as a general (we have a picture of him in this soldierly office) splendid in red silk and grave with jaundiced face and deeply-seeing dark eyes.

The business of that year and more has sides comic, horrible, and heroic. Its anecdotes have been told and retold a thousand times: How the soldiery was regularly confessed and communicated, how the officers chafed at clerical control, how the Cardinal filled the encampments with friars, how the slow engine of starvation did its gradual work.

To that will which beleaguered the town was opposed another will, worthy of it. The will of Guiton, made Mayor of La Rochelle after the first few months of the strain, in April 1628. That very short, broad-shouldered Calvinist had in him all the iron of his creed and inspired the legendary defence. One can see him almost alive to-day in his statute there. But no human will can make food from stones. They ate the grass of the streets and leaves of the trees; they boiled all the leather of the place for sustenance; they thought themselves fortunate in the last weeks to get rats in the cellars; and Rohan's old mother, remembering her Lusignan blood, starved with the rest for an example.

While there were still rations for the 4,000 militia and 2,000 troopers of the garrison (200 were English) on May 11th there appeared round the bend of the land a fleet of over fifty sail. It was under Denbigh, Buckingham's brother-in-law; it attempted its attack upon the mole, failed, and sailed away. The hunger increased. Guiton ruthlessly forced out between the lines some hundreds of non-combatants. They were not allowed to pass and masses of them died between the trenches and the walls. Still Guiton held. One last attempted succour from the sea by English ships necessarily failed as had the first, and on October 30th, 1628, the surrender came. Of the 28,000 men, women and children who had formed the "Republic" in its day when the trenches were completed, close on two-thirds were dead, and the living were too weak to handle arms.

Two days later, All Saints, the King rode in with splendour and Richelieu himself sang Mass in St. Margaret's.

Two monuments of that victor remain—one his own handiwork, the other built long after his death but proceeding from his victory. They are the mole—which you may see, a long line of darker hue, far out across the bay at low tide—and the gaunt cathedral, a huge vault of bare stone, naked of all ornament. It replaces the old beauty of the Middle Ages which the Huguenots had destroyed, and stands in ponderous emphasis proclaiming the downfall of its foes.

V

THE DAY OF DUPES

THAT whole business, which, so far as the internal politics of France are concerned, may be summarised under the title of the "Day of Dupes"—that is, the business which begins with the first expedition to Savoy, when the Queen Mother first began to show irritation against the Cardinal, develops during the second expedition, is advanced by the King's illness in Lyons in the summer of 1630, and ends with the execution of Montmorency in 1632—may be compared to the winning of a decisive battle. It is a comparison that Richelieu himself would have loved. I mean, not a decisive battle in his external struggle with Spain and Austria, (the decision in that affair did not come till 1639) but a decisive battle so far as his domestic power was concerned.

Before the episode "March 1629—August 1632" Richelieu is not what we now see him to be in history.

He is in possession of power, indeed, of power dominant over all others, but it is power from which any one of very many people may oust him at any one moment. After the episode, he is in power even greater, but (what is more important to a man of such a temperament) free from the caprice of many wills, subject to the choice of one alone—the King's—and that one reasonably sure to maintain him.

The "Day of Dupes" has come down to us as something striking to contemporaries and an origin in French policy; but to appreciate its full meaning we must read Richelieu's own view of it.

It is clear, from what he himself says, that between what came before and what came after there was the difference between ceaseless anxiety in the pursuit of his task, and a clear mind at liberty.

La Rochelle was the victory which broke the back of Protestant rebellion within the country. Richelieu's policy of complete toleration for the Huguenot religion and practice, confirmed that political victory at the expense of religious unity. His reasons for toleration we have discussed. The unforeseen consequences of it are to-day apparent to all in the religious chasm which cuts the French in two, paralyses their foreign policy, and menaces that political unity for the sake of which alone the Cardinal thus acted.

He was, then, from November 1628, when the great stronghold was entered, a man able to act unhampered. There remained, in the South of France, many walled towns Huguenot in government and therefore material for attempted trouble; but they could be dealt with at leisure. The strength of the faction was gone. And Richelieu henceforward could do all that he planned to do abroad free from the permanent menace of religious civil war at home.

But there remained another menace which he had not yet exorcised. His own power was not fully secure. At the King's side were influences, still very strong, which might depose him, or, failing that by peaceful means, attempt to overset him—and Louis too, if Louis supported his minister—by renewed *political* rebellion now that religious rebellion was at an end.

That menace matured. It was not till two years after the fall of La Rochelle—not till the November of 1630 —that he was master of opposition at Court and the peril of sudden fall; not till the execution of Montmorency in October 1632, two years later again, that he was free from armed rebellion within.

Meanwhile the diplomatic genius which had imposed the settlement of the Valtelline and the military genius which had triumphed at La Rochelle, were, both combined, to be put to a new test in Italy, and Richelieu was to come forth from that test with a success which was, morally, the main cause of his narrow escape from disaster at home in the chief crisis of his life.

It was some seven weeks after Buckingham's defeat in the Isle of Rhé, in the midst of the siege of the port and fortress which Buckingham had attempted to save, that there fell an accident upon the consequences of which turned all the Cardinal's future career, and upon which also were to be tested two things: his judgment and his good fortune. For it was upon the morrow of Christmas Day, 1627, that Vincent II, Duke of Mantua, died without leaving issue.

Now let us appreciate the position created by such an event at such a moment.

The two fiefs of Mantua and Montferrat united under the one head of the Duke of Mantua, were technically held at the will of the Empire. Though many centuries had passed since such a tenure had been a reality, yet

these were the very days in which the Emperor was re-
viving the full traditional claims of his crown. What a
little earlier would have seemed mere pedantry—the
Emperor's interference—was, in such a moment, a possi-
bility of action, and a dangerous one. The House of
Austria could speak upon the succession to Mantua and
Montferrat.

But there was more than this. The dead Duke had a
niece, the daughter of his elder brother, who was also
the granddaughter of Charles Emmanuel, Count (that
is, Sovereign) of Savoy. It could be claimed in the same
shadowy mediæval manner that the fiefs were female
fiefs of Montferrat and Mantua and should descend
through the nearest female heiress. Spain, acting with
Austria, possessed the Duchy of Milan. The Duchy of
Mantua lay east and south of the Milanese, and Montferrat lay squeezed between Milan and Savoy. It was a
small territory, but at this juncture of vital importance,
because upon it would depend the attitude of Savoy in
the great rivalry between France and Burgundy. Spain
of the Hapsburgs; and Savoy held the Alpine passes
whereby Spain could reach France and Burgundy. Spain
was acting with Austria. Spain would support any claim
which weakened France, and would do anything which
might tend to drag Savoy into the orbit of her own
power and that of the Empire. The next male heir of
Duke Vincent was a man wholly French in training,
residence and the rest: that same Duke of Nevers whom
we have seen pestering Marie de Médicis during her

wretched regency. Further, Vincent of Mantua had left the Duchy in his will to this same Duke of Nevers.

Such was the legal situation—arguable by lawyers, like any other one of these feudal anachronisms surviving into the seventeenth century—with the balance of the old fuedal law probably in favour of the female claim against the Duke of Nevers, which claim Spain supported.

But in practice the conflict was between the French monarchy and the House of Hapsburg in its two branches of Spain and Austria. The Empire, that is Austria, was rising to the height of its power and was soon to appear supreme over all the Germanies.

So long as the French Crown was caught in the net of rebellion, the fate of La Rochelle still undecided, Richelieu could only look on at the dispute upon the Mantuan succession. He could not act save at the expense of compromising with the Huguenots in arms. This he would not do, and the event justified his delay. That delay imposed by the fine resistance of La Rochelle, might have been fatal to Richelieu's plans in Italy, but good fortune aided him.

Had the Spanish support of the female claim succeeded, the Duchy of Mantua and Montferrat would have thenceforward existed dependant upon Spanish power, and the hesitating policy of Savoy would have at once been drawn into the same current. The encirclement of France while still plunged in civil war would have been complete.

This it was which gave the crisis its decisive character.

If a sufficient force from the armies of Louis XIII could prevent the Spanish seizure of the Duchy of Mantua and Montferrat, Savoy would be separated from the Spanish power and the French would have a bastion, as it were, against that power in Northern Italy. Should the French King fail to support the claims of Nevers, he was wholly surrounded.

At this point it is necessary to recall once more the convention of that age which, if it is not grasped, renders it unintelligible to the modern reader: the convention that auxiliary aid given by a third party to one of two belligerents did not count as an act of war by that third party.

In all that we are about to follow up to 1635, all the energy of Richelieu is directed to *avoiding* the "open rupture" with Spain. He acts as an auxiliary to the enemies of the Hapsburgs, never as a principal, and thereby postpones to a day of greater strength the risk and expense of war on a national scale. He postpones *that* till the last moment, when his other action had undermined the supremacy of that great double Hapsburg power which he had faced at first as something far too strong for him—to be manœuvred against with skill in a perilous defensive. He saw it, before he died, fallen back into a failing defensive against the new domination of the Crown he had so well served.

To return to the Mantuan affair. Nevers, immediately upon the death of Duke Vincent of Mantua, had occupied the Duchy under the will of his cousin and by claim of hereditary right. But he had no offensive force sufficient to meet the Spanish armies close at hand in the Duchy of Milan, nor even sufficient to meet those of the Duke of Savoy acting in the plains of Piedmont from his capital at Turin. Only one point—but a good one—could be held by Nevers, and that hardly. It was that fortified town of Casale.

Now it may justly be said that the future history of Europe turned in this critical year upon the fate of Casale, and if we forget the modern political map of united Italy and remember the political map as it was then, we at once see why.

The fortified town of Casale, with its hill of Montferrat close at hand, covered the wasp-waist of that sort of hour-glass shape which the Duchy of Montferrat filled. Further, it commanded the only permanent bridge over the river Po for a day's march and more, above and below. If Casale could be held, and so long as it could be held, the whole policy of Spain here was kept in suspense and the Duke of Savoy was left undecided as to whether he had to fear or expect most from the King of Spain or the King of France.

The first step in the business was an understanding between Savoy and the Spanish power in January 1628. The troops of Charles Emmanuel of Savoy occupied everything north of the Po up to the river Stura, and Gonzales of Cordova, the Spanish governor of Milan, laid immediate siege to Casale, which a small volunteer garrison of Frenchmen held in the interests of the Duke of Nevers. That was in February 1628.

I have said that the garrison of Casale was a small

one: the forces of the besieging army were much larger. But the place was strong—perhaps the strongest place in North Italy—the troops were good, and after the repelling of the first assaults it was clear that the results would probably depend more on blockade than on direct attack.

It therefore became a race between the siege of La Rochelle and the siege of Casale. And of the many such dramatic time-limits in European history, this is one of the most absorbing.

So long as La Rochelle held out Richelieu could do nothing to succour Casale. So long as Casale held out, Richelieu could pursue his chief domestic business, the reduction of La Rochelle. Should Casale surrender before La Rochelle, the French influence in North Italy would crash, Savoy would go Spanish, there would be uninterrupted facility of communication between the Spanish Hapsburgs to the south of the Alps and the Austrian Hapsburgs to the north, and no threat against the former power in the Lombard plain. Should La Rochelle fall before Casale, leaving time for the relief of Casale, then strong French action across the Alps with the army released from La Rochelle would change the situation wholly in favour of the French Crown.

What Richelieu did at this moment was characteristic of his will; it was also characteristic of his good fortune.

He steadily pursued the siege of La Rochelle, neither raising it nor even detaching a force for the relief of Casale. No doubt he had advices that Casale was sufficiently provisioned to last for many months, perhaps a year; but then provisions are not everything: with the increase of scarcity there might be illness or disaffection, and the little garrison might find it impossible to hold out. It was for Richelieu to judge whether the risk of concentrating at La Rochelle was worth while. He took the risk, and he succeeded.

In what followed the fall of La Rochelle, the advance over the Alps into Italy, the famous forcing of the Susa Gorge, and the relief of Casale, you again find something in Richelieu which touches upon Napoleon. There is the same simplicity, the same rapidity, the same power of making others work—those who had, until the Commander's appearance, lain apathetic. There is the same command of detail, the same sharpness of focus in judgment, the same refusal to be daunted by physical obstacles.

The situation in the January following upon the capitulation of La Rochelle, that is in the January of 1629, was dangerous, partly from the growing exhaustion of Casale, but more from the, as yet but half reformed, maladministration of domestic affairs.

When it was already decided to bring the army right across France, in mid-winter, from the Atlantic to the frontiers of Savoy (the Spaniards besieging Casale thought it was no more than a threat), the sums set aside for the purchasing of wheat were, more than nine-tenths of them, unused. Two hundred thousand livres —£100,000—had been set aside for the purchase of wheat for that force; only 15,000 livres—£7,500—had been spent; and the commissariat work had been given, by favouritism, to a young incompetent man who had purchased at absurd prices, perhaps by corruption. It must be remembered that Richelieu was not yet fully in control at home, and the hangers-on of the Queen Mother and of the King's brother and other magnates still had power. Even of that purchase nothing was made until it was heard that the King was as far down as Dijon on his march towards the Savoyean frontier.

Richelieu, himself at Dijon, ordered and purchased the remaining necessary wheat and sent it down at once by water to Valence, whence it was to be taken up into the mountains by carts and mules. When the Cardinal and the King, whom he accompanied, were already within a day of the frontier, no plan of the further day's march into the foreign territory had been made, nor, consequently, was there any provision for the troops at the end of each day's march, or any arrangement for billeting. None of the guns were mounted. There was only one officer trained to handle artillery, and he was too old for his work. Of 1,100 mules that should have been purchased and present before the end of February, none had yet appeared.

It was under conditions of breakdown like this—of breakdown due to Richelieu's not yet having full control at home—that the stroke for the relief of Casale was undertaken. And Richelieu did exactly what Napoleon would have done in the same straits. He made men work at a sudden new pressure, by his own personal presence, activity and supervision of detail: and also, it must be admitted, by that lavish expenditure of money which was his trump card in every critical point throughout the great eighteen years of his domination. He speaks amusedly in his Memoirs of how he got the guns mounted at Grenoble within three days by "money grease." For a month and more there had been tripartite negotiations between himself and the Spaniards and Savoy, which had clearly pointed to the determination of the powers beyond the Alps—Savoy in Turin and commanding the roads to Casale: Spain besieging Casale —to delay the French expedition until the garrison should be starved out. As determined was Richelieu that by a certain date, and no later, the garrison should be relieved. He was not going to delay that relief beyond the middle of March; for it was after that date that, by his advices, the situation would become perilous.

What follows is one of the most dramatic military operations in history.

It was mid-winter, the twenty-second of February, that the King left Grenoble. There had been exceptionally deep falls of snow, and the whole country was covered. Debate as to which of the passes should be used was decided by a determination upon that which was lowest and led most directly to the goal, the Mont Genèvre, and even that at such a season was five dreadful marching days from the starting place. One had to go right up into the heights of the Pelvoux and over the pass at La Grave, or round, miles further, by the Croix Haute. It was on the last day of the month, the twenty-eighth, a Wednesday, that the army lay (under heaven knows what conditions of shelter for so many thousand

men in such a season and at such a height) at the foot
of the Mont Genèvre. On the Thursday, the first of
March, 1629, Louis XIII leading the vanguard, it crossed
the pass and came down upon the Italian side, the King
sleeping that night at Oulx. The snow upon the further
side of the range was as deep as upon the nearer, and,
probably because it balled so in the horses' hoofs, nearly
all that heavy stage was done by the King himself on
foot.

Here, then, with not many days to spare if Casale were
to survive and the task to be accomplished, were Richelieu and the master whom he served and directed, on the
right side of the mountains, having accomplished this
feat in weather which had made his opponents believe it
to be impossible.

With the French on his own territory Charles Emmanuel of Savoy proposed further negotiations.

The situation was a plain one—would he act as a
friend, allowing passage of the French army through
Susa down to the plain and on to Casale: in other words,
would he come down frankly on the side of the French
in the quarrel and as their ally, or at any rate as a
friendly neutral, virtually admitting the claims of the
Duke of Nevers? Or would he join the Spanish power?

In number of troops Charles Emmanuel was far inferior; perhaps in quality as well. On the other hand,
by the route which the Cardinal himself had chosen, the
direct road down on to the Italian plain runs through
the gorge just above Susa, where there is no room to
deploy, where attack must be made in column, and where

a few men, as it seemed, could hold up ten or a hundred times their number—at any rate for a sufficient time to defeat Richelieu's object.

The attempts at delay over negotiations—which took place at Chiomonte—lasted three days, the second, third and fourth, and through the greater part of the fifth of March.

It must not be imagined that Charles Emmanuel's procrastination was due to any loyalty to the Spaniards or any fixed policy upon his part supporting them. All he desired was to aggrandise his estate, to increase his revenues, to strengthen the position of his House, closely allied as it was with the French reigning family.[1] He wanted leave from Louis XIII to attack either Genoa or Geneva, or both. (What a revolution in history had a Catholic power seized Geneva!) His true motive in causing such delay in negotiations was to strike as good a bargain as he could with the Cardinal and Louis. It is probable or certain that he felt himself secure in thus dragging out the palaver. Every hour added to the anxiety of those who were advancing in great force to relieve Casale, and made Charles Emmanuel's position stronger as a bargainer. The gorge in front of Susa seemed impregnable, the narrow way was defended by successive parallel dry walls of stone and barricades of wood between. The first attack would presumably be repelled, if attack should come; it would be more likely that there would be no attack unless a mere blunt re-

---

[1] Christine, Louis XIII's sister, had married Charles Emmanuel's son and heir.

fusal were given to the Cardinal's demands for a passage: and such blunt refusal Charles Emmanuel had no intention of offering. All he was asking for was a higher price.

He was offered, for the renunciation of his claims upon Mantua and Montferrat (claims which he could never realise fully, because he would only have held them under the shadow of Spain) 12,000 livres a year and the town and district of Trino. The Cardinal was even ready to bargain, and the 12,000 livres were raised to 15,000.

Even as late as the morning of Monday, March 5th, the heir to Savoy, the Prince of Piedmont, acting as envoy, tried to prolong the delay. He talked of being given French towns in pledge or hostage to prevent Susa remaining in French hands. Richelieu, never brusque until the last moment, and always desiring to achieve what had to be achieved at the least expense of energy, had determined that this day should be the last. He met the demand for French hostage towns with laughter— a thing rare in him; good-naturedly offering Orleans and Poitiers by way of a jest. He then more seriously told the Prince that if this day went by without a decision, no more negotiations would be attempted but the barricades would be attacked. "For," said he, "I know my master." It would be more accurate to have said that his master knew him. Brave as was Louis XIII, and even more impassive than brave, ready to bear the extremities of every season, yet the force behind that drive was the will of Richelieu.

The Prince returned to say that he "had not been able to find Charles Emmanuel in Susa," and the short winter day concluded.

Then came the stroke. The Cardinal and Louis mounted between ten and eleven that night. The troops were set in motion in the darkness, a vanguard of some 7,000 men with only three pieces, the mass of the guns following. The Guards went first, 4,000 in number, then 2,000 Swiss, and a mixed force of cavalry and infantry, 1,000 all told, from Chiomonte, the last stage where the negotiations had been taking place.

The troops, in movement all night (from three in the morning, when the King and the Cardinal joined them) did not attack till after sunrise. What a stand to arms, at such a height and in such weather! The final orders for the charge were not given till eight in the morning.

It had to be delivered with a spear-point of 200 picked men only in that deep funnel of a mountain gorge: 100 of the King's Musketeers with 50 of Navarre and 50 of the Guard on either side. Behind them 300 from each corps; behind them again a column of 1,000 with one culverin and two small pieces. Why the attack was not made with artillery we do not know—probably there was no emplacement in view and range of the barricades. A small party which knew the mountains had gone round by paths on the heights to the south of the gorge in an attempt to turn the position.

But all these preparations, manœuvres, and whatever discussions there may have been as to the possible use of the three poor pieces of ordnance available, meant nothing in the issue, for at the first stroke the barricades were forced against sharp musket fire which hardly checked the charge. There were not thirty dead in the attack, and only half-a-dozen of the leaders wounded, two of them gravely.

The comedy inherent in history showed its head here as it always does. Charles Emmanuel, all but captured in that rush (and having had a man killed at his stirrup), galloped backward through his flying troops, and found himself checked by some of them—mercenaries, French in origin—cried: "Let me pass! Let me pass! *Your* people are very angry!"

Such was the forcing of the "Passage of Susa," certainly due to Richelieu himself and to no other, small in scale, vast in consequence. It was all over before nine o'clock on Tuesday, March 6th, 1629. Ten days later the siege of Casale was raised as the large organised forces of the French approached, and the provision train was thrown in to the relief of the starving garrison. Savoy had abandoned the Spanish alliance and was in a new league with France, with Venice, and with the newly secured Duchy of Mantua and Montferrat. In other words, the Spanish power in North Italy was again threatened upon both sides.

But a new and more tangible strategic advantage had resulted from that campaign. The Duke of Savoy was constrained to admit a French garrison into Susa and to let it hold the citadel, nominally as a temporary guarantee for the provisioning of Casale, but really as a permanent post.

Now mark the advantage. There was one pass across the Alps, in that day upon the French frontier; one passage by which a force could be on the summit of the main chain without leaving French territory—this was the Mont Genèvre. To reach any of the others you had to invade Savoy or to ask leave of its Government, or to go round by the Swiss Cantons equally by invasion or permission. But the Mont Genèvre was a gate in French hands—and a low pass at that.

Now from the summit of the Mont Genèvre there are—not *one* road down to the Lombard Plain, as in other passes, but—*two* roads diverging like the branches of a Y and leading to the plains beyond the Alps, the one by the valley of the Dora, the other by that of the Chisone.

At the end of the Dora Valley is Susa—where the Mont-Cenis road comes in and joins the Mont-Genèvre road—so that the citadel of Susa blocks both approaches to Italy. At the end of the Chisone Valley is Pinerolo just at the foot of the Alps on the edge of the plain.

Richelieu having thus got hold of Susa, held it with a certain strategic and political purpose which we must clearly appreciate. He did not intend annexation of Italian land. He was aiming only at restoring the natural frontiers of France, the Gallic line, the "square field" which ends at the Alps. But he did intend to hold bridge-heads by which he could advance against external enemies and their possession in enemy hands gave *them* the power of entry against *him*. Such a bridge-head was Susa: a stronghold beyond the defiles of the two passes, commanding both, and so placed that from it an army could debouch on to the Italian plain when occasion should arise. He envisaged the flat land beyond the Alps in Lombardy as he later envisaged Catalonia beyond the Pyrenees and the right bank of the Middle Rhine, not as country to be conquered but as a belt of protection beyond a frontier, a belt in which French influence could be felt. He used these "penumbræ" of power as France at this moment, in 1929, is using, physically, their occupation of the Palatinate and the Reich, morally the disaffection of Alsace.

From this success he brought the King back into France, to settle the last possibilities of Huguenot resistance in the South. Privas, which resisted, was sacked, the other towns surrendered. A peace "of Grace" was granted. Fortifications and walls were destroyed, but the Edict of Nantes was re-issued and full toleration of Calvinism solemnly reaffirmed. Richelieu's own policy, imposed once more against the opposition of personal enemies, of simpler minds, of those few who felt in their bones what the distant results would be and dreaded them.

By the autumn of that year, 1629, he was back with the Court at Fontainebleau—but the menace of Casale was renewed. The armies of the Empire had come down through the Alps in aid of Spain, they held the Duke of Mantua blockaded in his capital.

Once more Richelieu set out, this time alone. He would not risk the life of the ailing King in a second winter campaign. The Cardinal left Paris two days before the end of the year, he crossed the Alps for a second time at the head of a large force, and challenged Charles Emmanuel of Savoy to abandon his secret negotiations with Spain and the Empire: for it was still the old Duke's obvious plan to play France against the Hapsburg, and between them increase his territory. It was as obviously the plan of Richelieu to make him take sides definitely with the succession of Nevers.

The campaign was Richelieu's own. He led it as a General and was as much the personal victor in it as any commander in history. He took Rivoli and then, unexpectedly, doubled back southward by forced marches, captured and held Pinerolo (at the end of March 1630)—and with that held his second bridge-head across the hills.

It was a master-stroke. No one could now turn a French advance towards the plains, and there was choice of entry by a French army along three roads: the Mont-Cenis and the two roads from Mont-Genèvre. With the summer the King joined the Cardinal, Savoy was over-run, and though Mantua had fallen, Casale—defended by Toiras—still held.

There followed side by side, in the late summer and close of 1630, two movements of unequal importance to the future of Europe. The one that seemed of greatest moment was the least. For the one that seemed of greatest moment was the saving of Casale by negotia-tions in which young Mazarin, sent by the Pope, enters the history of France: the one that seemed no more than a domestic trouble was such that on it would turn the whole attitude of France in the succeeding years, and consequently the success or failure of the Hapsburg re-Catholicising of Europe: it was the last strong effort to be rid of Richelieu at home, his hair-breadth escape from that menace, and his final triumph.

Marie de Médicis, through whom Richelieu had risen, who regarded Richelieu as her own creation, and who had certainly during all his difficult years been his one support and promoter—he had climbed entirely through her favour—Marie de Médicis, who had nursed that career and fed it, one may say, and sustained it from the man's twenty-fifth year until now when he was in the middle forties, who had even made him Cardinal, was growing filled with a blind anger against this dependant of earlier days, this present master of affairs.

Now what was the cause of this anger? Extravagant causes have been invoked to explain what some have thought an odd revolution in affection. Yet the explanation is not far to seek. It was the anger of a woman limited and stupid, yet emotional, even violent, who felt that her most intimate rights had been invaded, and invaded by one who should be, by every title, a personal inferior: a sort of servant.

She was the mother of the King. She had ruled, and after a short fall from power she had risen to rule again. There could be no question in her mind but that she had a right to rule, or at any rate, if the King were to be the real ruler by law, the right to be his first adviser and to control his councils. She had of her royal kindness raised

to a prominent position in those councils a young man
of no very great eminence, to whom she had graciously
shown exceptional kindness. She had not had the dis-
cernment to discover the calibre of this young favourite.
And behold, he who ought to have been nothing but a
compound of subservience and gratitude, subordinate as
of course to her magistracy, was now not only governing
the country but taking the gravest measures without allowing her to be consulted and more and more according
to a policy she detested.

She was of Hapsburg blood and he was now openly
checking the Hapsburg power. She was sincerely and by
conviction, as well as politically, on the side of fully restoring the Faith in Europe; and here was a priest whom
she had made Cardinal, doing all he could to halt that
advance. She was surrounded by those—such as Bérulle,
recently dead—who saw that toleration for Huguenots
within France would be destructive—and Richelieu was
the prime mover in toleration.

He did worse: on what was surely her right and the
right of the royal family, the nomination of the heir apparent to posts of honour and high revenue, he had put
a veto. She had asked the King to give his brother Gaston the governorship of Burgundy or Champagne. Richelieu had forbidden the putting of frontiers into such
incapable hands. To Marie de Médicis it looked like an
insult with no motive save the exhibition of insolent,
upstart power. She could not conceal from herself that
in some way this man felt himself her superior; yet by

all her standards he was still as far below her as any other petty subject.

She saw things domestically as a mother; her right to control her son, her three daughters married to Savoy, England and Spain; yet in England abandoned, in Spain and Savoy attacked.

With all this there went the confused sourness which most of us have observed in those who perceive that someone of whom they are jealous is regarded by third parties as somehow above them, and is certainly so regarded by himself. For not even Richelieu's control of feature and gesture could quite conceal his profound conviction that this patroness of nearly twenty years' standing was a fool.

Now to all this you must add yet one more emotion, which was that of the poet's "woman scorned."

It is often suggested that Richelieu had been her lover, and that he had grown weary of the relation. Such a suggestion is quite baseless and false in psychology so far as *he* is concerned. With *her* it is a little more complicated. She had certainly felt some attraction for this man so much younger than herself, and this sentiment, lasting throughout at least fifteen years—perhaps longer, from the first interview at Fontainebleau—sharpened the intensity of her present resentment. It is not conceivable that she went further. But she took pleasure in his company, counsel, presence after a very personal fashion—and he had affected her also by his mastering intelligence.

So much for her. But it cannot be admitted that Richelieu ever accepted an intimate relationship with her. It would not have been in his character to do so; and if by some extraordinary calculation he had permitted himself even a close friendship, then certainly a man of his sort would not have abandoned it. What he *had* done was to flatter her continually and use what (in her) was something like affection. Therein, and therein only, had he co-operated with her—and it was for his own advancement only.

It is part of the striking contrast between the two characters that while she from smouldering rose to a ferment of hate, he steadfastly and even humbly tried to maintain her old feeling of patronage. He actually humiliated himself in the phrases he used; he offered to resign (though knowing that it was only a form); and the protest he made late in life that he had never swerved from the gratitude due to his original benefactress, that she had never found him wanting, was sincere. But he could not help knowing what he never said or wrote—for he could not write or say it—that her stupidity was a danger to the State.

He had no hand in thrusting her out. It was she who thrust herself out by challenging him and attempting to rid the King of a counsellor lacking whom his growing position in Europe and at home would have crashed.

How long had this feeling of Marie de Médicis been growing? Perhaps three years; hardly more. It was not till early in 1629 that the Cardinal himself was aware of it, and not till the next year that it reached its height; and in the summer of that year 1630 the opportunity of the incompetent woman came.

During that second campaign of Savoy, when Richelieu and Louis had again marched together in arms, the
King fell ill of dysentery. He had to leave the army in
July 1630. As he went back into France he got worse;
and by the end of the month, at Lyons, he was apparently dying. There were four days, from the twenty-
seventh to the thirtieth of September, when they gave
him up for lost, and on the last he was given extreme
unction.

The Queen Mother and the Queen Wife had the invalid to themselves. They nursed him tenderly enough
and he was so far modified in character for the moment
by his illness and their assiduity, that he gave them something like apologies for his recent indifference to their
rights in government, or at any rate to his mother's.
His apologies to his wife were perhaps rather that he
had neglected her.

In that mood they approached Louis with the caress-
ing demand that he should rid himself of the masterly
influence which so offended them, and, indeed, when
he examined his own mind, offended his own feeling of
independence. When Richelieu got back to Lyons he
found (I quote his words—they are not too modest)
"that the time which his fidelity, his courage and his
virtue, had made him employ so happily in the glory of
his master, had been equally employed by the envy,
jealousy and malignity of his enemies, to ruin him with
the Queen: so that he was in peril of losing all the fruit
of his labours."

That is a roundabout way of saying that the Queen

Mother, whom he well knew had long been turned against him, had succeeded in getting that promise from her son. The strain continued up to the return to Paris and beyond; and the crisis came that November.

On Wednesday, the tenth of that month, Marie de Médicis, properly in the saddle again, was discussing with her son, as was now their wont, in her own palace, the Luxembourg, the affairs of State that had come before them that day.

The two were alone in that large square room of the west wing, on the first floor (leading out of her state bedroom) wherein she was accustomed to give audience. The small, highly decorated Florentine room near the chapel on the floor below in the east wing, was only used for public occasions.

This large square room leading out of the great state bedroom has to-day three doors, as it had then; one giving on to the great gallery, which Rubens had filled with his famous pictures of her and her spouse; the second on to the great state bedroom, the third into what was then a sort of servants' passage running parallel to and behind the great gallery.[1] This passage ran the whole length of the building and communicated at the other end of the great gallery by a staircase with a landing from which one could go on to the servants' quarters or turn down into the chapel on the ground floor. The

[1] In modern times all this southern side of the Luxembourg has been added on to and the old passage is absorbed in the new wing. The description I here give is the best I have been able to make out from a close examination of the palace in its modern state. Perhaps further evidence would make me modify my conclusion.

Queen in that interview had persuaded the King to have done with the Cardinal once and for all. She had said that she could no longer work with him, nor bear the sight of him under her roof (she had already dismissed with violence Richelieu's niece, hitherto one of her principal ladies). She now assured her son that she would leave the Council herself rather than meet him there. The Cardinal must go, once and for all. She proposed to replace him by her adherent, the elder Marillac, at the moment Keeper of the Seals, brother to the Marshal Marillac who was with the army in Italy.

Did the King consent? Did he plead to keep his genius of a minister? Richelieu himself would have us believe it, and would have us further believe that when the King left his mother's presence he had given no pledge. But what means had Richelieu of knowing? His own part in that famous interview was as follows:

He had wind of what was toward. He went through the chapel up the backstairs, down that long servant's passage, and came in upon them with majestic suddenness through the service door. As he stood there before them, he said quietly: "I will bargain that your Majesties are talking about me?" And Marie de Médicis later swore that what had destroyed her chance was forgetting to bolt that side entry.

She had, at that moment, no doubt of her triumph. She proclaimed it when her son had departed, going off in gloomy temper to Versailles; and all the Court came flocking round to congratulate her and to pay their respects to one who was now in their judgment the permanent controller of the Throne. Richelieu, it would seem, agreed with them; he made to go off to his town of Pontoise, of which he was governor.

Next morning the King sent for him from that little hunting lodge (as it then was) at Versailles. He despatched his closest companion of the moment, St. Simon (the father of the chronicler), and bade him seek the Cardinal, riding with full speed. Thus did that great man return. During this Monday, the eleventh of November 1630, the news spread throughout Paris, so that the day when the courtiers and all others who had flocked to the Queen Mother's presence were thrown back in stupour of disappointment—or its morrow— has been known thenceforward as the "Day of Dupes." [1]

So sudden and a large a revolution as the "Day of Dupes" produced a series of consequent movements. It was like the turnover of an iceberg which, after the immediate upheaval, is followed by a series of waves.

To begin with, Richelieu cleared the board of physically removing a host of opponents, some whom he had

[1] Two points must here be noted: first, the comparatively unimportant one that the phrase, "Day of Dupes," may be indifferently applied to Sunday the tenth or Monday the eleventh. It is commonly, but not always, applied to the last. Secondly, the more important one, that the accounts of the affair, which are numerous, differ a great deal among themselves. Richelieu's own account is too brief, omits his intrusion into the Queen's room, and puts his reconciliation with the King on the evening of the same day. But there is too much evidence for the sequence of events as I have put them to permit us to accept Richelieu's abbreviated account. It is most probable that the reconciliation took place on the eleventh.

long known as such, some who had betrayed themselves by their clamorous salute of the Queen Mother before she was undeceived, and their open rejoicing at the Cardinal's downfall. He captured Michael Marillac—whom the Queen had designed to take his place—and replaced him, as Keeper of the Seals, by a dependant of his own, Châteauneuf; the King's confessor, who had pleaded for Marie de Médicis; her doctor even; the widows of Lesdiguières—formerly the head of the army—and a bevy of other women. Guise went off of his own accord.

The most curiously illuminating case, showing into what detail Richelieu entered, was that of Bassompierre: the most tragic that of Marillac the Marshal, the exiled Michael's brother.

Bassompierre, successful, handsome, smiling, well set up and well regarded, well preserved, the diplomat who had appeased the quarrel between Charles I and his wife, who had signed the treaty of Madrid, who had gallantly restored the Chevreuse to court, years before, who had commanded before La Rochelle (and had foreseen how the fall of the city would increase the Cardinal)—all that!—Bassompierre, the friend in youth of Henry IV and the typical magnate of those days (he was at the height of his career, just on the right side of fifty), had asked Richelieu to dine with him on that same day, November 10th. The Cardinal, all broken with his imminent disaster, saw him after the scene at the Luxembourg and told him in agitation that he could not dine—that he must leave Paris—that in future he was nobody. Bas-

sompierre dined with the Duke of Créqui, and there, at
table, made such comments as the great news of Marie
de Médicis' supposed victory seemed to demand. His remarks were doubtless witty and certainly not favourable
to the fallen minister. Next day he heard that Richelieu
was again in power, and soon after he found himself in
the Bastille: with the present from Richelieu of a fine
rosary on which to say his prayers.

There he stayed for twelve full years—until the Cardinal's death—to which not uncomfortable but monoto-
nous sojourn we owe his "Life" and reminiscences: often
false, usually entertaining. He came out an old man and
died four years later.

The case of Marillac is more perplexing and more
terrible. He was a marshal, one of those commanding
the army in Italy side by side with Schomberg. He was
the brother of that Michael who had been Keeper of the
Seals and was, as I have said, marked by the Queen
Mother to replace Richelieu.

In the instant of his success the Cardinal sent down
post haste to the camp beyond the Alps, and ten days
after the "Day of Dupes" Schomberg with his own hand
had arrested Marillac and sent him back to the capital.
After a trial which dragged on interminably he was put
to death, eighteen months after his fall.

Now why did Richelieu act so? Marillac was not a
personal enemy, he had not intrigued. I believe the answer to be this: he had troops under his command and
so might later be dangerous: he was of a family, the
head of which was destined to supplant himself, Riche-

lieu, and was the Queen Mother's creature. That other
Marillac, he could not kill; there was no pretext. Richelieu was determined to make an example "out of the
heap" and picked out this victim, against whom it was
possible to produce a charge of sorts and yet of whom
nobody could say that he had been persecuted from
jealousy. But I doubt whether his death was intended
by the Cardinal until the plots of the Queen Mother
against Calais had been revealed to him.

The vanquished of the "Day of Dupes" took their
losses badly.

The King gave his mother the government of the
Bourbonnais, and she should thus have taken up official
residence in Moulins, its capital. She would not go.

She lived on in the Palace of Compiègne full of loud
reproaches, and then, in July 1631, fled north suddenly
—presumably to attempt a new insurrection.

She counted on the little frontier stronghold of Capelle. It was under the command of a young soldier she
thought would receive her. Richelieu got ahead of her,
sent the young soldier's father (of whom he was sure)
to replace him, and Marie found the gates of Capelle
shut against her. She fled over the neighbouring frontier
into the Spanish Netherlands, and thence wandered for
the remaining dozen years of her life from court to court,
railing and intriguing impotently against her unworthy
son and his traitorous Minister. Her very doctor was in
that Minister's pay and repeated to the Cardinal all she
said and did.

Gaston was as futile. In the first months he began by insulting the Cardinal, then apologised; then gave his royal brother a memorandum of Richelieu's crimes—saying (among other fatuities) that he had poisoned Bérulle. Then he made a first attempt at rebellion in Orleans, failed, and in his turn fled to Lorraine; thus voluntarily ridding his enemy of a grave anxiety—as had his mother. For the Blood-Royal were intangible (and bitterly does Richelieu in his Memoirs regret the fact that it was so).

But at last, after Marillac's death and the doom of the Queen Mother's plans, Gaston made one last effort, the defeat of which concludes this episode of the "Day of Dupes."

He came into France from Lorraine (whose Duke winked at anything that would weaken France) with 3,000 foot, 1,500 to 2,000 cavalry (this cavalry was the best of his force: mercenaries, Spanish, Croatian, Walloon), and three guns. He passed down the east through Burgundy, tried to take Avignon and failed, made for the other side of the Rhône. There he proposed to effect his junction with the man who should make all the difference to this new civil war, Montmorency.

Montmorency was still well under forty, looked younger than his years, was adored by women (in spite of a squint), and was, after the Blood-Royal (with which he was allied), the highest in rank of the kingdom: what we should call in England Earl-Marshal.

His sister, destined at first for Bassompierre, had married Condé, that cousin of the King who came next in blood and who not so many years before had been thought to be about to seize the kingdom.[1] He was of no great wit, but gallant, generous, and of a fine deportment. What was more important, he was thoroughly popular in the province of Languedoc, which he governed in hereditary fashion as his father and grandfather had done before him.

Languedoc was a kind of little kingdom, with its capital at Toulouse, its solid foundation upon the Pyrenees, its own southern tongue, and a long-standing separate tradition which still in some degree survives. It might almost be called the seed plot of Parliaments and "The Representative System" though that title perhaps more properly belongs to the Pyrenean valleys just outside its boundaries. At any rate it was the first of the great provinces to establish a fully developed House of Commons, and the example came straight from it to England through the agency of the Montforts. It had also its powerful group of hereditary lawyers and judges, the Parlement of Toulouse. And these Montmorencys, who had governed it for two lifetimes, were worthy of it; being of a nobility vastly ancient, rooted in the night of Time, springing from the Dark Ages, and for seven hundred years conspicuous in the story of their country.

When, therefore, Montmorency decided to support Gaston's rebellion, the moment was grave indeed. What prevented the outbreak of universal civil war was the

[1] Condé's plan during Louis XIII's minority was to pretend that the King was not legitimate, Henry IV's first marriage not having been duly annulled.

popular feeling for the monarchy, coupled with the refusal of the considerable Huguenot faction below the
rank of noble to move.

Had Montmorency been Huguenot himself, he might
have started yet one more of those religious rebellions
which Richelieu seemed to have destroyed for ever: but
he and his family had always been strongly on the Catholic side and the young man himself had already done
good service against the Protestants in arms and against
Spain. The only measure of support he got from the
Huguenots was some recruitment in the Cévennes Hills
from which he gathered three regiments. But the Protestants of the towns in the plains did not rise as he had
expected, not even in Montpellier.

His action was thoroughly disloyal, in spite of his
chivalric character. In order to get leave to raise a force,
he pleaded to the government in Paris the danger of a
Spanish attack, and meanwhile he was soliciting financial help from Spain itself for his projected stroke against
that government. He got very little (ridiculously less
than he had expected—£75,000) but the paltry size of
the subsidy does not excuse the treason.

What was of very high moment was his first step, the
summoning of the Estates of Languedoc. They met at
Pezenas and sanctioned the rebellion.[1] That was indeed

[1] The fight was opened on the twenty-second of July, Feast of St.
Mary Magdalen, and Richelieu was careful to note that St. Mary Magdalen has a special affection for Languedoc, and for all France, for that
matter. "Therefore did she bring the whole thing to naught, as she
had upon the same day shown her powers before La Rochelle, five years
before."

serious; such a thing had not been yet known in all
those rebellions against central authority which had been
the fruit of religious division. There had been plenty of
rebellious or semi-rebellious decisions on the part of con-
stituted bodies, and of course any number of them on the
part of bodies elected to represent the Huguenot faction;
but this was a true provincial assembly of most ancient
authority, speaking for the whole of Languedoc; and it
defied the King.

Nevertheless the Huguenot towns, as a whole, continued to refuse their aid; and even when Gaston of
Orleans had effected his junction with Montmorency
at Lunel, he failed to hold the greater part of the cities.
He got Albi by the action of the bishop; he fortified
Agde, and Brescou, and the two armies were in support
of one another by the thirtieth of July. Nîmes not only
refused to surrender, but its loyalty for the King was
specially emphasised by its leading Huguenot, Lagrange;
and Gaston's attempt at Beaucaire—which, had it succeeded, would have made all the difference—failed.

Beaucaire, had he been able to hold it, would have
been, what all men called it in the language of the day,
the "seat of the war." This idea of a *sedes belli* which is
always cropping up in these days (notably in the plans
of Gustavus Adolphus) is something unfamiliar to modern times. The conception is that of a stronghold from
which one can advance and to which one can retire, so
placed that it blocks the enemies' defensible entry against
the territory one desires to keep, and is convenient to
other defensible places sufficiently approachable from it.

For instance, anyone who held Stirling under the conditions of the seventeenth century would have such a "seat
of war" for holding the Lowlands against forces working
from the Highlands. The conception disappeared with
the raising of large regular armies; its value depended
upon what we now-a-days should call "irregular" conditions of recruitment.

The armies of the early seventeenth century were mer-
cenary, rapidly levied, disbanded again, haphazard. A
man with a "scat of war" could lie behind its walls when
recruitment was at a minimum, gather towards it new
forces, sally forth from it, make it a depot for provision
of all kinds.

Now Beaucaire was just that necessary place for the
rebellion. It stands opposite Avignon, dominated by a
huge feudal castle which has been renovated and is conspicuous to-day. Anyone who held it under the military
conditions of 1632, could stop all attempt to cross the
Rhône at that point, the northernmost point of the territories which Montmorency desired effectively to hold;
from it he could extend up into the Cévennes, and down
the river bank towards the open plain round Nîmes—a
town which, it will be remembered, had refused him
admittance. But if he could hold Beaucaire, Nîmes would
not long remain independent; and the fight at Beaucaire
was typical. The castle was betrayed to him, but the populace got hold of cannon and even mounted some of the
lighter pieces on church towers, heavier ones in the
higher parts of the town. At the expense of great dam-
age to their own houses they managed to turn out the

rebels. And thenceforward Montmorency had bad luck with all the other towns except the three which he held.

The news of the rebellion had been in Paris some days, but its gravity was only just recognised, when the Cardinal, on the sixth of August, gave the King his admirable advice of "the Lion and the Fox." It was the moment to show strength and ruse combined—and yet the event did not depend upon anything that Richelieu or the King did. The King did indeed make his declaration as a matter of course, five days later, and ordered the somewhat unwilling Parlement of Toulouse to ratify it (they did not do so until two days before the defeat of the rebels). Then Louis went down to Lyons.

There he heard, just before entering upon the campaign, that the work had been done for him. On the first of September in front of Castelnaudary, Schomberg, though with an inferior force yet with a force of well-trained men, and by a clever tactic, had destroyed the rebels. Montmorency himself, charging desperately, was captured—but with seventeen wounds in his body.

Gaston went to pieces. He surrendered abjectly, signed a document at Béziers within a month of the battle—on the twenty-ninth of September—that he would particularly cherish his cousin the Cardinal Richelieu.[1] In that document the Duke of Orleans wholly abandoned Mont-

[1] The word "cousin" in the mouth or from the pen of a royalty signified a recognition of rank superior to nobility and inferior to royalty itself. (Royalty itself is "brother.") Hence "dukes" (Royal-Blood) were called cousins, and the princes of the Church also. I am told that the word cousin is still used in those dead formalities of summoning an English duke to Parliament.

morency. The Duke did take the trouble to go and see the King at Tours some days later to plead for Montmorency's life, but he did nothing more. His prayer was not granted. Louis, with Richelieu behind him, insisted on the Parlement at Toulouse trying the prisoner; they were very reluctant, but they were compelled, and Richelieu's creature Châteauneuf, the Keeper of the Seals, presided. There could be no question of the facts; the man had been taken in arms and in full rebellion. He obtained leave to suffer in private, and he was beheaded in the courtyard of the castle on the thirtieth of October —after indignant protests from all the great families, from some few foreign courts and from the populace who roared all night in the streets for a reprieve.

With the fall of Montmorency and his execution, following upon that of Marillac, the capital episode which might be named after the "Day of Dupes" is closed.

But those two deeds of blood demand a special examination if we are to sound the depth of Richelieu's soul. The executions of these two men, Marillac and Montmorency, give us opportunities of particular value for estimating the true nature of his motives, character, and manner, which are among the objects of this study.

I propose, therefore, to go into each in some detail, and to attempt a conclusion in the matter. They are of particular value because each was in its way highly exceptional, though the victims differed in origin, in social, and in political importance, and still more in the nature of the crimes for which they suffered.

First let us consider the case of Marillac.

It has been almost universally condemned as an outrage, from that day to this, and the condemnation is,
upon the whole, just. It was an outrage against the
hitherto fairly fixed conventions of procedure, and it was
an outrage against apparent justice: that is, the man was
put to death for reasons other than the reasons apparent
in Court. We have three points to examine: (1) How
the thing looked from Richelieu's own point of view;
(2) How far his own excuses (for he has left behind
elaborate excuses) justify him even if that point of view
be accepted; and (3) How far it may be justified from
an impartial survey of the circumstances apart from
Richelieu's own interests.

From the point of view whence Richelieu regarded
the events of those eighteen months between his victory
over the Queen Mother and the beheading of Marillac,
that tragedy was not in itself necessary.

It was indeed necessary to secure Richelieu's position
that both the brothers Marillac should be put out of
action once for all. But both could have been put out of
action by close custody, as the elder in fact was. Whether
the death of the elder Marillac in prison can be ascribed,
as many contemporaries and some in our own day
would ascribe it, to the Cardinal's action, whether the
death of that man in prison, like that of not a few others
—Ornano, for instance, and Vendôme—was in fact murder by Richelieu, we have no proof; and in the absence
of proof history has no right to assume. The coincidences
are striking, the advantages of their deaths to the Car-

dinal obvious; but I would point out that, when we have made all allowances for the inflexibility of the man's conduct and his native indifference to all save the end which he had in view, secret murder is not consonant with his character. Had it been so, there are other occasions on which he could have earned more by that practice. Apart from this, one must judge men by the whole stuff of which they are made; and the more intimately you know the stuff of Richelieu, the less the popular melodramatic accusations of poisoning attune with it.

We know that he was a man strongly attached to what he regarded as honour—when once he had so far raised himself as to be able to afford that luxury. We also know that he was a man who argued things out to their last detail within his own mind, not only on the pros and cons of expediency, but also on the pros and cons of a certain moral code which he did not abandon. Moreover, that very coldness which would make the thing possible in him makes it improbable, just as the current, vague guesses at amorous intrigue upon his part are so improbable as to be negligible.

Custody, then, would have sufficed to guarantee Richelieu's own power, and that which in his mind was inseparable from it, the good of the State and the salvation of the monarchy, and of the particular prince upon the throne. Yet with custody he was not satisfied.

Note, however, the interval which elapsed between Marillac's arrest and his death. There was no haste; and, when the thing was finally decided on, the decision was

not the mere end of a necessarily long process, but a special conclusion come to under special circumstances peculiar to the summer of 1632 and not present eighteen
months before, when Marillac was first seized. These
special circumstances were the renewed intrigues of the
Queen Mother and Gaston of Orleans.

They were intending to strike from the Low Countries, where Marie de Médicis had taken refuge; and
their intention undoubtedly aimed at seizing one or more
strongholds in the neighbourhood of the then frontier
between the Spanish Netherlands and France. In particular, they aimed at the seizure, certainly of Calais and
also probably of St.-Quentin. It was essential for the
maintenance of Richelieu's new position and obviously
as essential for the King's power over France that no
success should attend these attempts. In other words,
the *execution* (as distinguished from the arrest and trial)
of Marillac was an example made for striking terror into
those who might lend themselves to the plots of the
exiles; and granted Richelieu's identification between his
own interests and those of the King and the State (which
was sincere), to have kept Marillac in custody only would
not have given a sufficient example. This is amply proved
by the fact that the imprisonment of the two brothers
had not prevented continued plotting against the Crown.

But the pretext was insufficient and the trial legally
scandalous.

As far as mere example goes it would have been a still
more striking example to have put to death the elder
Marillac, who was the direct though unsuccessful rival

of the Cardinal, and whom the Queen Mother before her fall had specially designed to take Richelieu's place. But, as I have said, there was no pretext upon which he could put the elder Marillac to death by public sentence. He put the younger Marillac to death upon a pretext which at any rate was sufficient to be the basis of an indictment, though not sufficient for the sentence pronounced on conviction.

Therefore the excuses which Richelieu makes at great length, and displays for his exculpation before posterity, are of high interest—and we can only conclude upon an examination of them that these excuses are wholly insufficient. They are the excuses of a man who is troubled in conscience and still more troubled by the fear lest his reputation after death should be tarnished; who casts about for means to make his act less odious, but who fails to make his defence good. Let us see what sort of things he brings up against Marillac in his lengthy self-pleading.

He tells us that Marillac was of low birth and therefore not only beneath the dignity of the places he filled and the honours he achieved (the command of a great army, the title of Marshal of France, the management of great financial transactions in connection with the campaign) but also, on account of his base blood, an unworthy soldier.

Now all this is ridiculous. Richelieu always exaggerated the importance of rank and of the distinction between the nobles and the middle-class. It was an illusion which he cherished and in which he was in some

degree self-deceived, but not in the degree implied by
this first count against the character of his victim. It was
absurd to pretend, in the first third of the seventeenth
century, that a man of Marillac's social rank was un-
suited to the places he held. His father was of no great
origin, but of reasonable birth, from Auvergne, had
held important posts under the treasury, and had brought
up his sons into the way of public service, as had scores
of such men for more than a century past. The passage
from such service into the highest nobility was a commonplace.

Next he brings forward against Marillac a host of accusations of cowardice, with hints that sometimes that
cowardice is treason. He tells us that the man suspi-
ciously failed to discharge his duties in the attack at La
Rochelle; but, after all, it was Richelieu himself who
had put him there. He says he behaved badly in the
attack on the Isle of Rhé somewhat earlier; but he puts
it vaguely, and there is no contemporary corroboration
that I know of. He tells us that Marillac having been
charged by Marie de Médicis to make the fortifications
at the bridges before the "tomfoolery" of the Ponts-de-
Cé, was the first to abandon them, and hints that his
abandonment of them was deliberate. He says that Marillac did everything he could to delay the execution of
the order he had received to take his army into Italy.
And so on. The whole thing is thin for there is no confirmation.

He cannot escape from the fact that he himself, Richelieu, had put the man where he was; he makes it the

work of the Queen Mother, but then Richelieu at the
time of Marillac's promotion was the right hand of the
Queen Mother and serving her with all his might. He
contradicts himself by telling us on the same page that
Marie de Médicis had advanced Marillac by marrying
him to one of her maids of honour because she was perpetually pushing his fortunes, and yet that she only
forwarded the marriage because she wanted to do the
girl a favour and feared that the young woman might
not get a husband at all.[1]

Now no one can miss the obvious fact that these accusations, even if they were true, had nothing to do with
the catastrophe. Marillac might have been the most
arrant coward, and of the basest origin, insufficient, and
advanced entirely by court intrigue, yet, all that would
have nothing to do with his trial and condemnation.
He was tried for malversation in the course of his duties
of furnishing the army he commanded, and the stronghold and garrison of which he was the governor,
Verdun.

Here Richelieu is on surer ground. He piles up a great
mass of counts for indictment, probably all true, though
perhaps too much emphasised; how the man comman

[1] I would here point out to the reader who may be interested to turn
to the long account of the affair in Richelieu's *Memoirs*, that he must
beware of the misprint on the last line of the first column in the
original Michaud, second volume of the *Memoirs* (numbered Vol. 8
in the Series), p. 377. The following line, which should make the first
line of the second column, has been transposed to the end of that
column: a printer's error which makes nonsense of the passage until
it is pointed out.

deered goods from the peasants and then sold them for his private profit; how he put the government purchases at prices higher than those he paid and kept the differ-ence, etc., etc.

But the point for us to remember is that these irregularities were of common practice. It is the first accusation made against any military commander during the seventeenth century and somewhat later, that he put in his pocket part of the sums which passed through his hands. The accusation is nearly always true, as it was eighty years later in the case of Marlborough, yet it is unjust because it was not universally condemned by public opinion, nor, in the nature of the times, easily avoidable. Everything was farmed out, especially military things. Everyone was interested to make *some* profit from his place—and indeed there was no method of raising or conducting armies save on the supposition of some such moderate profits; from the small gentleman who volunteered to raise a troop if the king would give him a lump sum of money, up to the commander-in-chief, everybody worked "on a margin of profit." It is no doubt true that Marillac exceeded the conventions; but it is not true that his excess merited any very severe condemnation, still less that it merited death. And it is most emphatically untrue that these peculations were the true motive of the prosecution.

There is, however, in Richelieu's long explanations a worse feature, which is the suppression of essential truths. For instance, the venue of the trial was changed from Verdun to Rueil, a suburb of Paris. Richelieu mentions that fact in one colourless sentence as being the decision of the King, "in order that the Keeper of the Seals, who was to preside at the tribunal, could conveniently attend." But he omits to tell us that the Keeper of the Seals was a creature of his, and that the place at which the trial was held at Rueil was his (Richelieu's) private house! He also omits to tell us that when the judges voted, the condemnation of the unfortunate man was only arrived at by a majority of one. He tells us truly enough that no doubt some pressure was put upon this exceptional Court of Justice, that the exiled Queen Mother and her son had the insolence to threaten the judges, and that one of her messengers boasted that he would shoot any one of them who condemned Marillac. But if he tells us all that, he ought also to have told us the other circumstances which he suppresses.

Again, by all precedents a Marshal of France should be tried by the Parlement of Paris. (It would not have condemned him.) Instead of this, Marillac was tried by a special commission. Richelieu defends this on the plea that the King must be all-powerful. He knew very well as he wrote the words that "the King" meant himself. It was he who had decided to take the thing out of the hands of the regular judges, he who had the commission sitting in his private house, and he who changed the venue.

In a word, Richelieu comes out very badly on the chapter of the excuses he puts forward. He had not really satisfied himself by them, and he has certainly not satisfied history. It cannot be forgotten that even these special commissioners debated the matter for two days before finally deciding the fate of the unfortunate man—by that majority of one.

But on the third point, which is the core of the affair, we must decide that, Richelieu or no Richelieu, the execution of Marillac in that critical moment of the spring of 1632, was imperatively needed.

Marillac was put to death in order to strike terror into those who proposed the seizure of Calais. Any determined government would have had to do what Richelieu did or risk the realm. The admirable secret service which the Cardinal had already organised left no doubt upon that. Calais was being "managed," the governor of the garrison was in secret touch with Gaston and with Marie de Médicis. Calais was of first-class importance. La Rochelle had shown what strength could be shown by a rebellious stronghold based upon the sea, and the kingdom could not afford a second siege of La Rochelle with a probable failure. Moreover, Calais lay right open to England, and the English succour which might come to it would be a very different thing from the abortive efforts to rescue La Rochelle.

Putting Marillac to death at that moment meant that any one of the Queen Mother's agents caught in secret treason would die. So poor Marillac was like the owls and stoats which the gamekeeper nails to the barn door; a terror for the rest. In general it was an iniquity of State of the sort called necessary iniquity, and not personal to Richelieu and his régime.

Now let us consider the case of Montmorency. The putting to death of Montmorency raises a problem of quite another kind, to wit, how far Richelieu dared to go in executing a particular criminal upon whose crime there was no doubt but whose position was exceptional. We judge by this case his exact judgment of the limits to which he could go and also of his luck. For it was a very near thing whether the death of Montmorency might not upset the minister (and King?) responsible.

As to the question of right, to debate that, we must put ourselves back into the conditions of the time.

We are at a turning point between the old power of the great nobles within the nation and the modern state governed by central authority; but it is only the turning point because it is the epoch of Richelieu. It was Richelieu who made the change. Did he on this particular occasion go beyond what the ideas of the time and its morals could tolerate? Was this act of justice also an enormity?

Most men thought that he did; most men thought it was. And, when Montmorency's head fell, it affected the people of that day as something so extreme in the exercise of a new power that they could not pardon it.

Yet we must decide that upon the whole Richelieu was right; and we further must remember that he did not proceed in this particular and very grave case with precipitation, nor even with instant resolution.

On the facts of the case there was no doubt whatever. The man had been caught in open armed rebellion against the Crown, levying war against it and committing overt treason against the State. But then he had acted in support of the King's own brother—whom there could be no question of putting to death—and in support of a great faction which, in the eyes of many, was an alternative government; in support of the heir apparent who would almost certainly be King, and that, in most people's judgment, within a short space of time; and in support of various grievances all of which centred upon the detested rule of an all-powerful minister standing between the monarchy and the people.

I have said that the thing was not done without deliberation and without a long balancing of advantages and disadvantages. Richelieu has told the whole story at great length, and I think that no one can read this section of his Memoirs without agreeing that it is history; that the things which he describes, though they passed in private, really happened. It has quite a different ring about it to the long and confused excuses put forward in the Marillac case from the same pen.

When, upon the fourth of October, 1632, immediately after his wretched surrender, the Duke of Orleans came to Tours to plead with his brother for the life of Montmorency, he certainly found the King hostile. A whole week passed before Richelieu closeted himself with his sovereign and thrashed the matter out. For it was on the eleventh of the month that, behind closed doors, he put every possible argument for and against; and he says, (I think truly) that he left it with the King to decide—though of course it cannot be denied that the King was under his persuasion.

To begin with, he tells us (and this is undoubtedly true) that from the beginning of the conversation the King was determined upon the execution of the rebel. All that Richelieu desired the King to consider was whether the advantages of sparing Montmorency's life were sufficient to counterbalance the obvious advantages of the King's carrying out his determination. He put the advantages which would follow on the sparing of Montmorency very fully and convincingly. The man could be held as hostage against any further movement on the part of Orleans. Orleans had made his peace, and would be restored to his estates. It was an act of clemency which had struck the popular imagination, which was perhaps dangerous but which at any rate was accomplished. What was not accomplished was any guarantee that the trouble would not begin again.

Had Richelieu been by a shade a weaker man than the very strong man he was, he would have allowed another consideration, not indeed to appear in his open speech with the King, but to gather in his own mind. Upon the King's death (it was not two years since he had been at death's door) Gaston would reign, and the man who had executed Montmorency would be arrested—to be an exile or killed. This precarious position which the Cardinal held is too often forgotten. We know the end, and we forget that *he* did not know it. We know that the King was to survive him, that he was to have a complete triumph and to end his life at the very height of his power. But *he* did not know anything of that.

He took the risk of putting the counter-arguments,

and they were sufficient to convince. The King had no
child. Everyone believed his health to be wretched (here
Richelieu remarks, with sound judgment, that popular
rumour, and even Court rumour, exaggerated). The
tendency to further rebellion was very strong. The presence of the Queen Mother abroad and of the untamed
factions within, were like an ulcer which must be lanced;
with one very striking, indeed (for that age) almost in-
credible, act of government, the lancing would be effected.

It was probably, perhaps certainly, the *quality* of the
support given by Montmorency to the rebellion which
had had the greatest effect upon Richelieu's mind. It had
been a territorial affair, the act of an hereditary house
which was a sort of little kingship of its own; frontiered
with Spain, even subsidised by Spain; and it had behind
it, if not the active support of the province, at any rate,
the old local liberties in opposition to the new centralised
government. This rebellion in Languedoc had been an
affair of a different colour from the others. It was not
even religious, but very largely moved by the semi-
autonomy of a great province. All that Richelieu made
it the business of his life to do was in peril if elected
local assemblies and hereditary local judges could withstand the Crown.

Yet it must not be forgotten that in his long debate
of reasons for and against the very grave decision, Richelieu concluded by returning to a further consideration
of the policy of compromise. He gave the last word, as
it were, to the defence, lest he should seem to be forcing

the hand of the King. I have no doubt that by his tone of voice and his manner, any third party present would have seen that Richelieu had decided for death; but it must not be forgotten that the King also had so decided before Richelieu began to speak.

It was an enormity to put to death such a man at such a time. It was an enormity, the justification of which would lie in its future effects, and the success of its effects did, in fact, justify it. But it was very near the line. The carrying out of that sentence marks the furthest advance made in the new establishment of absolutism, of deciding that national monarchy should triumph and the great Houses be reduced to the authority of the popular Crown.

The execution of Montmorency is in France the counterpart to the execution of Strafford in England nine years later. For the death of Strafford set the seal upon the conquest of the English Crown by the English upper class; the death of Montmorency set the seal of the conquest of the upper class by the French popular monarchy.

It was, in Richelieu, an act of the highest daring. It challenged every force at once. But it succeeded.

When on that fourth anniversary of the surrender of La Rochelle he put to death the first noble in France, victor by sea and by land, heir to seven centuries of fame and the last of his line, he killed in the same stroke the last chance of oligarchy.

He had himself but ten more years to live.

VI

GUSTAVUS ADOLPHUS

THE execution of Montmorency ends the crisis of Richelieu's affairs at home and begins his henceforward unquestioned supremacy.

We have now to follow the great business of the Cardinal's remoulding of Europe, and for this purpose we must go back in time: for Montmorency's death is of October 1632, Richelieu's moves in German affairs date from 1631.

There are three consecutive decisions in Richelieu's wrestling with Hapsburg power after the first skirmish in Italy.

First came the letting loose of a high military genius, the King of Sweden. Richelieu hires him to attack Austria, although that genius, Gustavus Adolphus, represented all that was anti-Catholic in Europe, all that was blindly opposed to the re-unison of our civilisation and the recapturing of Europe for the Faith. This stroke of policy, long played with, was accomplished in the first days of 1631, that is, only a few weeks after the "Day of Dupes" at home, while all that we have been describing in the last section was still proceeding in France. But once that hired soldier took the field, Richelieu found that he had called up the devil and that the devil was too much for him. He had the good fortune to get that devil exorcised by death—for Gustavus Adolphus fell in battle at the end of one year; but Richelieu had loosed

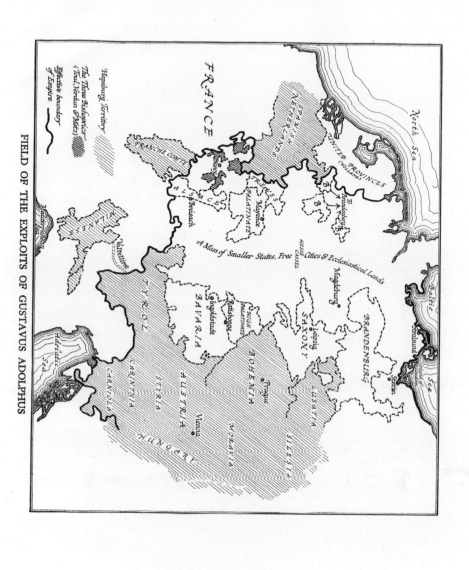

FIELD OF THE EXPLOITS OF GUSTAVUS ADOLPHUS

forces stronger than he could deal with, and he was almost mastered by the storm. He had intended to check
the advance of the Austrian Hapsburgs by paying a
new captain to fight them, but he had not intended to
weaken Catholicism. He discovered that he had almost
ruined it in the Empire and had in any case left it permanently unable to recover its old supremacy there.

The second chapter beginning in 1635, is that of a
most perilous war upon a full national scale. His long
and indirect subterranean offensive against Hapsburg
domination had come to its inevitable conclusion, and,
after 1635, there must be open conflict, and there was.
In that conflict he was compelled, in spite of himself, to
ally himself with the interests which desired to stamp
out the Faith. He so struggles during four years, until
the end of 1638, and beyond—indeed, until the July of
1639. Though many things in the last year of the four
were beginning to go his way, Richelieu, until almost
the end, struggled handicapped.

With July 1639, opens the third phase, which is the
gathering of the harvest. Fortune serves him as well as
do the fruits of his long tenacity in plan, and for the
remaining three and a half years, up to the moment of
his death at the end of 1642, Richelieu accomplishes for
France all he had set out to complete in youth, a lifetime
before.

The men who change the history of the world are
always making mistakes, as do all other men. They seem
to differ from other men chiefly in four things; first,
that they have better fortune; secondly, that this good

fortune works upon exceptional ability (coupled with a strong desire to rule and direct the world; thirdly, that they are continuous in action; fourthly (at which I beg the reader not to smile), that they live long enough —which may be accounted by some a part of their good fortune, by others of their ill.

We begin, then, with the summoning and hiring of the King of Sweden.

All those who follow the career of Richelieu must feel —and it is the sober verdict of history—that they are dealing with something which has no parallel. There is a point after which a difference in degree involves a difference in quality, and there is a difference in degree between Richelieu's power of handling an indefinitely varied situation and that of, say, Metternich or Cavour, or even Kaunitz. This difference in degree of diplomatic talent seems to put the Cardinal into a different category from others, and one in which, I suggest, will be found no one standing next him, save Bismarck alone—and the complexities of Richelieu's problems were greater than those of Bismarck.

Now this sentiment, which we all have touching the man, is especially aroused by our knowledge that, in all the earlier part of his public life, he was achieving his results not only in foreign policy, but in the wretched and torturing business of political intrigue against him at home; and it is most significant that it is just when that intrigue is at its very worst, seems certain to destroy him, and indeed, is such that he only escapes from it by that element of good fortune which attended him always, that he does the most striking work abroad. Just that moment when he is almost lost at home, and barely wins his decisive battle of the "Day of Dupes," is also the period when he is carrying to success the beginnings of that formidable diplomatic victory which was the foundation of all that followed: I mean, the formation of his covert alliance against the House of Austria and the launching of Gustavus Adolphus.

The domestic business of the "Day of Dupes" and its sequel was contemporary with the foreign combination whereby was permanently ruined the great plan for reducing all Germany to one Catholic state under Hapsburg obedience ruling from Vienna.

That is why, in following this great business abroad, we have to go back in time and deal with it as a parallel to what was going on in France against Richelieu's ministry. The first approach to Sweden is contemporary with Richelieu's first fears of the Queen Mother's enmity. The King of Sweden accepts French pay just after the "Day of Dupes." He wins that decisive battle of his by Leipzic at the moment when the Cardinal is anxiously watching Marie de Médicis' and Gaston's plots, he is ravaging Catholic Bavaria just while Orleans is raising rebellion in Languedoc. He falls at Lutzen a week after the execution of Montmorency.

In the year 1629, the power of the Emperor Ferdinand II was at its height. He had mastered the Palatinate and confiscated the patrimony of its foolish young Calvinist rebel, solidly planting there the power of Catholic Bavaria; he had beaten off the effort of Christian of Denmark. He had behind him the great unconquerable army of Wallenstein, some hundred thousand men, mercenaries drawn from all nations, and handled by a general of the first class; he had not yet lost the support of the Catholic League with their army under Tilly. There seemed nothing that could oppose him with success, or his plan for a centralised German state hand in hand with his cousin of Spain and mastering the world for the Catholic Church.

Ferdinand had also behind him, one may say, all the strength of the Six Electors; the three ecclesiastical ones, of course, Bavaria of course, and even Protestant Brandenburg and Protestant Saxony. For Brandenburg (in the hands of a man of no great decision) was divided into three separate parts: one, the fief of Poland, (whose king was Ferdinand's brother-in-law and a secondary champion of the Catholic cause), one to the east of the Lower Rhine, and one isolated from either of the other two. The Elector of Saxony supported his imperial chief partly from the old German tradition of loyalty to the Kaiser, much more because, as a strong Lutheran, he hated the Calvinists even more than he hated Rome; but also through a certain gratitude and a certain interest: he had actually fought for Ferdinand, and Ferdinand had largely rewarded him.

The French ministry which Richelieu directed was far too occupied and embarrassed, abroad with Italy, at home with the increasing interferences of the Queen

Mother, to pursue its will, even covertly, beyond the Rhine.

Now with the early months of this same year, 1629, Ferdinand did that which was necessary to the re-establishment of the Imperial power and of religion, but which meant the running of a great risk. He proposed to undo the loot and ruin of the Reformation. He did exactly what, on a small scale, Charles I of England had attempted in Scotland three years before, and half accomplished four years later: and what Mary Tudor, a lifetime before, had not dared to do. He claimed the stolen ecclesiastical lands.

In the case of Charles I, it was the beginning, and the ultimate cause, of his ruin and violent death. In the case of Ferdinand II, it was the beginning of his decline —but not the cause. Of himself, he would have won through. The reason that he failed to win through, was that in due time the figure of Richelieu was to stand up pitted against him.

It was on the sixth of March, 1629, that the Emperor issued his Edict of Restitution; charged with explosives.

So long ago that only the very old men could remember the year, and that all who had then been in active public life were now dead, there had been concluded between the legitimate Catholic authority and the religious rebellion of the Reformers, a pact called the Peace of Augsburg. It was a compromise. The wholesale plunder which had taken place between the first upheaval and the year 1552—half a lifetime of loot—was secured to those rich nobles who had profited by the

religious tumult, and to those cities which had confiscated, to the advantage of their rich merchants, the
endowment of religion.

It had been sworn by those just thus permitted to keep
what they had taken, that henceforward there should be
no more plundering of any kind; but for a whole long
lifetime they had been breaking their word. The Edict
of Restitution did not propose to go behind this original
Treaty. It left the original loot, prior to 1552, in the
hands of the spoilers. But it proposed that all *since* pur-
loined should be given back—at least a hundred great
abbeys, and the endowments of a dozen bishoprics. Ferdinand was careful to make an exception for the Elector
of Saxony—on account of the help that Prince had given
him in the past—and he relinquished to him three of the
bishoprics; but one big fragment of revenue, the endowments of the archbishopric of Magdeburg, was to go
back to the Church—and Saxony was not wholly
content.

It cannot be denied that there was an element of pre-
scription attaching to most of this property. It had been
possessed for all their lives by its present owners. There
were not a few of the Emperor's supporters who doubted
the wisdom of a decision founded on justice rather than
policy; and Wallenstein himself, who had to carry it out,
treated it at first as fantastic.

From that moment there was a stronger reason for
uniting against the imperial power than ever there had
been before, and though Ferdinand seemed to have made

himself at last invincible, he had given his enemies a hold.

When Richelieu was no more than twenty-six years of age, a young provincial bishop consecrated barely three years, there came to the throne of Sweden a lad of sixteen, in whom the hereditary madness of his family had turned to genius, Gustavus Adolphus by name. The shameful history of his immediate ancestry, with its cynical usurpation of the throne and betrayal of religion for money, do not concern us here.

It is enough to remember that there was madness in the blood—a madness which turned to genius in this lad, and again much later in the less sane Charles XII.

In spite of his cant—mixed with a most sincere hatred of Catholicism—in spite of his foolish boasting of a nice honour (with such a record!)—in spite of his megalomania, there are admirable things in this big, red-headed soldier in the height of his fame (1629-32).

He was just in his dealings with his conscripts. He was a good barrack-room companion. He knew good ale, and loved it with all his soul—comparing it to the pure Gospel, and sour, muddy beer to Papistry. He had a genial comic swagger which his fatness (rapidly increasing) made very amiable to behold. He had also simplicity. And he was wonderfully courageous: not only against death, but against all hardships, and even against the loss of friends.

He was not the legitimate king. The legitimate king was his Catholic cousin, Sigismond, whom Gustavus' father had expelled, usurping his nephew's throne, and supported in the usurpation by the great landowners, who, here as everywhere, had shared out among themselves the property stolen from the Church. Sigismond, the legitimate and expelled king, had been elected to the throne of Poland, and was married to the Emperor's sister.

Against this Sigismond of Poland, in this year 1629, Gustavus Adolphus was waging war—for the genius of that young man of thirty-four was a genius for arms. His father had already conquered Esthonia, cutting off the Russians from the sea; *he* proposed to conquer Livonia and Courland, and the Baltic fringe of Poland, as well, so as to weaken his cousin as a claimant to the throne of Sweden.

In the fighting, which he had carried on for these many years, he had so distinguished himself as to make some impression upon neighbouring courts, but especially upon one very acute observer, Hercules Girard, Baron of Charnacé, a Frenchman who had travelled in those parts; and already, while the siege of La Rochelle was still proceeding, Charnacé had spoken to the Cardinal of the new power in the North that might be brought into the game against the Hapsburgs.

The country of Gustavus Adolphus was poorly peopled—perhaps two million souls—it had but a small revenue, and no great accumulated wealth; but its men were very fine material for infantry, they had become unitedly loyal to their leader, and he had given them a tactic, and especially a use of artillery, far superior to anything else in Europe.

Such were the man and the force now sought by the Cardinal—and the Capuchin. For, with the bringing in of Sweden, Father Joseph had a great deal to do. But there is a certain divergence between his aim and that of his great colleague, which it is important to notice. Richelieu brought in Sweden under the impression that a clever captain who would not do too much but would do something, might be employed as a sort of mustard plaster against Austria, drawing away the Emperor's forces from those in rebellion, neutralising his efforts at making a united Germany. He had no idea that Gustavus Adolphus would sweep the board and would appear within a few months as a Colossus, bestriding Central Europe. He had in mind a minor, though important, operation, and an operation purely political. Hence his determination to make that one more Protestant alliance, and to purchase it at the price he did.

Now Father Joseph lived on a plane somewhat higher in Christian morals, and for him the use of Gustavus Adolphus (whose genius perhaps he had divined earlier than had Richelieu) was to be the instrument in reducing Catholic Austria, indeed but only so that Catholic France should achieve her natural headship of the Catholic culture in Europe. Christendom was still his ideal.

Anyhow, both men combined had made the plan. The Swedish King must be brought in against Ferdinand— and for this, the first step was to arrange a peace between Gustavus Adolphus and his cousin of Poland, in order that the former should have his hands free for the use to which Richelieu intended him. Richelieu sent Charnacé out to handle that situation.

In the use Richelieu made of Charnacé there is once more a parallel to Napoleon. It something resembles Napoleon's use of talent in his marshals. The Cardinal managed to put his own spirit into his envoy, and so filled him with the spirit of his own policy that Chanacé's dealings might almost have been those of Richelieu in person acting at the other end of Europe. He was subtle, he watched carefully, he calculated, and he carried all through with that tireless persistence which was the exceptional characteristic of his master.

Charnacé's first step, in that summer of 1629, was to go to Königsberg to see the Marquis of Brandenburg. He got to the town and Court early in July.

Now the whole business of Charnacé, the great idea which he had been sent to emphasise and bring into action, was Richelieu's plan of getting the Protestant northern princes, like Brandenburg, to accept the support of the *Catholic* League in helping Denmark against the Empire. In this way the main thing Richelieu had at heart—the prevention of German unity under the single Crown of Austria—would be achieved, and yet the lessening of Catholicism in Europe would be averted. Brandenburg would hear nothing of this. When Charnacé spoke of stopping the Polish war, he was all in favour, but he jibbed at alliance with the Catholic League.

Well, on such a check the envoy showed all the suppleness of the man who had sent him. He turned his efforts into a new channel, accepting the second best, saying, as it were, "Since you cannot stomach the Catholic League, at any rate accept the idea of peace between Gustavus Adolphus and his cousin the King of Poland, and, what may follow, we shall see."

Brandenburg was agreeable; but here came in another difficulty. Charnacé must be very careful to offend neither Gustavus Adolphus nor the King of Poland. Whichever he went to negotiate with first, the honour of the other would be wounded. If he went to see Gustavus first, the King of Poland would say that a usurper had been approached before himself; if he went to see the King of Poland first, Gustavus would say that the recognition of the French monarch was being given to a claimant and pretender. Yet clearly the ambassador could not at the same moment see the two heads of the two armies opposed in war.

The solution of the puzzle is interesting and ingenious. Charnacé put it about that he had intended to see the King of Sweden first, but that Brandenburg, the King of Sweden's own brother-in-law, had dissuaded him from this and had said, "I will not countenance your helping him until you have first seen the King of Poland." Thus the French envoy had all the credit with Gustavus Adolphus of intention to give him the greater honour, while in action he gave it to the King of Poland.

Then came a third difficulty. The Poles were in a state of exasperation: it was essential not to let that exasperation destroy the work which Charnacé had in hand. They did not trust the motives of France, and on the top

of that, they were exalted upon punctilio. When Charnacé arrived at Thorn (he had left Königsberg on the
twelfth of July) he heard that the King had gone with
his army to Marienburg. When he got there and sent
his compliments to the general, he was told that he must
wait two days before getting an audience. When he got
an audience, he was asked why he came with only a
dozen or fifteen followers: why the King of France had
not gone through the formality of announcing beforehand the sending of his agent, Charnacé, and why he
had not full ambassadorial powers.

When Charnacé gave courteous and conciliatory an-
swers to these grievances (that, there being war by sea
and land, he could not travel with a greater retinue;
that a preliminary embassy would have wasted essential
time, etc.) he was again checked by the demand to have
all this put down in writing, so that they could debate
upon it. He did not allow himself to be moved to anger
or to any expression of hostility by such irritants; it
might have been the Cardinal himself at work. He sat
down to draft in written form the substance of what he
would propose as a basis of peace between the two
Crowns of Poland and Sweden.

That peace was negotiated with success under the
name of the Truce of Altmark—the French broker
doing just what he twice did in Italy, and calling off the
victor by securing him a share of the spoils.

Next, Charnacé and his master must go forward to
make Gustavus Adolphus do what Christian of Den-

mark had failed to do, and become a weapon against Austria.

Now the one demand of Gustavus Adolphus was for money. He did not want it from avarice; he wanted it in order to make war, which was his trade, and partly also (though in what degree we never shall know) to support the Protestant cause. Of his own resources he could levy, and train with that genius of his, by far the best army of his time; but he had nothing like the revenue to keep it in the field against any first class antagonist. He had fished for money both from Denmark and from Charles I; each had promised supply, and neither had been able to give it sufficiently. He now found that money could be obtained from France.

In his pursuit of this new avenue of supply Gustavus showed considerable ability. Charnacé was told to offer him three tub-fulls of gold, each with a purchasing power of some hundred thousands pounds of to-day: three hundred thousand pounds in all. The letter was sent off from France by Louis XIII, that is, by Richelieu, at Christmas, 1629, shortly after the news had arrived in Paris of the successful truce with Poland, negotiated by Charnacé. Charnacé put the "proposition" a month later, in the third week of January 1630. Gustavus Adolphus, with a great show of virtuous indignation, refused to sell himself, protesting to his minister Oxenstierna that he would never be a lacquey to the French King for three miserable tub-fulls of gold. He manœuvred to get more.

Wallenstein, at the head of the victorious armies of Ferdinand, had reached the Baltic, and was besieging the free city of Stralsund, himself now entitled "Admiral of the Ocean and of the Baltic." Gustavus Adolphus raised an army much too large for him to keep long in the field. He conscripted by force all the able-bodied men in the country who were without property and therefore of no political power, and even got a small picking of the farmers. He made moving speeches to his people, sent help to Stralsund, and on the fourth of July landed at Peenemunde in the island of Usedom, off the coast of Pomerania.

His excellent troops, on such little provision as he had, made good upon the coast, and held Stettin within that same month of July, and during the winter months, the last weeks of 1630, showed their superiority to the Imperialists, but could go no further.

There, without money, they might permanently have remained, until, on the twenty-third of January, 1631, Gustavus Adolphus, that excellent soldier and most astute bargainer (who had so gallantly refused three tubs of gold, swearing that he would never be a servant of the King of France, that he, a Protestant crusader, could not respect and preserve the Mass where he might find it established, that he certainly would not promise to spare Catholic Bavaria, should God grant him victory, nor stand neutral to the Catholic League, etc., etc.) accepted *five* tubs of gold (half a million pounds of our modern English money) and for that consideration now professed himself most willing to be a servant of the King of France, to respect and preserve the Mass wherever he should find it established, to spare Bavaria, to observe neutrality with the Catholic League, etc., etc.

It took some time for even the first driblets of the money to reach him, and some more time for him to use it in the preparation of those 30,000 foot and 6,000 horse for which it was to form a year's supply; or at any rate, to meet the balance of such supply (a similar subsidy was to be renewed from year to year). Well entrenched —and in the open too, for that matter—he held his own while Tilly pursued the siege of Magdeburg. He hesitated to violate the territory of the Elector of Brandenburg, and Saxony still hesitated to join him. Madgeburg therefore fell, and the horror of its sack stands out abominably even in the abominations of the Thirty Years' War. We must not exaggerate the sentimental effect of that horror, but we must not diminish it either. Such things work both ways. In the dread of them men may either yield, or the more strongly resist. In the month after the sack Gustavus Adolphus was able to cross the hitherto closed territory of Brandenburg, and Saxony at long last joined him.

On the seventeenth of September, 1631, within sight of the walls of Leipzic, at Breitenfeld, he destroyed the army of Tilly at one blow, and, with it all, the strength of German Catholicism in the field.

On this field of Breitenfeld, three miles north of Leipzic, the full value of the Swedish King's new tactic was apparent. The new Swedish artillery shook the opposing Imperial foot to breaking point: the new Swedish tactic of the foot destroyed them.

We have not to deal with military details in this appreciation of Richelieu's international achievement. But, in passing, it should be remarked that this decisive occasion—which by its ultimate effects rendered the re-Catholicising of Germany impossible, and impossible at the same time the union of Germany—was due to that understanding of changing conditions which marks great captains in moments of tactical transition. Gustavus Adolphus was the first to apply three new rules: first, the restraint of cavalry in the use of it for shock tactics—a rule which Oliver Cromwell expanded and greatly improved. Secondly, he gave infantry more firing power by a system of retiring the muskets after each discharge and covering them with pikemen; the interval between any two discharges of a musket was long, and this simple piece of drill doubled the efficacy of the weapon, to which he added the cartridge. Thirdly, and much the most important change, he began the intensive use of artillery.

From that day to this the journey had been a long one; but it is to the credit of Gustavus Adolphus that he first managed, by concentrating upon that one point, to produce batteries in the field which fired two shots to the opponent's one, and on occasions it was noted that they fired three to the opponent's one. It was as though he had multiplied in that proportion the numbers of the most expensive arm.

A vast quantity of other things he did, such as to spend all his energy in giving unity to a mixed force (he is said to have been the first to introduce uniforms as a

general practice). He had, with all this, the general
character of an excellent leader, drawing his men
towards him, but it remains true that it is as a gunner
this great captain chiefly stands out, and it was by guns
that he won Breitenfeld.

Tilly had expanded his line, as was his wont, with
the purpose of envelopment. The cavalry of one of his
wings, under Pappenheim, charged the Saxons too soon,
too far, and too successfully. Tilly, high on his horse,
white-haired, beloved, saw that loss of connection between this body of horse and the rest of his line. He
cried out, in agony, "Fool! You have lost the world!"
—a good piece of prophecy. Then the new Swedish
musketry, and still more the new rapidity of Swedish
cannon fire, destroyed the opposing line.

Yet would Gustavus for all his talent not have conquered, had Wallenstein and his myriads been at hand.
For, apart from the excellence of that new Swedish instrument of war, there was another factor making for
the result—the weakening of the Catholic side through
political dissension. It accounts not only for Breitenfeld,
but for the flow-tide of Gustavus in the succeeding
months—and to understand that business we must go
back again to the summer of the year 1630, fifteen
months before Breitenfeld.

In June 1630, while Gustavus Adolphus was still bar-
gaining for higher French pay, six months before he
ultimately took that pay and was launched like a bolt
from a French (golden) bow against the Empire, Ferdinand had convoked a Diet of the Empire to Ratisbon.

His object was to get his son, who was later to be Ferdinand III, elected King of the Romans and heir to the Empire. The four Catholic Electors (the three Bishop Electors and Maximilian of Bavaria) came in person; Brandenburg and Saxony sent representatives only.

For this critical Diet met in a sullen spirit. Brandenburg and Saxony by not coming in person desired to emphasise the anger which the Edict of Restitution had raised in the Protestant states and cities. But the Catholics were also in a rebellious mood. The cruelty of Wallenstein's troops, a hotchpotch of reckless mercenaries, already huge in number and aiming at a total of 150,000 men, was one cause. And another was that already expressed in the phrase, "the peril to German liberties." The Catholic German princes and cities were for the restoration of religion, but they did not propose to fulfil Wallenstein's own prophecy that they, the princes and free cities of Germany, should be reduced to mere subjects of an absolute monarchy, like so many grandees of Spain.

Instead of electing the future Ferdinand III, King of the Romans, the Electors demanded the dismissal of Wallenstein from the Emperor's service, and Wallenstein consented to go. That strange genius was ridden by astrology, and perhaps the stars persuaded him. At any rate, from that moment the forces to be opposed to Gustavus Adolphus (of whose full striking power no one had as yet an idea) were halved.

Meanwhile Father Joseph and Brulart had come as French Ambassadors to Ratisbon, to treat of the affair of

Mantua. They wanted the Emperor to invest the Duke of Nevers, the French candidate, with his Duchy in North Italy, and they had orders to confine themselves to that, and to leave Richelieu's hands free for any other negotiations with Austria.

But the trick was too obvious, and the asset in the Emperor's hands too good to be thrown away. He answered that he would not treat about one isolated question, but only about a general peace, and before he could come to a decision about Mantua—on which he professed himself agreeable to French views—he would have a settlement of all the other questions between himself and France. For instance, with regard to the three bishoprics (Metz, Toul and Verdun) he would appoint a commission to examine the rights and the wrongs of it—acting, you see, as theoretical overlord, and in some contempt of the actual power there exercised by the French for now two generations. And so he would deal with any other matters at issue between the Cardinal and the House of Austria.

Richelieu's two envoys could get no answer out of their master. We must remember that those were the days in which the crisis between himself and Marie de Médicis was coming to a head, and that we are within a few weeks of the "Day of Dupes." Failing to get an answer, the two French envoys signed a general peace, including Ferdinand's claim in the matter of the three bishoprics. They signed on the thirteenth of October, but lest they should be accused of bad faith it must be remembered that they insisted at the time that they had not full powers, save in the matter of Mantua.

Four days later—too late—came Richelieu's answer, forbidding them to accept a general peace. Whether the delay was due to deliberate purpose on Richelieu's part— which is probable—or, what is less likely, to the worry he was in over the domestic battle he was fighting at the Court, delay there was. Hence the signature of an agreement which (had he honoured it) would have prevented him from taking any further action, even indirect, against the Austrian Hapsburgs.

The news that they had signed reached him late. He got it on the twenty-first of October, and he affected rather than felt a violent anger. He spoke openly to the Venetian Ambassador (with the object of having a witness) saying that the conditions were intolerable and that he had never accepted them. He insisted on revision.

Seeing that we are dealing with men so subtle, it is not impossible that Father Joseph himself had intended, in signing, to provoke this check and trouble later on. It is even possible, and has been maintained on high modern authority, that the whole business was pre-arranged between Father Joseph and the Cardinal. Father Joseph was to pretend that France wanted a lasting and complete settlement, and so to give the impression that she was not working against Ferdinand's power, and at the same time to get the advantage of the Emperor's confirming Mantua to the French claimant, the Duke of Nevers. The Cardinal was then to affect high indignation in order to leave the *other* points unsettled, so as to be free to continue intriguing against the Emperor.

It may be so. Anyhow, the treaty was revised, and meanwhile Father Joseph was working underground with the Electors to prevent the nomination of Ferdinand's son as heir to the Empire—and he was successful.

Now it is all this division of Catholic power in Germany, and especially the withdrawal of Wallenstein, which helps to explain the later successes of Gustavus Adolphus, and the enormous initial stroke of the Breitenfeld, a stroke more violent than the Cardinal, who had paid for it, desired.

The consequences of that stroke were more violent still.

In a few weeks Gustavus Adolphus was carving his way through the wealth of Western Germany towards the Rhine, with the drive of an overwhelming storm. Before Christmas the Spanish garrison of Mayence had surrendered to him, and he was on the eve of taking Spires and Worms. He held court at Mayence almost as a second Emperor might. He seized, against his pledged word, the Catholic endowments, he created a new Duchy of Franconia, for all the world as though he were master of the Germans; and when, under the terror of his sudden rise to apparent military omnipotence, the Emperor tried to treat, he made it a condition of peace that he himself, Gustavus, should be King of the Romans and heir to the Empire!

Can it be doubted that he desired, in a sort of megalomania which went with the insanity of his blood, to do now, in the early seventeenth century, what Bismarck only managed to do more than two hundred years later, and even then only partially: I mean, to create a Protestant German Empire in the place of the old Catholic one, with himself as Dynast at its head?

In that connection he made an offer to Richelieu which was of the highest moment to history. He suggested that this business of the Thirty Years' War should be ended now and forever by a partition. Let the French King take the left bank of the Rhine, Alsace, Luxemburgh, the Franche-Comté, perhaps the lower Moselle as well (recovering the ancient frontiers of Gaul), and in exchange leave the Swedish Emperor free to destroy (for it amounted to that) Catholicism beyond the Rhine.

By the dazzle of that irresistible march to the west, following upon that crushing victory (there was no army on the Catholic side in Germany but Tilly's, and Tilly's army had been wiped out at Breitenfeld) Richelieu himself was blinded. The proposal came before the French Council on the sixth of January, 1632, and there was taken a decision which to this day affects all our lives, no matter in what part of Europe we live, or to what modern European nation we owe our allegiance.

Father Joseph most urgently insisted that the offer should be refused. His reason was simple and straightforward. He desired France to be the leader of Catholic civilisation, but he thought it abominable that France should lend herself to such an overthrow of this civilisation throughout central Europe. In the perpetual strain between the new nationalism and the international duty of supporting the Faith he came down, when faced with so drastic a solution, upon the side of our common culture.

I think it may be decided that, acting for once with complete simplicity, he saved that culture—for he persuaded Richelieu.

Alternative plans had occurred to the Cardinal: [1] but that vast major alternative, to take or to leave the new prospect offered to him, to reach at a blow all that he had designed by so much slow calculation and effort which would need continuance long after his death, to effect in one act the end of the German, Italian, Spanish, English wars, to make peace throughout Europe—what a temptation was here! . . . But at what a price! No less than the betrayal in essence of that in which he was a prince, and to which he was sincerely loyal, the Catholic faith.

The Council separated without coming to a decision on the offer of Gustavus Adolphus. The Cardinal sat up all that night, meditating on loss and gain. In the small hours of January 7th, 1632, he had come to his decision. He sent for Father Joseph long before it was light—at six o'clock in the morning—and told him that he had made up his mind. He would refuse the left bank of the Rhine, he would refuse to countenance the destruction of German Catholicism. And he was right.

Gustavus Adolphus in this new-found, toppling power

[1] They may be read in detail. *Memoirs*, Vol. II, p. 364, col. 2, as he proposed them, just after, to the King.

of his, was approached by Maximilian of Bavaria. He was asked at least to evacuate the Rhineland, which was none of his. Gustavus answered by saying that he on his part demanded the restitution of all German things to the situation in which they had been in 1618 before the beginning of the Thirty Years' War; that is, to wipe out all the re-Catholicising of Germany, and especially to destroy the Church in Bohemia. He knew his power —or thought he knew it. He forgot that he was mortal. Maximilian of Bavaria turned to the Emperor, whom he had so recently opposed. He was desperate. Gustavus marched upon him, forcing the passage of the Lech in the April of this year, 1632. Following that action white-haired Tilly, over seventy years old, wounded, died a fortnight later in Ingoldstat, so ending a very glorious life. The ravaging of Catholic Bavaria by the Swedes began.

It was on the part of Gustavus a cynical breach of the word he had pledged when he took Richelieu's pay upon the campaign. But in his new-found, unquestioned power, he cared nothing for pledges. The French stopped their subsidies. Their local representative protested violently and threatened Gustavus with the entry of the King of France. Gustavus sneered his indifference.

But he over-estimated his own strength. Wallenstein had been recalled, and had re-formed an army. He followed up. He failed to dislodge Gustavus from before Nuremburg, but, by the autumn, the two great opponents clashed. Once more upon that same plain of Leipzic, upon the far side of the town from the Breiten-

feld, and no more than a long day's walk from the
ploughlands upon which had been fought, thirteen
months before, the battle which established Protestantism in Northern Europe, Wallenstein and Gustavus,
the Imperial Army and its chief opponent met.

The struggle was joined in front of the village of Lutzen upon the sixteenth of November, 1632. A mist descended upon the battlefield and there was no decision.
Wallenstein withdrew northwards upon Leipzic, the
Swedes remaining upon the field and in possession of
their enemy's guns and baggage train. Each side sang
its *Te Deum*.

At about noon on that same day, while the fighting
was at its hottest and the fog confusing all things, Gustavus Adolphus, not yet in his thirty-ninth year, his
horse being already wounded, his immediate supporters
by some accident dispersed, fell under many wounds. His
body was found later. There had happened to it what
happens to bodies with valuables upon them under the
conditions of human nature—what happened to the
body of Charles the Bold, in the frozen marshy land in
front of Nancy two centuries and a half before—the
wounded corpse had been stripped stark naked, and
some few poor Croat devils had got away with what
they could snatch from it in cloth or gold.

The great man had fallen just in that moment when
he was intending an attack upon the remaining power
of the Austrian House at its centre, and might, as he
thought, have decided forever the fate and religion of
the Germans.

It is difficult to exaggerate the after effects, in their various kinds, whether of Breitenfeld, the great victory, or of this strange accidental death in the mist. Richelieu himself wrote to Louis (with that ironic French choice of words which say less than they mean), "Had the King of Sweden postponed his death by six months, your Majesty's position would be more secure."

Was he right? Would not a great Protestant Empire have arisen in the midst of Europe? Had it so arisen, would it not have been a far greater danger to all that for which Richelieu was wrestling than Austria had ever been, or even both the Hapsburgs? Again, even had Gustavus survived, would it have been possible for that dream of the Swede to be realised, now that Wallenstein was again in the field?

During the paralysis of Austria under the sudden blow of Gustavus, the west, beyond the Rhine, stood derelict. Even while the Swede was ravaging Bavaria, the Elector of Treves had thrown himself under the protection of the French King; and already the French were seeping into Lorraine. Later they put a garrison into Nancy, taking advantage of that same paralysis of the Empire, and in the first days of 1634, Charles IV, Duke of Lorraine, had fled. His place was taken by his brother Nicholas, the Cardinal-Bishop of Toul, but that did not save Lorraine.[1]

[1] I would not digress, but I will add a note upon something amusing. Charles IV had married the daughter and heiress of the last Duke of Lorraine, who had a sister, a co-heiress. It was disputed whether the fief were in the male or the female line; if in the female, it fell under

In that same moment it is probable—it is almost certain—that Richelieu suffered one of his few considerable failures.

Wallenstein was playing fast and loose.

After Gustavus' death there had been formed a new Protestant League called that of Heilebron. Richelieu was coquetting with it, and Wallenstein, his independent power at the head of his great army more and more suspected by the Emperor, had, to say the least of it, a foot in both camps, Catholic and Protestant.

I say it is so probable as to be almost certain, that Richelieu in this moment, January, 1634, negotiated or was in the act of negotiating a treaty with Wallenstein whereby that soldier of fortune should have a million subsidy, and be supported in a sudden claim to the independent monarchy of Bohemia, as the price of attacking Austria which he served.

Among the Protestants who were holding out was Bernard of Weimar. He seized Ratisbon, he continued the ravaging of Bavaria, and Wallenstein did nothing to stop him. Wallenstein thus became more than suspect with his monarch and employer, the Emperor. He was

---

France, if in the male, under the Empire. Charles had married that heiress in order to make his position quite sure either way. Now that Charles had gone, Nicholas, Cardinal-Bishop of Toul, his brother, hastened to marry the *other* sister and secure his *own* new position, as Duke of Lorraine. But how could he do that, being a Catholic bishop? Why, he resigned his See, and *gave himself a dispensation to marry*. It profited him nothing. The towns of Lorraine were occupied by French forces.

certainly negotiating with Sweden and Saxony to betray that master. His commission was revoked in that same month of January, 1634, and Richelieu's planning, which may be presumed to have existed, came to nothing.

In the middle of the next month, Wallenstein's deprivation for treason was openly published, and on the twenty-fifth of February, 1634, at evening, abandoned by his captains, under what orders or anticipated orders we do not know, he was killed. Those who got rid of him were Butler's Irish Dragoons, under the captaincy of Devereux. But any others would have served.

Had his astrologers given him the date? Not beforehand.

There was, then, a recrudescence of Ferdinand's power. Breitenfeld had done the trick (if I may so express myself). Never again could there be a united Catholic German monarchy under the single power of Vienna. But the Hapsburg cause, granted that it compromised with its enemies, was once more in the ascendant. The Germans would remain half Protestant at least. The re-Catholicising of Europe as a whole had failed, and Richelieu was the man who had caused it to fail, though he had not desired that failure. But would the thing on which he was bent, the diminishing of the great Hapsburg rivals of France, also be achieved?

It seemed doubtful.

In a few months it became more doubtful still. It came to look as though Richelieu had ruined the cause and the Church without gaining the prize for which he had so acted. It came to look as though Austria, having compromised with the mass of her Protestant vassals, emerged a worse menace to France than ever.

On the sixth of September, 1634, the Protestant champions Bernard of Weimar and Horn, the Swedish General, commanding the Protestant army and pursuing the policy made at Heilbron, for keeping up the war within the Germanies against Ferdinand, were utterly overthrown in front of Nordlingen.

Their destruction was due to the arrival, in the very last hours, of reinforcements for Ferdinand. The still invincible Spanish infantry which had come marching up through the passes of the Alps under Philip IV's brother, the Cardinal Infante Fernando, conquered decisively.

Richelieu's Protestant German friends, whom he had covertly supported for so long, whom he had subsidised and upon whom his policy depended (though France herself had avoided open war) could no longer hold the field. All their artillery was taken, their forces were dispersed, and Nordlingen opened a new chapter.

It was becoming clear that the indirect policy so long maintained with doubtful success, so much too successful after Breitenfeld, was compromised. And the next year, 1635, made the necessity for open war glaring: that is, the necessity of open war if the French Crown were to maintain even the position it had. Nothing, I say, could restore the old hopes of a Catholic Europe. It was too late. And it was Richelieu who had made it too late. But it was not too late for the combined Hapsburg powers to overwhelm France.

In the spring of that year, 1635, on the twenty-eighth of March, the Spaniards seized Treves, bore away prisoner that clerical Elector who had put himself under the protection of Louis XIII, and with the events of those days Richelieu in his own mind determined upon overt hostilities, upon national war.

It was a very grave decision. Hitherto no very great armies had been raised on French soil, and, grievous as the taxation had become, and rebellious as men were under its burden, there had not arisen as yet the intolerable strain which would follow on the raising of really large forces. Moreover, there was in France nothing trained to fight upon a national scale.

But it had to be done. Ferdinand of Austria was treating with the German Protestants and he and his cousin of Spain would soon have their hands free. It was a sort of race between Richelieu's declaration of war and the settlement of Ferdinand's power.

It was still the policy of the Cardinal, since war it had to be, to declare it against Spain alone, to carry on the convention that he had not provoked any direct rupture with Vienna.

All through April, 1635, it was more and more certain that the Empire was going to make its peace with the great Protestant vassals, Saxony and Hesse-Darmstadt. In mid-May Richelieu was to declare war. Just before the end of the month, Ferdinand's compact with the Protestants was open and public. *The Edict of Restitu-*

tion was repealed.[1] Of Protestant Germany only Bernard of Saxe-Weimar and the Landgrave of Hesse-Cassel stood out.

Already a month before, acting under that pressure, seeing what was coming, Richelieu had taken what was morally the final step. In the Treaty of Compiègne, he had promised Oxenstierna, who spoke for Sweden, that he would abandon to that Protestant power the Catholic bishoprics of Mayence and of Worms, that he would support a settlement reverting to the conditions of 1618 —that is, abandoning the Catholicising of Bohemia. In a word, between the two ideals which he had constantly balanced, of the nation and of religion, the nation had forced him at last to the sacrifice of the religion altogether.

Morally, I think, that date, the twenty-eighth of November, 1635, is the most important in the life of the man who did so very much and in doing it, did so much more which he never set out to do.

Now was he pledged to that direct action which would lead at last to the Europe we know: divided, fallen into a ruin of angry nations and with religion mortally wounded—if indeed the Immortal can suffer mortal wounds.

[1] They called it "a truce of forty years," but it meant, of course, in practice, that the re-Catholicising of Germany was abandoned by the House of Austria, for the sake of preserving the Imperial name and its remaining powers.

VII

THE FINAL WAR

AS EARLY as the beginning of the year 1629, Richelieu had read a private memorandum to the King and his mother, on what he conceived to be the true foreign policy of France: it turned and harped upon—not Austria—but the encirclement of France by Spain.

It is of high interest because we can watch in every step of what followed how he maintained his programme. Nor would I adopt the convenient hypothesis that the thing was drawn up after the event. It is much more consonant with Richelieu's character that he should have planned all beforehand.

Now I do not say that in this memorandum he gave the whole of his thought. At the back of his mind, he undoubtedly held that reducing the power of the Austrian branch of the Hapsburgs was essential. He had so far done much more against Ferdinand by indirect action than he had against Philip, and he regarded the twin powers as inseparable. But if it came to formal hostilities between the French Crown and the Hapsburgs, with all the powers of the State involved, then the Hapsburg chosen for direct attack would be the Spanish, not the Austrian one. To prevent a solid, united and centralised German state from arising beyond the Rhine, or, when it has arisen, to work at undermining it, must necessarily be a permanent part of French policy. And we

350

may test the good or ill government of France at various periods by her success or failure in that policy.

But the Austrian House, sufficiently reduced, was no direct menace. Spain was such a menace, *and it was Spain which had won the Austrian victories;* notably Nordlingen—the action which had made it necessary for Richelieu to declare open war and which was the foundation of the Peace of Prague—had been decided by the Spanish steel. If Philip's general had a new first-class enemy on their hands, that would, of itself, solve the Austrian problem also for the Cardinal.

There was a last consideration. Austria was Catholicism at issue with the new break-up of Europe. To throw all his weight in against Austria was to imperil the future of the Church. Spain had no such domestic enemy to face within her vast dominions as Austria had in Germany; for one may say that, by 1635, the United Provinces were secure in their independence. To reduce Spain and exalt France in her place would not irretrievably wound the whole body of Catholic culture in Europe. To reduce Austria much further would so wound it.

Moreover why have two enemies to fight?

Therefore it is that, when at last, six and a half years after the reading of that original memorandum, he was driven to open war, Richelieu still acted on the convention that Spain alone was the enemy. Austria joined in, but he could plead that Austria joined in of her own accord, and that he was never himself guilty of "open rupture with the Empire."

When it was decided that France should make open war (and that war, though the result of her long indirect action, was at first defensive) forms were observed of the quaintest fashion, as though something of the Middle Ages still lingered.

The King's herald and the King's trumpeter rode in courtesy, state and splendour, up to the walls of Brussels, in that mid-May of 1635, and when they were refused an audience, threw the challenge across the great market place which we still admire.

As they crossed the boundaries of the realm on their way back, a defiant trumpet blast was blown—and all the rest of it.

Such stage shows introduced what was to prove a difficult and at one time a desperate pass. To find an excuse for the war, Father Joseph issued a document in the *Gazette* justifying the quarrel with Spain (and with Spain only) on the grounds of her having laid hands on an ally of the French, on a neutral, the Elector of Treves. But he need not have troubled himself with such formalities. It was going to be plain hammer and tongs, not only with Spain but with Ferdinand, that is, with all the united Hapsburg power; and that way which Europe has of settling into opposing camps when great things are threatened brought in the Protestant princes of Germany on the side of the Emperor.

The effort immediately made was considerable. Richelieu planned to raise the very great number of 150,000 men, one-seventh of them cavalry. But, though he would not perhaps have put it in that way, he knew two things:

first, that he had no real army ready, and secondly, the historical thing, that the Gauls are nearly always defeated in the first actions of their wars. What links these two truths together is the Gallic temperament, that same energy which produces their victories causes both lack of discipline in any but exceptional times, and civil conflict within their own frontiers.

By far the most useful portion as yet of the large body of men which Richelieu thus attempted to raise, were foreign mercenaries of every kind: many, of course, German-speaking, hired out by their masters or acting individually for pay; the best of these mercenaries were Swiss, not a few were from Ireland. As to the French themselves, numerically by far the greater part of these not yet mobilised hosts, Richelieu's own view was sound: "You can do nothing with them."

Well, that was the moment when the Cardinal began to create what remained after him for nearly three centuries, the French army.

Some months ago I had occasion to speak with a man whom I met during my travels, a quiet man of sober and sensible fashion, French in speech, and when we discussed certain matters I ventured to ask him what his profession might be. To which he answered (he was in civilian clothes), "I hold a commission in what was once the French army." *Ubi Troia Fuit*. I would not be so impertinent as to console him, yet I might have answered him, that, like English lyric verse, his particular factor of Europe would never be permanently out of action; it goes under the surface and then comes up again in unexpected fashion. To-day such men complain that "what was once the French army" has turned into a militia of boys; they are filled with memories that stretch from Rocroi (I mean Enghien's Rocroi) to 1914. But they should note that there are many interludes. There was a moment when the Roman legions of Gallic recruitment (were they on guard at Calvary? The Tenth Legion?) vanished suddenly and formless levies took their place. There was another when all that force of the soil in arms was dissipated in the agonies of the fourteenth century. There was another when it ceased to exist in the civil tumult of the sixteenth. That which modern French military tradition so regrets had a longer lease of life than any of its predecessors. The French army which became the model of Europe in the later seventeenth century, and whose traditions and whose songs fill history to within our own time, *that* French army of the last phase, was made by Richelieu.

There was, properly speaking, no such army at all when he thought himself compelled to take the field against those Spanish troops which had behind them an unbroken tradition of a century and still felt themselves to be the only true soldiers in Europe.

He did not complete the instrument—very far from it. The moulding of it into its permanent shape was for his successors, and was the creation of the minority and early manhood of Louis XIV; but he sowed all the seed, he did this very general thing, as he had done the lesser particular thing of La Rochelle—by minute industry: that industry which was the necessary complement to his vast general views, so that without it such views would have been worthless. He began to organise, and to work, by night and by day, at detail upon detail. He organised provisionment and munition, recruitment, grouping, and command. The hopeless recruits he attempted to form by intensive drill.

Unfortunately one cannot make an army by drill alone; and what was worse, there was no one trained in the handling of great numbers. There were very many great gentlemen who had fought in the religious wars, a few who had led divisional troops into Italy; none who had handled really large bodies of men. Richelieu, beginning the affair, had nothing comparable to the excellently forged weapon with which Gustavus Adolphus had startled Europe four years before. He had not even got such troops as the determination of the Princes of Orange, father and son, had put into the field. Perhaps the best unit in all his service was a body of close on 20,000 Germans whom Bernard of Weimar brought in under his own command before the end of the year; when he had been bought at an even higher price than Gustavus himself (not less than two million pounds), and, over and above that, the pledge that he should be independent Lord of Alsace if the fighting went well.

Richelieu also wisely used that blunt, brave, on the whole good, but stupid Huguenot Rohan, who, at any rate, knew all there was to know about giving and taking frank blows from the early times of the religious rebellions until now; and Rohan was sent into the

Grisons to hold the passes of those cantons and the Valtelline.

Before the formal declaration of war at the end of May, the Cardinal had made all his plans for alliances and upon the whole had made them successfully.

He had persuaded the Dutch to come out openly, and though the best thing they did in that connection was the saving of the poor remnant of the French army after its worst disasters at the beginning of the war, still, they neutralised and held the northern part of that long western line from the Valtelline to Flanders upon which Richelieu's originally defensive effort reposed.

He prevented the divergence of Swedish troops into a field where he had no interest by managing, with a diplomacy comparable to that of four years before, the continuation of the truce between the Swedish Crown and the Polish. The old truce was expiring when this new one was negotiated, with the French agent Avoux as its principal author: the Truce of Stumsdorf. It was to last nominally for twenty-six years. It was finally ratified on the twelfth of September, 1635.

In Italy, he achieved the League of Rivoli. He got Louis' brother-in-law of Savoy to leave the passes in French hands (France already held the entrances into the Italian plains by Pinerolo and Susa), and bribed the Duke to come in by holding out to him the prospect of new annexations right up to the sea coast. An entry by sea remained the ambition of Savoy for centuries, until it was achieved in our own time and formed the beginning of the new Kingdom of Italy.

Having Savoy thus well in hand, and Mantua as a matter of course, the Dukes of Parma and Modena joined in. Thus Richelieu at the outset of his perilous venture, had virtually the whole of Northern Italy combined against the Spanish power in the Milanese, and, with Rohan already in the Valtelline, a solid group working in Lombardy, Condé attacking the Spanish Franche-Comté, all the south of this line was engaged.

But the essential sector was the centre—Alsace and the Middle Rhine. And it was there that the hired services of Bernard of Saxe-Weimar were to do Richelieu's work.

Bernard was far the best general in the combination thus arranged against Spain by open declaration of war, and practically against Austria as well. He had learnt war in years of continued fighting, and, in spite of his recent disaster at Nordlingen, he was now a master in that trade. He may be called, in view of his talents and of his submission to French pay, the second Gustavus Adolphus of that campaign.

But the money promised him was not immediately paid, and the 18,000 soldiers which he should have had to handle were neither all present, nor those present sufficiently munitioned.

Sixteen hundred and thirty-five was but a beginning on the part of the French, and a bungled beginning; and, in connection with it, there is another check and difficulty of Richelieu's to be remembered. While Richelieu was negotiating with the Duke of Savoy, he had suggested a link of suzerainty between the Duchy and the French Crown—something corresponding to the link between Bouillon's territory of Sedan and the French Crown in the previous reign.

Now, if Victor Amadeus, the new Duke,[1] had accepted those terms, we should have had a changed Europe. The effect would have come quickly, because the Duke was not destined to live long, and in the succeeding minority the French grip would certainly have been tightened. The policy of getting hold of Savoy, or at any rate of its French-speaking part, remained at the back of French diplomatic tradition right on till the nineteenth century, and, under Napoleon III, was, in the main, achieved.

But had the bargain been struck in 1635, there would have been, long before the nineteenth century, a solid French establishment over all the western Alps, and full entry into the plains of Italy—with all the consequences of such frontiers.

Victor Amadeus refused the bargain. Richelieu had calculated that the brilliant prospect of access to the sea and of a very wide extension of territory would make the House of Savoy agree. After all, he only thought it a turning of suzerainty virtually acquired into one legally corroborated. He miscalculated, and his miscalculation has affected history profoundly from that day to this.

[1] His father, the old Duke, who had attempted to resist at Susa, and in the Pinerolo campaign, was dead. This new one was the former Prince of Piedmont, his heir, who had married Christine, Marie de Médicis' third daughter, Louis XIII's sister.

It is yet another example of the checks which Richelieu's policy continually received, and of the way in which he had to swerve round suddenly to meet an unexpected situation, due to his own miscalculations, that the position of the Low Countries turned out quite other than that upon which he had gambled. Richelieu had gambled, had staked the success of an advance into the Spanish Netherlands, upon a Flemish revolt against the Spanish power at Brussels, and a French-speaking revolt of the Walloons in favour of the French invasion. He had planned that there should follow a partition of all that flat land between the rebels of the United Provinces and the French Crown: the Flemings to go to the first, the Walloons to the second. But there was no sign of revolt in the Southern Netherlands. The ringleaders of the plot were caught, no one followed them, and, as for the numerically large French force facing that frontier, it dissolved.

The bad disappointments of 1635, and what were to be the worse ones of 1636, were not only due to the deplorable condition of the French army—which indeed as yet was hardly an army at all—nor only to the fact that the Cardinal's generals were untrained for war; but also to the further fact that he had to be sure of his lieutenants. He might have had better men under his hand, men whom he judged to be superior in the conduct of a campaign; but he was compelled to use men whom he could trust. He probably did not know how severe the strain was going to be, but he did know his own very great unpopularity; and he was also aware that though his domestic enemies were for the most part mastered, there was within the country plenty of material for a new attack upon him. Therefore he named such men as Condé, the Cardinal de la Valette, and Brézé, his own brother-in-law, and none of the three as yet did anything successfully. The Cardinal's army had gone to pieces in the Netherlands, and Condé failed before Dôle in the Franche-Comté.

So much for 1635.

Sixteen hundred and thirty-six saw something much more serious; the enemy came out of the Spanish Netherlands right into the heart of French territory, swept through Picardy, and captured Corbie; their Croat outriders watered their horses in Compiègne, and some few pushed to Pontoise. Now Compiègne and Pontoise meant the zone of Paris, and there arose in that capital and among the men of Northern France generally, such a mood as their history is familiar with. They began to swarm like bees under the influence of invasion, and that mixture of terror and anger which is the most fruitful of their violent emotions. It certainly looked at that moment as though all that Richelieu had hitherto done was in ruins. Huge printed manifestoes against the Cardinal appeared on the walls, and there were howls from dense throngs of the populace when his carriage went through the streets. Louis himself began to turn his face away—and Richelieu broke down within his own mind. For the first time in nearly thirty years he lost grip of his plans.

It was Father Joseph who saved the situation, by

succouring the brain at the centre of it and by bringing
back his colleague or superior (a sick man with intelligence for the moment, it is said, disordered) up to the
level of his duties. Richelieu appeared in the streets
again, impassive; a sudden enthusiasm for volunteering,
such as was to arise a century and a half later, during the
similar invasion of the Revolution, filled that ancient
hive. A great armed mob of men—the infantry hardly
an army yet, but with disciplined horse and with a strong
nucleus of the royal guard—8,000 men—went out into
the plains of the North East and recovered Corbie and
the whole situation in the North was restored—but it
had been a lesson!

How should a true army arise? It arose within three
years by dint of action—"If you wish to be a Carpenter
you must do carpenter's work." This repelling of the
invasion achieved, and Richelieu breathing again, the
Emperor, who had been actually fighting on the side
of the Spanish cousin for months, the noble, disciplined,
determined Ferdinand II, declared formal war—it mattered little whether he declared it or not, it was already
a fact. The Imperialist troops had for some time been
in the field. There had been troops of theirs at Corbie.

The French recovery in Picardy was, after all, only a
recovery against a swarm of light cavalry who could not
stand up against large forces provided with artillery,
even though those forces were of such raw recruitment.
It was followed by the recovery of the Burgundian frontier.

The enemy had got right into Burgundy; they had

reached Dijon under the command of Charles of Lorraine, and Woerth; they were checked before the little fortified place called St.-Jean-de-Losne[1] and, failing there, had to fall back. By the end of the year (November 3rd) all the invaders were beyond the frontier, save that the Spaniards had got hold of St.-Jean-de-Luz, just over the Pyrenees on the Basque coast—an irritant, but one that could have no permanent effect on the campaign, which was rather to be decided upon the Rhine. More serious was their capture of the Lerins Islands, which they could use as a base for their galleys and for holding the Mediterranean, just at the moment when Richelieu was building his great fleet.

With the opening of 1637, the strain was very great. There was no longer actual invasion, on any considerable scale; but there was the impression abroad that the French recruitment was worthless; and it was clear that the one really good general whom they had hired, Bernard of Weimar, was not being properly backed up. Richelieu had failed, with all his efforts, to persuade Maximilian of Bavaria to get himself elected King of the Romans and successor to the Empire. The House of Austria won in that bout, and Ferdinand's son was elected in due course. It was the Cardinal's third principal failure in this life and death struggle; and there was a fourth to come—in the Valtelline.

Nevertheless, what next followed was a piece of good fortune which, coupled with a later similar piece of good

[1] On the Upper Saône, about a day's march south of Dijon.

fortune, in the case of Bernard, ultimately turned all things in Richelieu's favour.

Ferdinand II died on the fifteenth of February, 1637. Now the son who succeeded him, Ferdinand III, had nothing of his father's intensity of purpose and little of his father's desire to unify the Empire. That grand policy of re-Catholicising Europe which had so nearly succeeded, and which, but for Richelieu's hiring of Gustavus Adolphus and throwing him into the battle, would have succeeded, belonged to the generation which was mature with the turn of the century. It was an ideal proper to the men of 1610-20, but it had no longer the same strength in 1630-40. Time had done its corrupting work.

And there was more than time. The Thirty Years' War which had now run two-thirds of its long course, and much more than two-thirds of its active waging, had destroyed the very body of the Germanics. The place was in ruins. The loss in population had been already enormous—before the business was over the German-speaking body was perhaps halved. The lassitude and incapacity for continuing which followed on such dreadful conditions might have been to the advantage of Austria and Spain some years earlier; now it was to their disadvantage. The struggle within the Germanies had reached that stage which comes in all long wars, when each party has become doubtful of being able to finish the affair, and when, therefore, a third party—in this case, the French Crown—is more likely to gather the fruits of fratricide.

Thus, the accession of Ferdinand III was a real asset to Richelieu's still desperate effort, and it was an asset which outweighed two considerable deficits nearly contemporary with it.

The first of these deficits was the loss of the Valtelline, and the second the break-up of what had been at first the excellent French position in Lombardy.

In the Valtelline, Rohan possessed the strongholds, well garrisoned; but he was insufficiently provided with money, and the Protestant Grisons were growing restive. They felt that the bargain with them was not being kept. At this point, there came in precisely what had come in with regard to the left bank of the Rhine and Gustavus Adolphus' offer of five years before—that handicap to the French national effort, the reservation upon religion. Richelieu could not use the anti-Catholic forces whole-heartedly because he could not sacrifice the Catholic position in Europe whole-heartedly. He did not desire to do so, and he would not do so; still less would Father Joseph do so.

Rohan, feeling the pressure beyond bearing, and the delays in receiving supplies still continuing, and being a Huguenot, made an agreement with the Grisons and submitted it for the approval of the Home Government. By this agreement the Grisons should recover their old rights over the Valtelline, including the nomination of governors over the towns; and that meant, of course, renewed persecution of the Catholic religion in the Valley.

Richelieu refused to allow it. Therefore Rohan, or rather Rohan's men (he himself was penned up on the other side of the mountains) could not longer hold, and the Valtelline was lost. Perhaps if Rohan had been a Catholic himself, and had proposed such a compromise, it might have been accepted; but, that he was a Huguenot, and a Huguenot who had fought as the head of the Huguenot rebellion, helped to turn the scale. It was felt that his plan was essentially an anti-Catholic plan rather than a purely military or diplomatic one; hence its rejection, and, with its rejection, the loss of the Valtelline.

But that loss was not nearly so severe as it would have been a few years earlier. It was by the Valtelline and on up through the Tyrol that the Spaniards had poured their men to the victory at Nordlingen, and it was by the Valtelline that their fine troops passed over to those successes which had ultimately compelled Richelieu to declare war.

But now that undefeated soldiery was beginning to show signs of an exhaustion only second to the exhaustion of the Austrian Germans in alliance with them; and the Valtelline, fallen into Spanish hands, would never again be of the capital importance which it had been for so many years in the immediate past.

The second piece of ill fortune which befell the Cardinal's policy in that year of special strain was the death of Amadeus of Savoy. He left a child on the throne, and the coalition of North Italy broke up. Parma submitted to Philip IV, Margaret of Mantua tried to give him Montferrat, and meanwhile the surest of Richelieu's Protestant allies in North Germany, William of Hesse-

Cassel, also died. And far to the north the Swedes were beaten back to the Baltic.

In such a vortex of struggle I seem to see the thin delicate body of the Cardinal bent over a desk dictating in that voice of a man growing old; but his spirit on horseback in crimson robes leading most furious charges through the clouds.

In this critical moment Richelieu raised another great body of men—under what strain to the French populace in blood and in treasure we hardly know, because we have no machinery for sounding the popular depths of that moment; but it was certainly a very close thing between success and failure when that large new recruitment was raised.

With 1638, the tide turned, so far as the advance and retreat were concerned: but not definitely as to assure the main objects of the war.

Bernard of Weimar was now properly paid, and his army in full equipment. He went forward through Alsace to seize the line of the Rhine, and he succeeded. Richelieu planned indeed at this moment a great triple scheme which came to nothing. While Bernard was advancing eastwards, he wanted the Swedes to come back again down southwards into Bohemia (which they could do with the pressure relieved by Bernard's advance); and he wanted the Prince of Transylvania, helped by the Turks, to come westwards and invade Hungary, so that from the east, the north and the west, a converging movement should be made against Vienna. Of all that over-large scheme, nothing came. The Swedes entered

Bohemia, but behaved so abominably that even that exhausted province checked them in revenge for their atrocities. The Transylvanian advance failed. Only that of Bernard succeeded. At first it had been checked before Rheinfeld, on the twenty-eighth of February, 1638; but immediately after, in March, he surprised the Imperial army in winter quarters, captured Woerth, with nearly all the enemy staff, and then proceeded to besiege Brisach.

Now Brisach was at that moment perhaps the most important geographical point in Western Europe. *If Brisach held, the corridor whereby Spanish troops could come up north along the valley of the Rhine and reach the Netherlands remained open. If it fell, that corridor was cut.* It is yet another example, just as was that of the Valtelline some years before, of the way in which political circumstance changes the geographical strategy of Europe. Brisach, which means nothing to-day, meant, in 1638, something as important as the lines before Verdun were in 1917. And after a long siege heroically maintained by the Imperialists on that steep rock, Brisach fell. The capitulation was signed on December 17th, 1638.

Father Joseph was dying. The Cardinal bent over the bed and called in his ear—perhaps he heard—"Father Joseph! Brisach is ours!"

There were two little errors in the triumphant pronouncement with which Richelieu designed to rally his failing friend. In the first place, Brisach had not fallen; it fell only a few hours before Father Joseph died, and the news did not reach Richelieu till nearly a week later.

It was but an intelligent anticipation. In the second place, Brisach was not "ours"; it was not Richelieu's, it was *Bernard's*—and Bernard had no intention of letting it go!

Bernard was an ally, it is true, and as an ally he had, by the capture of that stronghold, cut in two the whole Spanish power between the north and the south. It was the fall of Brisach that now compelled the Spaniards to send, or rather attempt to send, reinforcements to the Netherlands by sea, with the result that their fleet and convoys bearing 20,000 men the next year were attacked by the Dutch Admiral Tromp off Dover and broken in pieces—not a third of them reached Dunkirk.

But though Bernard's capture of Brisach paralysed Spain in the Rhine, it appeared not as a French but as a great *Protestant* victory. Though won by troops in the hired service of the Catholic French King and his Cardinal, the fall of Brisach had rung throughout Protestant Europe as a triumph of its own. It was not yet a French victory. Bernard held the solemnly attested document whereby Richelieu guaranteed him the Lordship of Alsace, and Brisach, which he had thus so gloriously seized, would be his, no other's.

Then it was that fortune came in once more upon Richelieu's side, and this time decisively. On the eighteenth of July, 1639, Bernard of Saxe-Weimar died. What followed this startling change was another change, more startling still.

Bernard had put in as governor of the captured town of Brisach, a Swiss, one Erlach; but the man who was his right hand and at the head of the active army in the field was a French subject, a young man adored by the soldiery, full of vigour and command, a cadet of a small Breton noble house, Guébriant by name. He persuaded Erlach to hand over the town to the French King. And in that act the plain of Alsace, already occupied, changed hands, became Richelieu's and with it the line of the Rhine.

On that day, Monday July 18th, 1639, or rather, just after, when Brisach and its army was handed to France from the relaxed dead hand of its fallen conqueror, the mortal crisis was over. Richelieu's victory was achieved. Nothing remained but to gather the harvest.

And in the last phase of the Battle, something else had happened. Anne of Austria, on September 5th, 1638, while Brisach was still holding out, gave birth to the child that was to be Louis XIV.

I say "It remained only to gather the harvest."

The gathering of the harvest was rapid indeed. No sufficiently strong adverse power now remained to halt the process.

England had ceased to count. Charles' attempt at building a fleet to match the Richelieu's naval armament of France had led to Ship money and Ship money to the first threat of civil war.

The Empire was held, Spain was on the eve of internal strain which halved her power.

The France of Richelieu which, not two years earlier,

had been at breaking point, tided over, and it was the rivals of France who now began to feel exhaustion. In Germany the results were confused, although after Brisach the French in a body for the first time crossed the Rhine and, with the army of Weimar, were in the very midst of the Germanies at Erfurth, yet an attempted peace failed. It was ding-dong, and all one can say is that by the time the Cardinal died, his ally of Sweden, after one strong victory, held Saxony. But though the gathering of the harvest in the Germanies was not dramatic, nor even conspicuous, it was there. The French policy held a position which was to have its effect after the Cardinal's death. The scales had turned.

It was the same in Savoy. Louis XIII's sister Christine had attempted to negotiate with the Spanish Government of Milan, but, after Brisach, Richelieu could act as her master. He compelled her to hand over the frontier districts to her brother Louis' tutelage; her Savoyean brother-in-law, uncle of the little count her son, rose against the French domination, and Piedmont rose with them. Thomas of Savoy besieged the French garrison in the citadel of Turin. But Richelieu's general, Harcourt, besieged the town from the outside, himself surrounded and beleaguered by the Spanish governor of Milan. Of this triple concentric siege the Cardinal had the fruits. On the eighteenth of September, 1640, Thomas of Savoy surrendered, and though there was no final settlement for two years, in June 1642, when that settlement was reached, Turin itself was held by a French garrison.

As against the Spaniards the luck ran fairly true.

Barely more than a year after Bernard of Weimar's death and the turning point of Brisach, Arras, the bulwark of Flanders, was in French hands. And though here again there were ups and downs, in French hands Arras remained—the beginning of that advance into the Low Countries which marked the next reign.

Of Spanish power to the south the same story is told —all in those last three years of the Arch-Designer's declining life.

Two years before the Cardinal's death, eighteen months after Bernard's, Portugal rose against the Spanish power. Though there was nothing definitive, the Portuguese revolt immobilised throughout 1641-1642 a mass of the Spanish military power, and the Cardinal at once allied himself with the new Portuguese party of independence.

But the greatest factor was the Catalonian. Catalonia rose against Spain in mid-December, 1640. And again, Richelieu acted at once. Before the end of the following January Louis XIII had been elected Count of Barcelona, and the French carried the war out beyond the Pyrenees. Richelieu had no intention of an extension of France too far south, but he did intend the frontier of the Pyrenees. The efforts south of those mountains were not fortunate. The French fleet was beaten away from Barcelona and the Rosas was not held. But, as in Savoy, so here in Catalonia, what lay beyond the natural frontier was but an advanced post in policy: the solid work to be achieved was the conquest of the Roussillon: that is, of Catalonia, on the French side of the hills. It was undertaken methodically, town by town. The capital, Perpignan, surrendered on September 9th, 1642.

I never gaze on that sharp descending edge of the final, lessening mountains falling, by lower and lower cusps, into the Mediterranean sea, but I think of a wall to the "Square Field."

That wall had been reached at last; but even as it was reached and his work accomplished, Richelieu, hearing the news in Lyons where he lay, wrote to his King: "Sire, your arms are in Perpignan and your enemies have perished." But, even as he wrote the words, he remembered that he was dying.

THIRD PART

THE EXIT

THE EXIT

WHEN the time came for Armand du Plessis to make his exit from the few hours of this high-lit, too glaring stage, he was permitted, or condemned, to depart from the scene in a fashion peculiar as was his life.

I might add "unique" as was his life, for I can remember no other getting away from the short business of living in which the last passage was so entirely consonant with all that had gone before.

A wise man will see in it something illustrative of the strange fate which had inspired such activities, had granted such immunity, and had used him as an instrument for such an end: the making of the modern world.

Even an unwise man will see therein some coincidence.

Such a curtain on life is as disturbing to the judgment as it is rare. Hardly ever—perhaps only in this case of all the great public careers the history of Christendom records—was there so completely mundane an ending, concluded exactly according to the earthly life of its hero.

For the life of Richelieu ends without preparation, without decline, abruptly, upon its full note; without that tragedy which should properly attach to all great human achievement. There is not even a drowsiness before sleep, but rather—in the last months, weeks and days—all that had signalised his life: all its characteristic marks in full activity: the miserable health: the intense industry: the personal triumph over enemies, and, with it, the triumph of the State: the plots, the threat of assassination, the implacable sentences, and the effusion of blood in a fashion more dreadful than ever; and, with it all, the pomp, the inflexibility, the service of the State, the recognition of religion, the contempt of consequence. It is one piece which ends absolutely and sharp like a sawn-off edge of ebony.

He dies in his palace (which he has built not without oppression, not without avarice—but bequeathed to the Crown) and receiving the largest of that gigantic revenue which he had amassed.

See how the approach of death carries on that tide!

Marie de Médicis, who had made him, who had then raved against him in her exile for so many years, was dying. She had needed money, and Richelieu had the supreme satisfaction of providing it. Twelve years before, she had insulted and humiliated his darling niece, that thing which he most loved on earth, and she it was now, the Duchess of Aiguillon, who interceded for the old woman with her uncle; and the Cardinal, even as he was envisaging his own end, could take the thousands from the public chest and give them with a thin smile by way of vengeance upon what he had suffered from her.

Or, again, see how this next thing is consonant with all his life. When he marries another niece to Enghien (who was to be the Grand Condé) he must needs draw up a minute scheme of expenditure: how the young man is to order his household: what to spend on this, on that: how to control, how to save, how to manage—and all this, not by the use of others, but with his own brain. The unparalleled industry working on such few hours of sleep is at it still: the long work before winter dawns and in the very early summer mornings before the town was awake. . . .

Or, again, the manner in which the going-off coincides with the reaching of the Pyrenees and the conquest of Roussillon. Or again, the domestic splendour in which he so delighted, maintained till the end, and in all the come and go of his huge new house.

Or, again, his imposing of his own plan upon those nearest to him while he still could breathe and forbidding that niece of his, who was his mainstay, to take the veil; rather enjoining on her to remain in the world and see to the just ordering of his inheritance.

But the matter which, in those last weeks, is most characteristic of all, that which makes the coming of his night more like a sudden eclipse than a sunset is this: that a chief conjuration against him and a threat of murder comes up again even now, within a few yards of the tomb—and is dashed down again and swamped in blood, as vigorously as all the others before.

The story has been told a hundred times, and, by most, too romantically. I would not repeat it here. But we must follow the main lines of it, to note how exactly true are the last actions of Richelieu, not only of his own will, but from fate, to all other actions of his life in power.

He had recommended to the king, to amuse that

hardly calculable nature, a young friend who he thought would make just such a favourite as Louis might welcome. Old Effiat, who had served the Cardinal and the State for so long, whom Richelieu had trusted and relied upon with something as near warmth as he had ever shown, who had gone for him on embassy to the English Court when Charles' marriage with the sister of Louis was being arranged, had left a younger son, who, after the fashion of cadets, was given a courtesy title of his own and called the Marquis of Cinq-Mars. He was a lad vivacious, running after women (he pleased most and particularly Marion de Lorme, who had experience enough to make a choice); he was a battler with unfailing energy, tall, ruddy, elaborately curled of hair; his impudent, brave eyes were not without subtlety. He wore excessive lace.

Being the son of that old friend and most trusted counsellor, and very well suited with his manly verve for the enlivening of that grey court, Richelieu thought himself sure of his man; he was wrong—and, as ever, repaired in the end his own misjudgment.—So had it been with Châteauneuf, for Châteauneuf had been Richelieu's own creature, made by him Keeper of the Seals after the "Day of Dupes," and obviously, condemning to death Marillac. He, at least, could be trusted, but he had been caught by that universal huntress, the Chevreuse, had babbled state secrets, had intrigued with Orleans. Yet, before it was too late, he was laid by the heels and under lock and key.

Young Cinq-Mars was nineteen when first Richelieu

had thrust him into Court in the end of 1638, a little
before the birth of the heir. He was now, in the last
months of the Cardinal's life, but twenty-two. He was
already horrible weary of the King. Louis, with his
sentimentalism, his violent short affections, facile jealousies and absurd comedies of reconciliation, was ill-
suited to the simplicity of the young and soldierly man.
And the young and soldierly man bore it because, by
the entry of a favourite, he might play some great part
—in particular he desired to marry Mary of Mantua,
that is, the daughter of one who was a sovereign in Italy,
and, within the realm of a nobility far higher than his
own, the Duke of Nevers.

The young fellow held a very great place; he had demanded and obtained the Mastership of the Horse, by
which right he rode in front of the King in a splendour,
during the provincial journeys, and had all the appoint-
ments of exalted office. He desired more. He thought
he should be of the Council; and Richelieu being consulted, laughed at the proposal.

It is a commonplace in the study of human nature
that men often turn against those who have raised them,
and the cause is clear: men resent constraint.

That Richelieu who had made him should also now
restrain him seemed intolerable. In the matter of the
Duke of Mantua's daughter, the Cardinal "hoped she
had not so far forgotten her rank" (for her marriage was
a matter of foreign policy to him). The words were reported to Cinq-Mars and he was the angrier. In the matter of the Council, Richelieu appeared to yield; but won

his point with a turn of the hand. When the young man appeared, nothing was discussed of any moment. Great matters were reserved, because, as Richelieu had said, they could not be debated before boys. And that phrase also was reported to the favourite, who did more—for he indulged the King's unchanging repugnance to the Cardinal's control, and the Cardinal's spies lost none of those jests.

The King, destined in a few months to die, had again fallen ill. His immediate death was feared. By a calculation most erroneous, a dozen lesser spirits imagined that, with Louis gone, Richelieu would be supreme. The Queen feared, lest her children should be taken from her; Gaston imagined he would have to fight for his own restoration.

Had they seen things as clearly as Richelieu did, they would have known that the Blood-Royal had in France too awful an authority for any such topsy-turveydom as the absolute rule of a minister, when the true master was no longer there. The mother and the uncle of the heir could not but be in power.

They were blinded by the immediate power of that intelligence and that will so indefinitely stronger than their own. In their blindness and terror of the future they intrigued with the Crown of Spain even in the midst of active hostilities. It was treason as plain as Montmorency's, and worse, because it was treason with the foreign enemy in time of war.

Gaston, seeking money and men to use when the expected crisis should come, had approached Bouillon (the son of that head of the Huguenots who has been described); Bouillon would not risk it; he had all the caution, though not the brains, of his father. He was commanding in Italy. Anne also may have approached him, in the hope that the principality and the stronghold of Sedan might afford refuge for herself and her children.

It was in these foolish flutters of suspense that the plot was formed. Because Cinq-Mars had the ear of the King he was dragged in, and Bouillon only half consenting, was kept in touch. The plot involved more than a secret treaty with Spain to send men and money against the actual government of France (that is, against the King himself). It, also, involved some dark plan for the murder of the Cardinal. Had they known the future they need not have plotted so on the ground floors of the Hotel de Venise. The Cardinal was already doomed by nature. His death was advancing. But still they schemed, and all that saved Richelieu then was that terror which he had inspired and which had already twice unnerved the would-be assassin.

For already the King had gone south towards the theatre of war against Spain in the Roussillon and the Cardinal was following him—woefully ill, ulcerated, paralysed of the right arm, indomitable. At this place and at that, on the journey to the Rhône and to Narbonne, the murder was to have taken place: but no one dared.

It was at Narbonne, in May, that Richelieu made his will. It was in those southern lands, under the heat of the summer, and he daily less and less in body (corrupting visibly), that he got proof—no one knows how—of the treason. The secret treaty with Spain had been conveyed to him.

He had gone back to Tarascon unable to bear the campaign. Louis, come south for the final conquest of the Roussillon, was warned, and Richelieu and his royal master, each too ill to leave his bed, discussed from those beds, one with the other, the necessary doom of Cinq-Mars. The Queen was intangible, Gaston was still intangible (and out of reach); but the young favourite was in Narbonne, drinking of the best. And as he drank one night, there was slipped into his hand a written message, warning him for his life. Already one minor accomplice had fled. He himself tried to escape; he found the gates shut; he passed the night with two farmer's wenches in hiding, and on the morrow was arrested.

In a famous picture, and in twenty famous exercises of the pen, the tragedy has been recorded. How the Cardinal, now far too ill to move, laboriously towed up against the slighter summer stream of the shallow summer Rhône, having on his barge that huge purple canopy as big as a great room (where he lay with table, chair and secretary at his side), dragged after his craft the young de Thou, who had indeed mingled in the conspiracy, but whose main fault was not to have betrayed his friend; how the two troops of cavalry followed by road along the bank, and how, on the further shore, Cinq-Mars went as a prisoner among them; how the two came to Lyons and were there tried.

It was upon the ninth of September that Perpignon fell, and the last aim of that great ministry was accomplished. It was upon the twelfth that the two young men died, with a gallantry not yet forgotten, upon the scaffold in Lyons. They had been condemned in the early morning of that Friday; they perished at noon—and Louis, watch in hand, asked "What sort of faces the Master of the Horse be making now?"

The Cardinal had reached Paris to die. It was Saturday the twenty-ninth of November—St. Andrew's Eve—and it would seem from the symptoms that have come down to us that what had immediately seized his moribund, pustuled body was pneumonia. Yet he remained himself, even into the very door-valves of death. On the Monday he obtained a declaration from the King relieving the Duke of Orleans of his remaining powers (Bouillon, arrested with the army in Italy, had been compelled to hand over Sedan); on Tuesday, the second, he entered into his agony.

The Vicar of St.-Eustache, the High Church close at hand (where fifty-seven years before he had received baptism), came to give him the Last Sacraments. To him it was that Richelieu made the famous answer to the ritual demand that he should forgive his enemies, "I have had no enemies, save those of the State."

See how he who had bowed down so continually to achieve mortal power would now stand unflinching before the Last Tribunal. "Have you forgiven your enemies?" Which of us will answer, "I have had no enemies, save those of the public good"?

And the King came in, and, finding the end so near, went out (they say) relieved; but first handed him with his own hand a cup with the yolks of eggs, all he could receive.

Upon Thursday, December 4th, which is the Feast of St. Barbara and of all Gunners, Father Léon the monk knelt by his bed, feeling a slight pressure of the hand only in response to the Adjuration to the Faith and Repentance for sin. They put a taper to his lips. The flame did not move. He was dead.

The Pope at Rome said, "If there be a God, the Cardinal de Richelieu will have much to answer for. If there be none, why, he lived a successful life."

They buried him in the Chapel of the Sorbonne, which his magnificence had built. In the Revolution, a butcher's boy, the grave having been rifled, stole his embalmed head. It had many adventures; but in our own time was purchased from its last collector and now is attached to its trunk most decently re-interred.

THE END

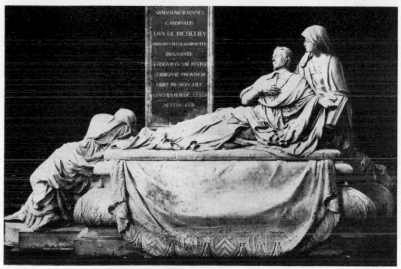

THE TOMB OF RICHELIEU IN THE SORBONNE
By François Girardon

INDEX

"Academy," Pluvinels, 153
Adda, 208, 212, 216
Adige, 208, 210
Adolphus, Gustavus, 41, 85, 97, 118,
  127, 225, 300, 318, 321, 325, 326, 329,
  330, 331, 332, 333, 334, 335, 336,
  339, 341, 342, 343, 344, 345, 355,
  357, 363, 364
Agde, 300
Aiguillon, Duchess of, 135, 376
Albi, 300
Alphonse, 154, 155, 165
Alps, 24, 44, 68, 85, 133, 138, 208, 221,
  222, 274, 275, 277, 283, 284, 285,
  295, 347, 358
Alsace, 39, 44, 284, 340, 355, 357, 366,
  368, 369
Amadeus, Victor, 358, 365
America, 53, 79
America, Central, 79
America, South, 79
American Colonies, 58
Amiens, 40, 229
Ancre, 193, 233
Angers, 203
Anjou, Duke of, 230, 231, 235
Anne, 180
Ardennes, 130
Ardillers, Lady of, 101
Armada, 75
Armand-Jean, 150, 155, 175, 188, 191,
  202
Arnauld, 241
Arques, 148
Arras, 371
Artois, 70
Atlantic, 42, 70, 79, 256, 275
Austria, 37, 70, 71, 73, 85, 118, 138,
  179, 210, 214, 215, 218, 220, 223,
  226, 267, 318, 321, 327, 328, 331,
  344, 345, 347, 350, 351, 357, 363
Austria, Anne of, 101, 111, 120, 122,
  191, 228, 229, 231, 369, 381
Austria, House of, 27, 29, 68, 73, 131,
  270, 271
Auvergne, 308
Avignon, 201, 202, 297, 301
Avoux, 356

Balin, 261, 262
Baltic, 138, 331, 366
Barbin, 195
Barcelona, 371
Barriades, 157
Basque Provinces, 258
Bassompierre, 294, 295, 297
Bastille, 295
Bavaria, 36, 320, 322, 332, 333, 342,
  344, 345
Bavaria, Duke of, 74
Béarn, 139
Beaucaire, 300, 301
Beauvais, 40
Bellarmine, 160
Bergamesque, 216
Berlin, 33, 43, 44
Bernard of Weimar, 345, 347, 349,
  355, 357, 362, 363, 366, 367, 368,
  371
Berne, 212
Bérulle, 287, 297
Besançon, 79
Béziers, 302
Blois, 198, 201
Bismarck, 30, 31, 33, 34, 35, 36, 37,
  38, 39, 40, 41, 42, 43, 44, 46, 95,
  109, 320, 340
Bohemia, 73, 137, 342, 345, 349, 366,
  367
Bordeaux, 55, 202, 240, 253
Bormis, 208, 213, 216
Bouillon, 135, 223, 358, 380, 381, 383
Bouillon, Duke of, 64, 111, 129, 130,
  131, 132, 181, 182
Bourbon, 75, 76, 78, 116, 187
Bourbonnais, 296
Brandenburg, 322, 328, 329, 333, 336
Breitenfeld, 333, 335, 339, 340, 343,
  344, 346, 347
Brenner Pass, 209, 210, 211
Brescon, 300
Brézé, 360
Brisach, 208, 367, 368, 369, 370, 371
Britain, 34, 36, 138
Brittany, 133, 234
Brulart, 336
Brussels, 352, 359

Buckingham, 120, 221, 223, 224, 226, 227, 228, 229, 230, 248, 251, 254, 255, 256, 257, 258, 259, 260, 262, 263, 265, 269
Burgundy, 132, 270, 287, 297, 362

Cadiz, 254
Cæsar, 42, 109
Calais, 253, 296, 306, 312
Calvi, 153
Canterbury, 39
Capelle, 296
Capetian, 43
Capuchins, 72
"Cardinal of the Huguenots," 102
Carlyle, 22
Casale, 29, 39, 222, 236, 273, 274, 275, 276, 277, 278, 279, 282, 284, 285
Caspéan, 159
Castelnaudary, 302
Cathedral of Orleans, 171
Catholic League in Germany, 118
Catolonia, 40, 284, 371
Cavour, 320
Cecils, William and Robert, 49, 50, 169
Centrale, Pharmacie, 151
Cévennes Hills, 299, 301
Chalois, 233, 234
Champagne, 182, 261, 287
Champaigne, 87
Channel, 59, 252, 255
Chapter, 165
Charlemagne, 66, 72, 236
Charles, 219, 223, 224, 225, 226, 228, 248, 251, 252, 254, 362, 369, 378
Charles I, 58, 294, 323, 331
Charles II, 49
Charles IV, 344
Charles XII, 325
Charnacé, 36, 326, 328, 329, 330, 331
Charter of Eleanor of Aquitaine, 243
Château of Meilleraie, 98
Châteauneuf, 294, 303, 378
Chesterton, Mr., 82
Chevreuse, 227, 228, 229, 231, 294, 378
Chiavenna, 213, 216
China sea, 42
Chiomonte, 279, 281
Chisone, 283
Christian, 322, 330
Christine, 279, 370

Cinq-Mars, Marquis of, 378, 379, 381, 382
Clément, 148
Cœurres, 215, 216
Coke, 252
Coligny, 249
College of Navarre, 152
Como, Lake, 208, 212
Compiègne, 296, 360
Comte, 22
Concinis, 183, 193, 194, 195, 196, 198, 206
Condé, 182, 191, 221, 232, 233, 234, 239, 297, 357, 360
Corbie, 97, 238, 239, 360, 361
Corneille, 108, 192
Corsica, 138
Council of Trent, 189
Courland, 326
Coussay, 173, 177, 185, 201
Créqui, Duke of, 295
Creuse, 147
Croix Haute, 277
Cromwell, 59, 97, 146, 334
Crusades, 53, 134

d'Albert, Charles, 194
d'Albret, Jeanne, 139
d'Ancre, Maréchal, 196
Danube, 44, 73, 137, 208
Dark Ages, 60, 298
d'Aumont, Hôtel, 151
Dauphiné, 221
d'Auvergne, House of La Tour, 129
"Day of Dupes," 36, 112, 235, 293, 295, 297, 303, 318, 321, 327
Déageant, 197
de Chevreuse, Madame, 229, 233, 234
de Chillon, Armand, 154, 192
de Condé, Madame, 233
de Givry, Cardinal, 161
de la Valette, Cardinal, 360
de Lavedan, Madame, 187
de l'Hôspital, Nicholas, 197
de Lorme, Marion, 378
de Luvnes, 115
de Marillac, Marshal, 104, 105
de Médicis, Marie, 101, 120, 122, 123, 128, 154, 175, 176, 180, 182, 187, 193, 198, 206, 214, 220, 232, 256, 270, 286, 287, 289, 291, 292, 294, 295, 296, 306, 308, 312, 321, 337, 376

de Montpensier, Mademoiselle, 150, 231, 232, 233, 235
Denbigh, 265
Denmark, 138, 322, 328, 330, 331
de Polignac, Anne, 146
de Richelieu, Madame, 154, 157, 158, 165
de Rohan, Henri, 133
de Thou, 105, 106, 382
Devereux, 346
Devon, 50
Diocletian, 42
Dijon, 55, 276, 362
Dole, 79, 360
Donauverth, 137
Dora, 283
Dori, Leonora, 193
d'Orléans, Madame, 186, 187
Dover, 248, 368
Dunkirk, 368
du Plessis, Armand-Jean, 20, 154, 158, 165, 375
du Plessis, Henry, 149
du Plessis, James, 165
du Plessis, Louis, 146
du Tremblay, François de Clerc, 136, 185, 186, 187
du Tremblay, Joseph, 136, 138

East Anglio, 156
Edict of Nantes, 47, 170, 181, 240, 284
Edict of Restitution, 323, 324, 336, 349
Egypt, 78
Elbe, East, 35
Elizabeth, 49, 65, 171, 180, 191, 223, 249
Ely, 156
Emmanuel, Charles, 270, 273, 278, 279, 280, 281, 282, 285
Enghien, 376
England, 32, 45, 48, 49, 51, 52, 55, 58, 59, 62, 63, 64, 65, 74, 76, 82, 84, 131, 134, 218, 219, 222, 224, 225, 226, 227, 229, 230, 233, 242, 250, 251, 253, 263, 288, 312, 317, 369
Epernon, Duke of, 205
Erfurth, 370
Erloch, 368, 369
Erlon, 257
Escorial, 81, 82
Essone, 148

Esthonia, 326
Europe, 136, 137, 138

Ferdinand, 73, 74, 210, 214
Ferdinand II, Emperor, 321, 322, 323, 324, 327, 331, 335, 337, 338, 339, 346, 347, 348, 350, 352, 361, 362, 363
Ferdinand III, 336, 363, 364
Feria, 212
Fernando, Cardinal Infante, 347
Flanders, 70, 356, 371
Flemings, 359
Foch, 24, 233
Fontainebleau, 176, 187, 284, 288
Fontenay-le-Comte, 162
Fontevrault, 185, 186
Formigny, 134
"Fort Louis," 241, 253
France, 25, 29, 30, 34, 37, 40, 45, 46, 47, 48, 49, 50, 52, 53, 54, 55, 57, 58, 61, 63, 64, 65, 68, 70, 72, 79, 81, 84, 85, 86, 91, 111, 114, 126, 128, 129, 130, 131, 132, 134, 137, 152, 157, 168, 170, 171, 181, 187, 189, 190, 202, 213, 214, 215, 218, 219, 221, 222, 223, 227, 230, 238, 239, 240, 243, 245, 249, 253, 254, 255, 256, 267, 268, 270, 271, 273, 275, 282, 283, 284, 285, 286, 287, 290, 297, 299, 306, 317, 318, 319, 321, 327, 329, 330, 331, 332, 337, 338, 340, 342, 346, 347, 348, 350, 351, 352, 356, 369, 370, 371, 380, 381
Franche-Comté, 79, 340, 357, 360
François, 146
Franconia, Duchy of, 339
Frankenthal, 74
Frederick, 223
French Revolution, 32, 34, 56, 58
Friars, Capuchin order of, 136
Fuentes, 212

Gabor, Bethlen, 74
Gaston, 26, 135, 232, 233, 287, 297, 298, 300, 302, 306, 312, 315, 321, 380, 382
Gaul, 340
Gazette, 352
Geneva, 279
Genoa, 79, 217, 279

Germany, 30, 32, 33, 45, 51, 69, 70, 72, 74, 75, 84, 131, 132, 137, 213, 214, 327, 334, 336, 339, 340, 351, 370
Gesport, 255
"Gesta Dei per Francos," 139
Girard, Hercules, 326
Gladstone, Mr., 151
Gonzales, of Cordova, 273
Granada, 75
"Grand Master of the Fleet," 108
Grande Chartreuse, 154
Gray, 79
Great Britain, 167
Great War, 18, 29, 31, 43, 100
Grenoble, 277
Grisons, 210, 211, 212, 213, 216, 217, 221, 356, 364
Guébriant, 369
Guise, 227, 231, 294
Guiton, 241, 265, 266

Hague, The, 221
Hannibal, 24
Hanotaux, 151, 160
Hapsburg, 131, 138, 139, 177, 179, 181, 196, 214, 223, 224, 270, 271, 272, 274, 285, 286, 287, 318, 319, 321, 338, 344, 346, 350, 352
Hapsburg, House of, 27, 28, 30, 46, 68, 70
Harcourt, 370
Hat, 91
Heidelburg, 131
Heilebron, 345, 347
Henneguin, 153
Henri, Duke of Bouillon, 130, 202, 203
Henry, 154, 175
Henry of Navarre, 170
Henry III, 26, 65, 148, 157
Henry IV, 26, 47, 65, 112, 120, 123, 130, 133, 134, 137, 148, 149, 154, 157, 160, 170, 174, 175, 179, 185, 194, 237, 239, 240, 297, 298
Hesse-Darmstadt, 348
Hohenzollerns, 33, 43, 95
Holland, 34, 83, 131, 132, 138, 218, 219, 242
Holland, Lord, 228, 229
Horn, 347
Hotel de Venise, 381
House of Commons, 66
Howard of Effingham, 249

Huguenot, 48
Hungary, 33, 68, 74, 137, 366
Hyver, 155

Iberian Peninsula, 138
Indies, 82
Ingoldstat, 342
Inquisition, 84
"Instruction for a Christian," 202
Ireland, 29, 168, 353
Italy, 32, 34, 79, 104, 137, 138, 217, 220, 269, 271, 272, 273, 274, 275, 282, 283, 292, 295, 308, 318, 322, 330, 337, 355, 356, 357, 358, 365, 379, 381, 383
Ivry, 148

James, Duke of York, 59
James I, 49, 74, 131, 159, 223, 224, 225, 226, 262
James II, 59
Jarnac, 239
Jeannin, 180
Joan of Arc, 140
John XXII, 155
Johnson, Dr., 152
Joseph, Pére, 40, 98, 140, 185, 186, 187, 195, 245, 327, 336, 338, 339, 340, 341, 352, 360, 364, 367
Juliers, 179
Jura, 70, 79

Kaunitz, 320
Kent, 50
King John of England, 134
King of Bavaria, 36
"King's ships," 58
Königsberg, 328, 330

La Croix, 160
La Fontaine, 151
Lagrange, 300
La Grave, 277
Landgrave of Hesse-Cassel, 349
Languedoc, 298, 299, 300, 316, 321
La Prée, 258
La Rochelle, 97, 133, 134, 153, 156, 236, 238, 239, 240, 241, 242, 243, 244, 245, 246, 247, 248, 249, 250, 253, 255, 256, 257, 260, 261, 262, 263, 264, 268, 269, 271, 274, 275, 294, 299, 307, 312, 317, 326, 354
Lazarus, 106

Lech, 342
Leipzic, 321, 333, 342
Léon, Father, 384
Lepanto, 82
Lerins Islands, 362
Lesdiguières, 220, 294
Les Roches, 185
"Life," 295
Livonia, 326
Lodève, Bishop of, 107
Loire, 203
Lombard, 274, 283
Lombardy, 284, 357, 364
London, 87
Lorraine, 39, 40, 64, 297, 344
Lotharingia, 132
Louis, 147, 155, 197, 199, 201, 206,
    268, 344, 356, 360, 378, 379, 380,
    382, 383
Louis XI, 213
Louis XII, 213
Louis XIII, 26, 47, 68, 94, 111, 112,
    114, 118, 119, 120, 124, 132, 135,
    139, 176, 178, 189, 214, 216, 217,
    223, 227, 229, 231, 234, 235, 236,
    242, 248, 251, 254, 266, 272, 278,
    279, 280, 290, 298, 303, 331, 348,
    370, 371
Louis XIV, 31, 52, 66, 76, 90, 96, 115,
    354, 369
Lourdes, 139
Louvre, 87, 196, 198
Luçon, 149, 154, 155, 156, 157, 158,
    161, 163, 166, 169, 170, 174, 176,
    177, 188, 191, 201, 204
Lunel, 300
Lusignans, 134
Lutzen, 321, 343
Luxemburg, 79, 291, 294, 340
Luynes, 194, 197, 198, 201, 204, 241
Lyons, 267, 290, 302, 372, 381, 383

Madrid, 29, 69, 70, 215, 223, 294
Magdeburg, 324, 333
Maillerais, 166
Malherbe, 152
Mansfeld, 215, 220
Mantua, Duke of, 269, 270, 271, 272,
    280, 282, 284, 285, 337, 338, 357
Margaret of Mantua, 365
Maria, Henrietta, 223, 224, 229, 252
Marie, 237
Marienburg, 330

Marillac, 292, 294, 295, 297, 303, 304,
    305, 306, 307, 308, 309, 310, 311,
    312, 314, 378
Marlborough, 310
Martha, 106
Mary of Mantua, 379
Matthias, Emperor, 73
Mayence, 339, 349
Maximilian, 336, 342, 362
Mazarin, 122, 250, 285
"Memoirs," 242
Metternich, 320
Metz, 39, 40, 41, 55, 337
Meuse, 133
Mezières, 182
Michael, 295, 296, 307
Michelet, 140
Milan, 79, 210, 221, 270, 273, 370
Modena, Duke of, 357
Mohammed, 42
Montauban, 215
Mont-Cenis, 283, 285
Montferrat, 269, 270, 272, 273, 280, 282,
    365
Montforts, 298
Mont-Genèvre, 277, 278, 283, 285
Montmorency, 234, 237, 249, 267, 269,
    297, 298, 299, 300, 301, 302, 303, 313,
    314, 315, 316, 317, 318, 321, 380
Montpellier, 299
Morbihan, 133
Moselle, 133, 340
Moulins, 296
Murat, 233

Nancy, 343, 344
Nantes, 234, 235
Napoleon, 9, 109, 145, 201, 275, 276,
    328
Napoleon III, 39, 358
Narbonne, 381, 382
National Gallery in London, 87
Navarre, 261
Néons, 147
Netherlands, 28, 29, 46, 69, 70, 76, 79,
    82, 84, 137, 219, 296, 306, 359, 360,
    367, 368
Nevers, Duke of, 192, 233, 270, 271,
    272, 273, 278, 285, 337, 338, 379
Ney, 233
Nicholas, 252, 344
Nîmes, 256, 300, 301
Nordlingen, 347, 351, 357, 365

Norfolk, 50
North American Republic, 84
Northern Earls, 64
North Sea, 71, 85, 133
Notre-Dame, 183, 227
Nottinghamshire, 50
Nuremburg, 342

Old Effiat, 378
Oléron, 245, 246, 248
Olivares, 85, 86
Orange, House of, 131
Orange, Princes of, 355
Orleans, 111, 113, 124, 128, 280, 297
Ornano, 233, 304
Orthez, 139
Ortler, 208
Oulx, 278
Oxenstierna, 331, 349
Oxford, 252
Oxfordshire, 50

Pacific Islands, 79
Palatine, 74, 131, 226, 284, 321
Pappenheim, 335
Paris Hôtel de Ville, 150
Parma, Duke of, 357, 365
Parthenay, 98, 134
Paulette, 183
Paul V, 159, 205
Paw, 55, 139
Peace of Augsburg, 323
Peace of Prague, 351
Peenemunde, 332
Pelvoux, 277
Perpignan, 86, 119, 372, 383
Petain, 233
Peter the Great, 32
Pezenas, 299
Philip, 350, 351
Philip II, 69, 74, 243
Philip IV, 74, 85, 210, 214, 347, 365
Philip, Jansenist, 87
Picardy, 360, 361
Piedmont, 138, 273, 280, 370
Pinerolo, 283, 285, 356
Plutarch, 31
Po, 273
Poitevin, 89
Poitiers, 155, 166, 177, 191, 280
Poitou, 98, 134, 136, 140, 147, 149, 156,
    170, 177

Poland, 29, 33, 137, 138, 322, 326, 327,
    329, 330, 331
Pomerania, 332
Pontoise, 293, 360
Ponts-de-Cé, 237, 308
Portsmouth, 254
Portugal, 371
Pragmatic Sanction, 51
Privas, 284
Prussia, 30, 32, 34, 39
Pure, 151
Pyramids, 81
Pyrenees, 28, 40, 70, 85, 86, 223, 284,
    298, 362, 371, 377

Quartre Bras, 257
Quatre, Henri, 177, 178, 180

Rabelais, 152
Ratisbon, 335, 336, 345
"Reich," 31, 33, 34, 40, 43, 45, 284
"Republic," 266
Renaissance, 59
Rennes, 55
Revelstoke, Lord, 97
Rhé, 97, 244, 245, 246, 247, 248, 256,
    257, 263, 269, 308
Rheinfeld, 367
Rhine, 29, 40, 44, 85, 98, 129, 132, 137,
    140, 284, 322, 323, 339, 340, 341, 342,
    344, 350, 357, 362, 364, 366, 367, 368,
    369, 370
Rhine Valley, 133
Rhône, 297, 301, 381, 382
Richelieu, 8, 9, 20, 25, 26, 27, 28, 30,
    31, 32, 33, 35, 36, 37, 38, 39, 40,
    41, 42, 43, 44, 45, 46, 48, 51, 52, 53,
    54, 55, 56, 57, 58, 59, 61, 62, 63, 66,
    68, 70, 71, 73, 74, 75, 78, 80, 81, 83,
    85, 86, 87, 89, 91, 92, 93, 94, 95, 96,
    97, 99, 100, 102, 103, 104, 105, 106,
    107, 111, 112, 113, 114, 118, 119, 120,
    121, 122, 123, 126, 127, 128, 131, 132,
    133, 134, 135, 140, 145, 146, 147, 149,
    150, 151, 152, 153, 155, 156, 157, 160,
    161, 167, 168, 169, 170, 171, 173, 175,
    177, 178, 184, 186, 187, 188, 190, 191,
    192, 194, 195, 196, 198, 199, 201, 202,
    203, 204, 206, 207, 208, 214, 215, 216,
    217, 218, 219, 221, 222, 223, 224, 225,
    226, 227, 229, 230, 231, 232, 233, 234,
    235, 237, 238, 239, 242, 245, 246, 247,
    249, 250, 252, 253, 254, 255, 257, 258,

259, 260, 263, 264, 266, 267, 277, 278, 279, 280, 282, 283, 284, 285, 286, 287, 288, 290, 292, 293, 294, 295, 296, 297, 299, 302, 303, 304, 305, 306, 307, 308, 309, 310, 311, 312, 313, 314, 315, 316, 317, 318, 319, 320, 321, 322, 323, 325, 327, 328, 331, 334, 337, 338, 340, 341, 342, 344, 345, 346, 347, 348, 349, 350, 351, 352, 353, 354, 355, 356, 357, 358, 359, 360, 361, 362, 363, 364, 365, 366, 367, 368, 369, 370, 371, 372, 375, 376, 377, 378, 379, 380, 381, 382, 383, 384

Ripa, 216, 217

Rivoli, 285

Robespierre, 56

Rochechouart, 107, 146, 149, 155, 157

Rocroi, 354

Rohan, 111, 133, 134, 135, 220, 228, 237, 265, 355, 357, 364, 365

Rome, 18, 160, 202, 224, 322

Ronsard, 152

Rosas, 371

Rouen, 55

Roussillon, 371, 377, 381, 382

Rubens, 87, 291

Rue de Jouy, 150

Rueil, 310, 311

Russels, 50

Russia, 37

Sardinia, 79

Saumur, 151, 176, 181, 237, 240

Savoy, 217, 218, 219, 220, 221, 222, 223, 267, 270, 271, 272, 273, 274, 275, 277, 280, 282, 283, 285, 288, 290, 356, 357, 358, 371

Savoy, Passes of, 153

Saxony, 322, 324, 333, 336, 346, 348, 370

Scandinavia, 138

Schomberg, 295, 302

Scotland, 46, 323

Sedan, 130, 132, 381, 383

See, 154, 155, 156, 157, 160, 161, 165

Sellier, 151

Sens, 183

Sèvre, 241

Sforza, Maximilian, Duke of Milan, 212

Sicily, 79

"Siècle" of Louis XIV, 31

Sigismond, 325, 326

Sillery, 180

Smith, Richard, 159

Soissons, 233

Sondrio, 208, 216

Sorbonne, 106, 161, 198, 384

Soubise, 133, 134, 204, 220, 221, 237, 244, 246, 249

South Africa, 78

Spain, 27, 29, 68, 69, 70, 74, 75, 76, 77, 78, 79, 80, 81, 82, 83, 84, 85, 118, 120, 127, 137, 138, 177, 179, 194, 210, 213, 214, 215, 217, 218, 219, 220, 222, 223, 224, 225, 227, 228, 233, 253, 267, 270, 271, 272, 273, 277, 280, 284, 285, 288, 299, 316, 322, 336, 348, 350, 351, 352, 357, 363, 368, 369, 371, 381, 382

Spires and Worms, 339

Splugen Pass, 217

Springs, 245

Stadtlohn, 74

Stelvio, 209, 210

Ste-Menehould, 182

Stettin, 332

St. Eustache, 150, 383

Stirling, 301

St.-Jean-de-Losne, 362

St. John, 106

St. Margaret, 266

St. Martin, 258, 259, 260, 261, 262

Stoke's Bay, 255

St.-Quentin, 306

Strafford, 317

Stralsund, 332

Strasbourg, 137

St. Simon, 293

St. Thomas of Canterbury, 158

Stuart, 32, 58, 227

Stura, 273

Styria, 73

Suffolk, 50

Sully, 134, 177, 179, 180, 181, 240

Susa, 236, 356

Susa Gorge, 275, 278, 279, 280, 281, 282, 283

Sussex, 50

Sweden, 30, 32, 73, 321, 324, 326, 327, 330, 346, 349, 370

Swiss Grison, 208

Switzerland, 137, 216

Tarascon, 382

Tarbes, 139

Thirty Years' War, 71, 74, 80, 131, 137, 333, 340, 342, 363
Thomas of Savoy, 370
Thorn, 330
Tilly, 322, 333, 335, 340, 342
Tirano, 208, 216
Toiras, 241, 258, 259, 260, 285
Tonale, 211
Toul, 337
Toulouse, 55, 188, 298, 302, 303
Touraine, 147
Tours, 303, 314
Trafalgar, 80
Transylvania, 72, 74, 366
Treaty of Compiègne, 349
Treaty of Madrid, 216
Treaty of Monzon, 218, 222, 253
Trembloy, Joseph du, 37, 53, 111
Trentino, 211
Treves, 344, 348, 352
Trino, 280
Tromp, Dutch Admiral, 368
Truce of Altmark, 330
Truce of Stumsdorf, 356
Tudor, Mary, 323
Turenne, Count of, 130, 131, 133
Turin, 273, 277, 370
Tyburn, 252
Tyrol, 210, 365

Umbrail, 209, 210
United States, 219
University of Paris, 152
Urban VIII, 216
Usedom, 332

Valence, 276
Valois, 26
Valtelline, 81, 85, 118, 207, 208, 210, 211, 212, 213, 214, 215, 216, 217, 218, 222, 226, 227, 269, 356, 357, 362, 364, 365, 367
Vendôme, 233, 234, 304
Venice, 27
Verdun, 309, 310, 337, 367
Versailles, 292, 293
Vienna, 27, 69, 70, 71, 72, 73, 75, 137
Vieuville, 215
Villeroi, 189
Vincennes, 233
Vincent II, 269, 270
Voltaire, 98
von Bismarck, Otto, 20

Wallenstein, 109, 322, 324, 331, 335, 336, 339, 342, 343, 344, 345, 346
Walloons, 259
Waterloo, 257
Wattignies, 261
Weimar, 370
Westminster, 221, 253
Westphalia, 76
White Mountain, 74
William of Hesse-Cassel, 366
William the Conqueror, 171
Woerth, 362, 367
Worms, 349

Zurich, 212